Grammar
Workbook
for the **SAT**, **ACT** and more

Grammar Workbook

for the SAT, ACT and more

Second Edition

George Ehrenhaft, Ed.D.
Former English Department Chairman
Mamaroneck High School
Mamaroneck, New York

BARRON'S

All inquiries should be addressed to:
Barron's Educational Series, Inc.
250 Wireless Boulevard
Hauppauge, NY 11788
www.barronseduc.com

Library of Congress Control Number: 2010010041

ISBN-13: 978-0-7641-4489-9
ISBN-10: 0-7641-4489-8

Library of Congress Cataloging-in-Publication Data

Ehrenhaft, George.
    Grammar workbook for the SAT, ACT—and more / George Ehrenhaft.—2nd ed.
        p. cm.
    Includes index.
    ISBN-13: 978-0-7641-4489-9
    ISBN-10: 0-7641-4489-8
    1. English language—Grammar—Examinations—Study guides. 2. SAT (Educational test)—Study guides. 3. ACT Assessment—Study guides. I. Title.
    LB1631.5.E465 2010
    378.1´662—dc22

                                                            2010010041

PRINTED IN THE UNITED STATES OF AMERICA
10 9 8 7 6 5 4 3 2

Contents

Preface: A Greeting from the Author   vii

Introduction: Grammar Q's & A's   ix

PART I   **GRAMMAR BASICS: AN ORIENTATION / 1**

Chapter 1 The Language of Grammar: Terms to Know / 3

     The Noun / 3
     The Pronoun / 5
     The Verb / 21
     The Adjective / 34
     The Adverb / 38
     The Preposition / 43
     The Conjunction / 46
     Answer Key / 48

Chapter 2 Sentences / 57

     A Note to the Reader / 57
     Sentence Basics / 57
     Clauses / 60
     Types of Sentences / 61
     Sentence Problems / 62
     Sentence Structure / 70
     Sentence Expression and Style / 74
     Sentence Mechanics: Punctuation and Capitalization / 81
     Answer Key / 88

PART II   **GRAMMAR TESTS / 93**

Chapter 3 Grammar Pitfalls / 95

Chapter 4 SAT Grammar Questions / 103

     SAT Questions for Practice / 108

Chapter 5 ACT Grammar Questions / 141

ACT Questions for Practice / 151

Chapter 6 Grammar Tests for High School Graduation / 197

Practice for High School Exit Exams / 198

PART III ESSAY WRITING ON THE SAT AND ACT / 227

Chapter 7 Writing a Grammatical Essay / 229

An Essay-Writing Process / 229
Sample SAT Writing Test Topics / 230
Sample ACT Writing Test Topics / 231
Making Every Second Count / 231
Essay Scoring / 245

Index / 247

Preface

A Greeting from the Author

Dear Reader,

Most people would rather be stuck in traffic than study grammar. Nevertheless, the book in your hands invites you to cast aside your prejudices and dare to discover the joys of grammar—although some will say "No way!"

Yet, here's a fact that can't be refuted: Grammar skills help you speak and write better, and if you happen to be a student, good grammar can lead to higher scores on the SAT, ACT, high school exit exams, and any other standardized tests you meet along the way.

This book is user-friendly. It acquaints you with the terms you need to know and shows you how to avoid grammar pitfalls that give many people headaches. You'll learn to write complete, effective sentences, say exactly what you mean, and even put commas in the right places.

Maybe you feel clueless about grammar, or maybe your grammar skills are rusty from disuse. Either way, take heart. You probably know more than you think. Be confident that you've made the right move by picking up this book, which starts with grammar basics. Begin by reading . . . no, begin *by studying* Part I, an introduction to the grammatical terms and concepts you need to know. Keep track of your progress by doing the exercises, called "Checkpoints."

If you're already well-versed in grammar and on the verge of taking college admissions tests, begin with Part II, a collection of the grammatical issues you're most likely to be asked about on the SAT, ACT, and other exams.

On the other hand, if you're preparing to retake the SAT or ACT to raise your score, turn to Part II, which is a compilation of sample SAT and ACT questions, as well as thorough analyses and explanations to help you nail down the right answer to each question.

Part III takes you deeper into the SAT and ACT with an account of the essay questions on both tests. Don't even think of taking either test without reviewing Part III beforehand.

Whatever your purpose or goal, use this guide regularly and often. Keep it by your side as a ready reference. Browse its pages in your spare time or read it intently from cover to cover. Whatever you do, let the book work for you. Let it help you sharpen your skills and build your confidence as a speaker, writer, and test taker.

Meanwhile, I'll keep my fingers crossed and avidly root for your success.

Good luck and best wishes,

George Ehrenhaft

Introduction
Grammar Q's and A's

Why is grammar important? What's all the fuss about?

If you want to send a verbal message to someone, good grammar helps. Without it, you can never be sure that your words say exactly what you want them to. Ideas shaped in faulty language may be crystal clear to you, but you can never know exactly what they'll mean to somebody else. Using good grammar increases your chances of accurately getting your message across.

Why do so many people find it hard to learn grammar?

The reason is that it <u>is</u> hard. Grammar is a jumble of abstract rules and principles, easy to memorize but awfully tricky to apply because the language doesn't always cooperate. Exceptions to nearly every rule cause no end of trouble and even make some people feel dumb.

Nevertheless, billions of people—not all of them brilliant—have learned grammar without whining about it and have spent a lifetime speaking and writing standard grammatical English.

What's the difference between "usage" and "grammar"?

Although some people say "usage" when they mean "grammar," and vice versa, the two words are not synonyms. *Usage* describes actual spoken and written language. "Standard" usage is the level of language embraced by literate people who, in a general way, occupy positions of leadership and influence in society. Grammar, on the other hand, is a set of rules that are followed when you speak and write "correctly."

Why do some rules force you to use language that sounds weird?

Because the English language keeps changing, old rules often become obsolete. It's always been correct to say, "*It is I*," but today, "*It is me*" is perfectly acceptable, especially in informal speech. Once upon a time, a question like, "*What's all the fuss about?*" was considered poor English because of a taboo against ending a sentence with a preposition. In the 21st century, however, no one would seriously say, "*About what is all the fuss?*" In short, the rules of grammar bend to fit the circumstances, but sometimes not quickly enough to keep up with our evolving language.

How will studying grammar help on the SAT, ACT, and other tests?

Let's make one thing clear: You won't be tested on the rules of grammar on either the SAT or the ACT. Instead, you'll be asked to identify mistakes in sentences and paragraphs. A sense of language—let's call it an "ear" for what is right and wrong—could steer you to the correct answers. But that's not enough. Very often, knowledge of the rules can help you spot grammatical errors in an instant and answer the questions with the confidence of an expert. There's another advantage to knowing the rules: You're less likely to make a grammatical mistake as you write your SAT or ACT essay, and an error-free essay will work in your favor when the essay is scored.

Even so, it's possible to answer all test questions on grammar without memorizing all the rules. But knowing the rules helps—a lot.

How does this book differ from other grammar books?

Instead of handing you a long list of grammatical rules to be learned and followed, this book zeroes in on common errors in grammar and usage. It shows you first how to track down everyday mistakes in speech and writing, and then how to fix them.

Part I

Grammar Basics

An Orientation

Chapter 1

The Language of Grammar

Terms to Know

People in every line of work—from bankers to beauticians, from stargazers to gurus—share a language special to their jobs. Grammarians are no exception, which means that you and I can't talk grammar without a vocabulary we both understand. So, what follows is a chapter full of the words used whenever people talk and write about grammar. Hard-core, essential terms are printed in boldface capital letters like **THIS**. Less crucial words appear in boldface italics like *this*. Learn the first kind cold. The second kind you can probably muddle through without—at least until you get serious about grammar and start wallowing in the stuff. That's no joke. There are countless grammar lovers out there—and not all of them are kooks.

This chapter on grammar terminology has been pared to the bone—first, to keep you from being overwhelmed, and second, because grammar contains countless mystifying terms that, although nice to know, don't necessarily help you become a more effective user of English.

> **Hint:** Read these pages slowly, digesting a few bites at each reading. Don't get bogged down trying to memorize every detail. Like everything, grammar takes time to learn. Perseverance helps. Expect to go back again and again until you're satisfied that you haven't missed anything.

THE NOUN

NOUNS (Remember: **BOLDFACE CAPS** indicate the most crucial words.) **Nouns** are the names of things, the labels we apply to everything we can see, touch, taste, and feel. They name the places we go (*school, work, the mall*), our means of getting there (*subway, legs, an SUV*), and what we pass by, pass through, and pass over (*the park, downtown, a bridge*) on our way. Nouns name the solid, concrete, tactile words of our language, the infrastructure, so to speak. But they also name:

- people (*Loretta, the mail carrier*)
- activities (*swimming, kissing*)
- concepts (*sportsmanship, love*)
- conditions (*mess, poverty*)
- events (*9/11, prom*)
- groups (*Microsoft, SADD*)
- feelings (*enthusiasm, headache*)
- times (*morning, curfew*)

Some nouns such as *Detroit* and *Hewlett-Packard* are capitalized. Those are ***proper nouns*** and refer to specific places, groups, things, events, and so on. The nouns that begin with lower-case letters go by the name of **common nouns**.

All the nouns listed above are **SINGULAR**. That is, they name only one person, one place, one thing, one activity, and so forth. By adding either *–s* or *–es* you make many nouns **PLURAL**, meaning more than one. Thus, one *woodpecker* becomes two or more *woodpeckers* and a *box* increases in number into as many *boxes* as you can count. Some nouns increase their **number** (a term that refers to singular and plural) with various combinations of letters other than *–s* or *–es*. For example: *sky/skies, knife/knives, ox/oxen, child/children, alumnus/alumni, goose/geese,* and *mouse/mice.*

Several nouns are the same in both singular and plural forms, among them: *deer/deer, scissors/scissors,* and *moose/moose,* as well as a handful of nouns with Latin endings, such as *data* and *media,* which are technically plural but have become singular through constant repetition.

English also contains nouns that come only in singular form. These include *news, garbage, happiness, information, physics, air, laryngitis,* and *honesty.*

Identifying singular and plural nouns is usually no problem for native speakers of English, but some people stumble over ***collective nouns***, nouns that stand for groups or quantities or masses of things, such as: *family, class, mob, orchestra, jury, team,* and *audience.* Although these nouns name collections of more than one individual, they are still considered singular most of the time, as in The class is in the gym. When you refer to individuals in a group, however, collective nouns may be used as plurals, as in The class were divided in their feelings about the poem. This is more common, however, in British English than American English.

Believe it or not, there are many more intriguing facts to learn about nouns:

- Nouns can indicate possession, as in *Harry's* nose and the *day's* end.
- A noun is an essential component of a complete sentence (more about that later).
- Some nouns look like verbs and are called *gerunds*, but they still function as nouns (more to come on that, too).
- Many nouns are not always nouns. They change identities when the context changes. Take *love,* for instance:

  > Susan is the *love* (noun) of my life.
  > I *love* (verb) her dearly.
  > I wrote her a *love* (adjective) song.

These, among many other wonders of English grammar, await you in the pages ahead. For the scoop on verbs, turn to page 21; punctuation, page 81; sentence structure, page 70; and modifiers, page 34. If you're just dying for a sneak preview of these and other matters, don't hold back. Just turn the pages and go for it!

The Article

If you're ever unsure whether or not a word is a noun, here's something to try: Put one of three articles (*the*, *a*, or *an*) in front of it. If the article + word sounds like a combination you are apt to hear or even use yourself, chances are that the word in question is a noun, as in <u>the</u> alphabet, <u>a</u> lobster, <u>an</u> egg. Because you wouldn't say

> The label "article" applies to only three English words: *a, an,* and *the*.

"*the me*," "*a destroy*," or "*an of*," you can be sure that *me, destroy,* and *of* are not nouns, but some other part of speech.

An **ARTICLE** is one of the traditional **PARTS OF SPEECH** (see next paragraph). It is a label that applies to only three English words: *the, a,* and *an* —and no others. *A* and *an* are called **indefinite articles** because they are used to refer to nouns that are not clearly specified, as in: *a truck driver, a river, an explosion. The* is called a **definite article** because it refers to more specific, identifiable people, places, or things, as in: *the old truck driver, the Mississippi River, the first explosion.*

PARTS OF SPEECH is a general term that refers to eight types of words, each playing a different role in speech and writing. You've already met the **NOUN** and the **ARTICLE.** The others are the **PRONOUN, VERB, ADJECTIVE, ADVERB, PREPOSITION,** and **CONJUNCTION.** You'll get to know all of them in the pages ahead. You'll also come to see that, in spite of different names, the parts of speech do not live in isolation. Rather, they work together like the instruments of an orchestra, each influencing the other to create a unified and often melodic language.

But wait! There's one missing—the **INTERJECTION.**

Not to worry. *Interjections* are minor words and phrases, mostly one-word utterances tacked onto or inserted into sentences to heighten emotion or express feelings. *Uh oh!* is an interjection. So are *alas, well, oh, wow, good grief, shhh!, for Pete's sake!, damn!,* and a host of other expressions, including any number of colorful expletives that can't be printed here. Although interjections serve a rhetorical purpose, they hardly matter grammatically. When you write, use them sparingly—with or without exclamation points.

THE PRONOUN

Simply put, a **PRONOUN** is a handy word used as a substitute for another word, usually a noun. Without pronouns, we'd be stuck using the same nouns over and over again, as in this passage:

> On the way home, Dot sat next to Dan on the bus. Dot didn't say much, but Dot offered Dan a stick of gum. Dot also let Dan use Dot's iPod, which was Dot's way of saying thanks to Dan for helping Dot with Dot's math homework.

Thank God for pronouns! They spare us from mountains of such monotonous repetition. Look how three everyday pronouns transform the passage into something far more readable:

> On the way home, Dot sat next to Dan on the bus. Dot didn't say much, but *she* offered Dan a stick of gum. *She* also let *him* use *her* iPod, which was *her* way of saying thanks to *him* for helping *her* with *her* math homework.

Using the pronouns *she, him,* and *her* as substitutes for *Dot* and *Dan* makes all the difference.

Choosing the Correct Pronoun

It would be hard to prove, but adult speakers and writers of English probably use the correct pronoun ninety-nine out of a hundred times. Well, maybe ninety-eight out of a hundred, but still a very high rate of accuracy. Total compliance with the rules of pronoun usage may be out of reach, but you can do your part by knowing how to choose the right pronoun at the right time.

To begin, you should know that faulty pronoun usage occurs most often:

- When pronouns in the wrong "case" are chosen
- When pronouns in the wrong "person" are chosen
- When pronouns fail to agree in number or gender with the noun for which the pronoun is a substitute.
- When the pronoun reference is unclear or ambiguous

The pages that follow will illustrate these pitfalls and show you how to avoid them. Along the way, you'll also find checkpoints—places where you can check your understanding of the grammar that governs pronoun usage.

The "case" of pronouns

He, she, and *him,* along with *I, me, her, it, they, them, we, us,* and *you* are called ***personal pronouns.*** Most of the time, you can depend on your ear to tell you which pronoun to use. For example, because you'd never tell the bus driver, "Let *I* off at the corner," you'd use *me* without even thinking about it.

Unfortunately, pronoun choice isn't always that simple. For instance, which pronoun—*I* or *me*—should complete this sentence?

Philip is a faster runner than _____.

Half the people would probably say *I,* the other half *me.* Which half is correct? Read on, and you'll learn how to figure it out.

When you can't depend on the sound of the words, it helps to know that personal pronouns fall into two groups:

> It helps to know that pronouns fall into two groups: *subject* pronouns and *object* pronouns.

Subjective	*objective*
~~Group 1~~	~~Group 2~~
I	me
he	him
she	her
they	them
we	us
you	you

Group 1 words are called **SUBJECT** pronouns and are in the ***nominative case,*** whereas Group 2 words are called **OBJECT** pronouns and are in the ***objective case.*** They've been given different labels because pronouns in the nominative case function differently from pronouns in the objective case, and vice versa. Therefore, the word **CASE** refers to the role each pronoun plays in a sentence.

1. Subject pronouns are used in two ways: They name the people, places, or things being described by the sentence, as in:

   > *She* is weird.

   Or, they name the performer of some sort of action, as in:

   > It was *he* who turned off the light.

   In each sentence a pronoun serves as the grammatical **SUBJECT**. (For details about sentence subjects, turn to page 57.) It also happens that the verbs used in both these sentences are forms of the verb *to be*, a fact worth noting because so-called ***being verbs*** (sometimes called ***linking verbs***)—such as *is, was, were, has been, had been, will be*, and so on—are always paired with subject pronouns and never with object pronouns, even when the pronoun is not the subject of the sentence, as in:

   > The only students (subject of sentence) who failed the quiz *were* (verb) Donald and *he* (pronoun).

   For the record, the pronoun *he* in this sentence functions as a ***predicate nominative***, a term that refers to words that identify, define, or mean the same as the grammatical subject (details about *predicates* on page 58).

   One more thing: *Object* pronouns don't ever belong in sentence subjects, because you may end up saying things like, "*Them* are going to be late" or "*Him* and *me* walked to the diner," constructions suggesting that the speaker is, to put it mildly, grammatically challenged.

2. Object pronouns. In contrast to subject pronouns, *object* pronouns refer to people, places, or things being acted upon:

   > The music carried *them* (object pronoun) away.
   > He asked *her* (object pronoun) to call him (object pronoun) on his cell phone.

   Pronouns that function as receivers of action are called ***objects of the verb***, as in:

   > Terry invited *him* to the prom.
   > (*invited* = verb; *him* = object of the verb)
   > The waiter gave *her* and *me* a menu.
   > (*gave* = verb; *her* and *me* = objects of the verb)

   Object pronouns are also used in ***prepositional phrases***—that is, phrases that (as their name suggests) begin with **PREPOSITIONS**, as in:

   > between *you* and *me*
   > to Sherry and *her*
   > among *us* women
   > at *us*
   > from *her* and *him*
   > with *me* and *you*

   (For details on *prepositions*, turn to page 43.)

> Avoid mixing subject and object pronouns in the same phrase, for example: *she and them*.

Using pairs of personal pronouns

You'll never go wrong if you avoid mixing subject and object pronouns in the same phrase, as, for example, in *she and them* or *they and us*. When you're uncertain about which pronouns are used to make a pair, here's what to do: If you know that one pronoun is correct, pick the second one from the same group. If you're not sure of either pronoun, substitute *I* or *me* for one of the pronouns—if *I* seems to fit, pick the pronouns from Group 1; if *me* fits better, use a Group 2 pronoun. For example, decide which pair of pronouns fits the following sentence:

> Elvis asked that (he, him) and (she, her) practice handstands.

If you insert *me* in place of one of the pronouns, you'll get:

> Elvis asked that *me* practice handstands.

Because that language comes from another dimension, *I* must be the word that fits. So, pick your pronouns from Group 1:

> Elvis asked that *he* and *she* practice handstands.

Pairing a noun and a pronoun

When using a phrase made up of a noun and pronoun, such as *Charles and I, my canary and me, he and Jimmy, them and my uncle*, choose the appropriate pronoun as though the noun didn't exist. That's right, ignore the noun and then decide whether you need a subject pronoun or an object pronoun. For instance:

> The teacher and (*she, her*) argued about the test grade.

Whichever pronoun you choose, it's going to be part of the grammatical subject of the sentence. Therefore, forget *teacher* and insert *she* or *her*. Because no one ever says *Her* argued about the test grade, *she* must be the correct pronoun.

Similarly, if the noun/pronoun pair is the object of a preposition, as in A bond developed between Sarah and (*I, me*), let the noun and pronoun swap places in the sentence. Then the correct choice becomes perfectly obvious:

> A bond developed between *me* and Sarah.

Using pronouns in comparisons

To find the correct pronoun in a comparison that uses *than* or *as*, complete the comparison using the verb that would follow naturally:

> Jackie runs faster than *she* (runs).
> My brother has bigger feet than *I* (do).
> Carol is as tough as *he* (is).
> A woman such as *I* (am) could solve the problem.

Noun/pronoun combinations

When a pronoun appears side by side with a noun (*we* boys, *us* women), deleting the noun will usually help you pick the correct pronoun:

> (*We, Us*) seniors decided to take a day off from school in late May. (Deleting *seniors* leaves <u>We</u> *decided to* . . .)
>
> This award was presented to (*we, us*) students by the faculty. (Deleting *students* leaves *award was presented to <u>us</u> by the* . . .)

Checkpoint 1. CHOOSING PERSONAL PRONOUNS

Circle the correct pronoun in each sentence below.

1. Judith took my sister and (I, me) to the magic show last night.

2. We thought that Matilda and Jorge would be there, and sure enough, we saw (she, her) and (he, him) sitting in the front row.

3. During the intermission, Jorge came over and asked my sister and (I, me) to go out after the show.

4. Between you and (I, me) the magician was terrible.

5. It must also have been a bad evening for (he, him) and his assistant, Roxanne.

6. Trying to pull a rabbit out of a hat, Roxanne and (he, him) knocked over the table.

7. When he asked for audience participation, my sister and (I, me) volunteered to go on stage.

8. He said that in my pocket I would find $10 in change to split between (I, me) and my sister.

9. When the coins fell out of his sleeve, the audience laughed even harder than (we, us).

10. After the show, (we, us) in the audience thought that the magician needed lots of practice before his next performance.

Answers on page 48

Pronoun "person"

Have you ever noticed that everyday conversation is overwhelmingly about a single topic—namely, **people**? I tell you about myself; you tell me about yourself; we tell each other about someone else. To help you keep straight who is talking about whom, our language conveniently categorizes pronouns, both singular and plural, by **PERSON**:

    First-person **pronouns**—*I, we, me, us, mine, our, ours*—refer to the speaker(s) or writer(s).

    Second-person **pronouns**—*you, your, yours*—refer to the reader or listener, both singular and plural.

    Third-person **pronouns**—*she, he, it, one, they, him, her, them, his, her, hers, its, their, theirs*—refer to people and things written or spoken about, both singular and plural.

Third-person pronouns also include ***indefinite pronouns*** such as *all, any, anyone, each, none, nothing, one, several, many,* and others.

To avoid getting lost in this web of pronouns takes some doing. One way to stay on track is to make sure that pronouns agree with their **ANTECEDENTS**—the words they refer to. When you form a sentence cast in the second person, for instance, keep it in the second person. Consistency is the key.

INCONSISTENT: When you walk your (second person) dog, I (first person) must carry a pooper-scooper.
CONSISTENT: When you walk your (second person) dog, you (second person) must carry a pooper-scooper.

For some reason, the pronouns *one* and *you* tend to be switched more often than others:

INCONSISTENT: The more *one* watches television, the more *you* turn into a vegetable.
CONSISTENT: The more *you* watch television, the more *you* turn into a vegetable.

Actually, the guidelines for using the impersonal pronoun are more like suggestions than strict rules. That's why, in all but the most formal writing, you can properly combine the antecedent *one* with *he/she* and *his/her*, as in:

FORMAL: *One* must take into account *one's* ability to pay.
LESS FORMAL: *One* must take into account *his* ability to pay.

Pronouns and antecedents should agree in number and gender.

Pronoun/antecedent agreement in number and gender

Here's a straightforward rule about pronouns and antecedents: Pronouns and antecedents should agree in number and gender. Despite its simplicity, this rule is widely ignored. In fact, the use of plural pronouns to refer to singular antecedents is so common, that flouting the rule has almost become the norm:

Everybody (singular) is sticking to *their* (plural) side of the story.
Anybody (singular) can pass this course if *they* (plural) study hard.
Neither (singular) teacher plans to change *their* (plural) policy regarding late papers.
If *someone* (singular) tries to write a persuasive essay, *they* (plural) should at least include a convincing argument.

Such agreement errors occur because certain antecedents—chief among them *neither, everybody, everyone, nobody, no one, somebody, someone, anybody,* and *anyone*—sound plural. But they're singular and always have been. In standard grammar, therefore, the sentences should be:

Everybody is sticking to *his* side of the story.
Anybody can pass this course if *she* studies hard.
Neither teacher plans to change *his* policy regarding late papers.
If one tries to write a persuasive essay, *one* should at least include a convincing argument.

> **Note:** Some people object to the use of male pronouns when referring to people who might be of either sex. They prefer the more politically correct phrase "he or she," but because seasoned writers regard that usage as ungraceful and tacky, they use gender-neutral plural pronouns, as in
>
> > AWKWARD: During a college interview, a *student* should avoid griping about *his* or *her* high school teachers.
> > REVISED: During a college interview, *students* should avoid griping about *their* high school teachers.
>
> Or they might simply restructure their sentences to avoid the problem altogether:
>
> > A college interview is not a place to gripe about high school teachers.

Context determines whether the rule for pronoun-antecedent agreement applies to collective nouns (discussed on page 10). That's because words like *jury, class,* and *family* are sometimes singular and sometimes plural:

> The jury (singular) will render its (singular pronoun) verdict on Tuesday.
> The jury (plural) will return to their (plural pronoun) homes after the verdict.

Clearly, a noun that names a whole group is singular (*police, family*), but when it refers to its members acting individually, consider it plural, as in:

> The police had *their* photos taken for the newspaper.
> After the funeral the family thanked everyone who had sent *them* sympathy cards.

Checkpoint 2. PRONOUN SHIFT AND PRONOUN AGREEMENT

Some of the sentences below contain shifts in pronoun person or errors in agreement between pronouns and antecedents. Make all appropriate corrections in the spaces provided, but revise only those sentences that contain errors.

1. The English teacher announced that everyone in the class must turn in their term papers no later than Friday.

   _____ *his/her*

2. When one is fired from a job, she collects unemployment.

   _____ *one*

3. The library put their collection of rare books on display.

   _____ *its*

4. Each of my sisters own their own car.

   _____ *her*

5. In that class, our teacher held conferences with us once a week.

   No change _____

6. In order to keep yourself in shape, ~~one~~ *you* should work out every day.

   _____

7. The individual chosen as team captain will find ~~themselves~~ *himself* working very hard.

   _____

8. Each horse in the procession followed their ~~rider~~ *its* down to the creek.

   _____

9. The school's chess team has just won ~~their~~ *its* first match.

   _____

10. When one is visiting the park and ~~you~~ *one* can't find a restroom, they should ask a park ranger.

   _____

Answers on page 49

Pronoun references

Pronouns should refer unambiguously to their *antecedent*s. Vague or nonexistent references leave readers scratching their heads. Here are three practical tips for avoiding pronoun-reference traps:

- Double-check every pronoun you use to make sure that it doesn't refer to more than one antecedent:

   > The teacher, Ms. Taylor, told Karen that it was *her* responsibility to hand out composition paper.

   So, who's responsible? Ms. Taylor or Karen? It's impossible to tell because the pronoun *her* could refer to either of them. Corrected, the sentence reads:

   > Ms. Taylor told Karen that it was *her* responsibility as the teacher to hand out composition paper.

- Be wary of sentences that contain two or more pronoun references, such as:

   > Mike became a good friend of Mark's after *he* helped *him* repair *his* car.

   Huh? Whose car needed fixing? Who helped whom? The answer lies in a revised sentence:

   > Mike and Mark became good friends after Mike helped Mark repair *his* car.

   This is better, but you still can't be sure who owns the car. One way to clear up the uncertainty is to write more than one sentence:

   > When Mark needed to repair his car, Mike helped *him* do the job. Afterward, Mike and Mark became good friends.

Ah, now it's clear: Mark owns the car, and Mike pitched in to fix it.

- Watch out for words or phrases that may be mistaken for the antecedent, as in:

    Dave was taken fishing by his father when he was ten.

Because the words *he* and *father* are almost next to each other, *father* may seem to be the antecedent of the pronoun *he*. But, unless Dave's father holds a record for being the world's youngest dad, the sentence needs revision:

    When he was ten, Dave was taken fishing by his father.

By now you probably get the idea: Clear meaning depends on pronouns that refer unmistakably to particular nouns or other pronouns. But you also need to know that in some sentences, pronouns can refer not to single-word antecedents but to a phrase or an entire clause. The pronoun *it* in the following sentence, for example, refers to an eight-word clause.

    The storm named Katrina washed the bridge out, which made *it* impossible to get to Mobile on time.

Here, *it* refers to the clause The storm named Katrina washed the bridge out. In such cases, the pronoun can be a personal pronoun such as *it, they,* and *you,* or a **relative pronoun** such as *which, that,* and *this.* For details about relative pronouns, see page 16. Be careful when wording such sentences to avoid referring to something too general or too ambiguous, as in:

    Homeless people allege that the mayor is indifferent to their plight, *which* has been disproved.

Whoa! What really has been disproved? That people made an allegation against the mayor? That the mayor is indifferent to the plight of the homeless? No one can be sure, because *which* has no distinct antecedent. To eliminate the uncertainty, revise the sentence:

    Homeless people allege that the mayor is indifferent to their plight, but the allegation has been disproved.

Checkpoint 3. PRONOUN REFERENCES

The sentences below suffer from faulty pronoun references. Please revise each sentence to eliminate the problem. Use the blank spaces to write your answers.

1. When we teenagers loiter outside the theater on Friday night, they give you a hard time.

    _____

    _____

2. I answered the test questions, collected my pencils and pens, and handed them in.

    _____

    _____

3. Barbara told Ken that she wanted only a short wedding trip to Florida, which lies at the root of their problem.

   _____

   _____

4. His father let him know that he had only an hour to get to the airport.

   _____

   _____

5. During Mrs. Clinton's tenure in office, she traveled more than any other secretary of state.

   _____

   _____

6. Henry, an ambulance driver, disapproved of war but drove it to the front lines anyway.

   _____

   _____

7. After the campus tour, Mike told Todd that he thought he'd be happy going to Auburn.

   _____

   _____

8. Peggy's car hit a truck, but it wasn't even dented.

   _____

   _____

9. Within the last month, Andy's older brother Pete found a new job, broke his leg skiing, and got married to Felicia, which made their parents very happy.

   _____

   _____

10. She wore her new jacket to school, which was black and made of leather.

    _____

    _____

Answers on page 49

Other Types of Pronouns

Until now, these pages have focused on ordinary, everyday *personal pronouns*. But pronouns come in a handful of other varieties:

Nov 30 {
Possessive pronouns
Relative pronouns
Reflexive pronouns
Interrogative pronouns
Demonstrative pronouns

Here's some good news: These types of pronouns, although just as common as personal pronouns in everyday speech and writing, cause fewer grammatical problems.

Possessive pronouns

The ***possessive pronouns***—*my, mine, his, her, hers, your, yours, our, ours, their* and *theirs*—indicate ownership, as in *my* hair, *your* sister, *his* house, *their* party, and so on. They are in the ***possessive case*** and always answer the question "whose?"

> "Whose cat is that?"
> "It is *hers* (possessive pronoun)."
> "Are you sure?"
> "Well, no, maybe it is *theirs* (possessive pronoun)."

Unlike possessive nouns, possessive pronouns are spelled without **apostrophes**. Therefore, never write *her's, their's, your's*. And don't confuse the possessive pronoun *its* with look-alike cousin *it's*, a **contraction** meaning *it is*.

Use a possessive pronoun (*my, our, your, his, her, their*) before a **gerund**, a noun that looks like a verb because of its *–ing* ending.

> *Her* asking the question shows that she is alert. (*Asking* is a gerund.)
> Mother was upset about *your* opening the presents too soon. (*Opening* is a gerund.)

Not every noun with an *–ing* ending is a gerund. Sometimes it's just a noun, as in *thing, ring, spring*. At other times, *-ing* words are verbs; in particular, they're **participles** that modify pronouns in the objective case.

> I hope you don't mind *my* intruding on your conversation (Here *intruding* is a gerund.)
> I hope you don't mind *me* intruding on your conversation. (Here *intruding* is a participle.)

> **Note:** Frankly, gerunds and participles tend to cause students a good deal of grief, especially at first. But wait. You'll become better acquainted with them later—on page 63 to be exact.

that — essential to the sentance
Which — not crucial for understanding of sentance

Relative pronouns

Like all other pronouns, **relative pronouns** (*which, that, who, whom, whose,* and *what*) refer to nouns or other pronouns, as in:

Those are the dishes *that* I washed this morning.

Here the relative pronoun *that* refers to *dishes.* Simple, right? Yes, but that's not quite the end of the story. If you study the sentence some more, you'll see that the word *that* comes before the words *I washed yesterday*—words that describe the dishes. That is, the dishes are not just any old dishes but specifically those dishes that the speaker washed yesterday. Why is that important? Well, for one thing, it helps you use the correct relative pronoun—not always a slam-dunk matter because in everyday English, the relative pronouns *that* and *which* are often used interchangeably. They shouldn't be. Instead, use *that* when the subsequent words define or describe something essential to the meaning of the sentence, as in:

Those are the dishes *that* need to be put away.

On the other hand, use *which* if the words that follow give information that isn't crucial to the meaning of the sentence, as in:

Those dishes, *which* once belonged to my grandmother, need to be put away.

Here, the fact that the dishes once belonged to the speaker's grandmother may be interesting, but the information is not crucial to the main message of the sentence.

You should also know that the words that come after relative pronouns are called **relative clauses.** Or, put another way, *relative pronouns* introduce *relative clauses.* For example, here are two sentences with their relative clauses underlined:

1. The store *that* sold used bikes went out of business.
2. The backpack, *which* Belinda takes to school, disappeared.

> Commas precede relative clauses starting with *which* but not before relative clauses starting with *that.*

Notice that Sentence 1 contains no punctuation, whereas Sentence 2 uses a comma both before and after the relative clause. Why? Because in the comma-free sentence, the clause is important to the meaning of the sentence. In the other sentence, it's not. How a sentence is punctuated, then, indicates whether the relative clause is essential to the meaning of the sentence. If ever you're torn between choosing *that* or *which,* determine whether the relative clause needs to be punctuated with a comma. If so, use *which;* if not, use *that.* To reiterate: Commas precede relative clauses starting with *which* (or one of the other relative pronouns), but not before relative clauses starting with *that.*

> **Note:** You're not alone if you are puzzled by any of this material on relative pronouns. For one thing, we haven't disussed clauses yet. Moreover, the twists and turns of English grammar can drive some readers nuts. But please don't throw up your hands in frustration—not yet, anyway, because you'll find ample opportunities to work out the kinks in Chapters 4 and 5, where you'll meet actual SAT- and ACT-style grammar questions.

By the way, if you studied grammar in the past, you may have run into the terms *restrictive clause* and *nonrestrictive clause*. These labels are little more than other names for types of relative clauses. Restrictive clauses don't need commas; nonrestrictive clauses do.

Before we move on, one more detail deserves mention: In certain contexts, you can leave out relative pronouns without altering meaning. In the following two sentences, for instance, the bracketed pronoun is optional:

> The doghouse [*that*] Duke lives in is in the backyard.
> The guests [*whom*] we expected at six o'clock arrived at seven.

It's very common to omit the relative pronoun in everyday speech and informal writing, but not in more formal communication.

Who or Whom?

The notorious *who/whom* question baffles many people. Even more baffling, though, is its reputation as a tough nut to crack. The solution is reasonably simple:

Use the relative pronoun *who* as the grammatical subject of a sentence or as a pronoun that stands for the subject, as in:

> *Who* (subject) ordered a pizza to go?
> That (subject) is the woman *who* (subject stand-in) ordered it.

Use *whom* following a preposition or when it functions as the object of a verb, as in:

> ✸ To (preposition) *whom* should this fish be given?
> ✸ The detective found (verb) the thief *whom* he'd been seeking.

While weighing the use of *who* or *whom*, ask yourself whether the pronoun is performing an action. If so, use *who*. If the pronoun is being acted upon, use *whom*. Also, you can depend on prepositions. They are always followed by *whom*, as in *with whom, in whom, before whom, around whom, between whom*, and so on.

Who, That, or Which?

1. Use *who* and *whom* to refer to people.

2. Use *that* to refer to things, animals, and people, but use *who* when referring to a specific person, as in:

   > This is Corporal Powder, *who* fought in Afghanistan.

   Either *who* or *that*, however, may be used for more general references, as in:

   > Those are the pilots *who* flew the plane./Those are the pilots *that* flew the plane.

   Take your pick; both sentences are valid.

3. Use *which* to refer to things and nonhuman creatures, but never to people.

> Use *who* to refer to people, *that* to refer to things, and *which* to refer to things and nonhumans.

Reflexive pronouns

Reflexive pronouns stand out among all other pronouns because they end with *self* (singular form) or *selves* (plural form):

First person—*myself/ourselves*
Second person—*yourself/yourselves*
Third person—*herself, himself, itself/themselves*

Reflexive pronouns refer to the noun or pronoun that is the grammatical subject of the sentence in which they appear:

We will be going to the city by ourselves.

In this sentence, the reflexive pronoun *ourselves* refers to *We*, the grammatical subject. Because both the subject and the reflexive pronoun must be present in the same sentence, reflexive pronouns can't be subjects:

FAULTY: *Myself* wrote every word of the paper.
CORRECT: *I* (subject) wrote every word of the paper by *myself.*

Nor can they be object pronouns:

FAULTY: Mimi gave M&Ms to Margie and *myself.*
CORRECTED: Mimi gave M&Ms to Margie and *me.*

Interrogative pronouns

Interrogative pronouns are often called question pronouns. Their name derives from their function:

Q. *What* is their function?
A. To ask questions, make inquiries, and seek information.
Q. *Who* uses them?
A. You and everyone else.
Q. *Which* is better to use, *who* or *whom*?
A. It all depends.
Q. *Whom* must I ask to get a more specific answer?
A. Well, you could ask an English teacher, or you could just turn back to page 17.

And there you have them—*what, who, which,* and *whom*—four of our language's most popular *interrogative pronouns.* Others include *whose, when, where, why,* and *how.* Have you noticed that some of these words are also *relative* pronouns? In that incarnation, however, they serve a different function.

Demonstrative pronouns

Demonstrative pronouns also get their name from their function: They point, like arrows. *This, these, that,* and *those* point to nouns, phrases, clauses, and even whole sentences. The pronoun *this* points out an object close by in space (*this book*), time (*this year*), and thought, (*this idea of yours*). The pronoun *that,* on the other hand, points to distant objects (*that star, that time, that theory*).

Like other pronouns, demonstrative pronouns need to point to clear antecedents. When a writer or speaker expects too much from the demonstrative pronoun, ambiguity results:

> The zoo features more than 1,500 mammals, reptiles, and birds kept in tiny cages. In the primate area, eleven species of monkeys, gorillas, and apes live in a small space no bigger than your average schoolroom. All the animals are fed only twice a day, even though some require nourishment several times in 24 hours. *This* bothers me.

What does *this* refer to? The irregular feeding of some animals? The conditions described throughout the paragraph? It's hard to tell. Fix the problem with a new pronoun and a more specific antecedent:

> *These* (pronoun) *conditions* (antecedent) bother me.

Checkpoint 4. REVIEW OF PRONOUN PROBLEMS.

Correct any faulty pronoun usage you find in the following sentences. Some sentences may be correct.

1. My dog Rosie and myself took a long walk in the woods.

   _____

2. Teachers who I like best have a good sense of humor.

   _____

3. When you're specifically instructed to cross only at the light, one should not jaywalk.

   _____

4. The candy bar was split between Stacy and I.

   _____

5. Jim, Dan, and Elizabeth were swimming in the ocean when suddenly a giant wave appeared and scared him out of his wits.

   _____

6. The book, that once belonged to President Kennedy, was sold at auction for $5,000.

   _____

7. When myself and a friend took the subway, we got lost.

   _____

8. To be a successful musician, one must be so dedicated that you practice your instrument at least six hours every day.

   _____

9. Him and me are planning to go to a show this weekend.

   _____

10. Everyone should put their seat belts on.

   _____

11. To who should I give my change of address form?

   _____

12. The reason early paintings are so often an artist's most interesting work is that it was done with a fresh and youthful perspective.

   _____

13. Amy provided a room with twin beds for him and me.

   _____

14. Anyone with an airline ticket had better confirm their reservation online.

   _____

15. A person which needs to pay for their own health insurance is out of luck.

   _____

16. The meeting was not planned by Fiona and I, so don't blame we girls for its failure.

   _____

17. At the shipyard entrance, the police have been granted great authority. These include stopping any car they wish to, asking them for ID's, patting them down, and arresting suspects without stating their reasons. This policy was put into effect after 9/11.

   _____

18. Of all the teachers which give homework, Ms. Thomas gives the most.

   _____

19. I like Carol and he the best of all my classmates.

   _____

20. Even though the mountain peaks are among the highest in the world, it had no snow on it last summer.

   _____

   Answers on page 50

THE VERB

VERBS are words that name actions: *study, shout, dance, laugh, jab, think, decide, stand, deliver.* The list goes on and on and on. Some people claim that verbs are the most important words in the language. Whether or not that's true, the fact is that every complete sentence needs a verb, and without verbs we'd end up grunting things like:

> Sarah downtown this afternoon.
> When a fire drill?
> If you too much pepper, the sauce spicy.

> Every complete sentence needs a verb.

With verbs we can turn these utterances into sentences that others will actually understand:

> Sarah *plans to go* downtown this afternoon.
> When *will* a fire drill *be scheduled*?
> If you *add* too much pepper, the sauce *will taste* spicy.

In other words, verbs help us communicate with each other.

Not every verb describes an action like shouting, dancing, or laughing. Some simply express a **state of being**. Instead of telling you what the subject does, they tell you what the subject is or was, as in:

> Charlotte *is* a fast runner.
> The tomato *is* ripe.
> Emile *was* out to lunch.

Notice that state-of-being verbs function much like equal signs in an arithmetical equation: Charlotte = fast runner; tomato = ripe; Emile = someone who is out to lunch.

The verb *is* happens to be a form of *to be*, the basic state-of-being verb. Other forms include *are, am, was, were, will be, has been, have been, had been,* and *will have been.*

Verb tenses

Verb tenses are a blessing in disguise because they instantly tell you when actions took place. Think of the verb *climbed*, for example, as in Clare *climbed* the ladder. Clare, the subject of the sentence, performed an action, and because of the *–ed* ending, signifying **past tense**, you know that Clare climbed the ladder at some time before this moment.

On the other hand, if the verb had been *climbs* instead of *climbed*, the *–s* ending, indicating the **present tense**, tells you that Clare is climbing the ladder right now, or at least that she climbs it as part of an ongoing routine, as in Clare *climbs* the ladder whenever she paints ceilings.

Changing the tense of active verbs often involves changing their endings. But it sometimes also involves adding so-called **helping verbs**, such as *has, had, have, will, and will have.* Using various verb endings and helping verbs, English offers six basic tenses to indicate the time that actions take place:

PRESENT:	I *cook* pizza every day.
PAST:	Whitney *cooked* a pizza yesterday.
FUTURE:	Ellie *will* cook a pizza tomorrow.
PRESENT PERFECT:	Lucy *has cooked* a pizza every day for the last month.
PAST PERFECT:	Lilah *had cooked* so many pizzas she got tired of them.
FUTURE PERFECT:	They all will have cooked a thousand pizzas by now.

The same six tenses apply to state-of-being verbs:

> PRESENT: *is, are, am*
> PAST: *was, were*
> FUTURE: *will be*
> PRESENT PERFECT: *has been, have been*
> PAST PERFECT: *had been*
> FUTURE PERFECT: *will have been*

Tenses allow us to express time sequences very precisely. Take, for example, the following sentence:

> When Susie *walked* (past tense) into the store she *realized* (past tense) that she *had forgotten* (past perfect) her wallet at home.

The two verbs—*walked* and *realized*—indicate that Susie's mishap took place in the past. But the verb *had forgotten* tells us that Susie's act of forgetfulness occurred before her discovery of what she had done. In other words, changes in verb tense can tell us which events happened first, which ones second, and so on.

Meaning determines which tense to use, but someone not tuned in to the purpose of various tenses might say something like:

> There was a condo where the park *was*.

The intent of the sentence is probably to say that a condo now stands in a place that once was a park. But what it really says is that the condo and the park were in the same place at the same time—a physical impossibility. Stated more precisely, the sentence should be:

> There was a condo where the park *had been*.

Using the past perfect verb *had been* conveys the meaning more accurately: The condo replaced the park.

By and large, people use correct verb tenses most of the time. But to eliminate errors completely, it helps to know the differences in meaning that each tense conveys.

- Present/Present Perfect: Present tense verbs refer to actions currently in progress; verbs in the present perfect tense refer to actions occurring at no particular time in the past and that may still be in progress.

  > Adam *is* (present) captain of the wrestling team and *has* held (present perfect) the job since sophomore year.

- Past/Past Perfect: Past tense verbs refer to action completed in the past; verbs in the past perfect tense refer to actions completed before some specific time or moment in the past. The past perfect is needed to indicate which action occurred first.

  > Before George *arrived* (past), Lenny *had killed* (past perfect) the rabbit.

- Future/Future Perfect: Verbs in the future tense refer to actions that will occur in the future; verbs in the future perfect tense refer to actions that will be completed at some time in the future, but before some other action or event.

  > Ellie will arrive in San Diego on the 15th, but by that time, Dave *will have been gone* (future perfect) for two weeks.

These distinctions may strike you as nitpicking—but knowing such subtle differences separates people who use English precisely from those who don't.

Notice how verb tenses affect meaning in the following pairs of sentences:

1. a. Benjamin *was* in the army for two years. (Benjamin is no longer in the army.)
   b. Benjamin *has been* in the army for two years. (Benjamin is still in the army.)

2. a. Dinner *had been* on the table for two hours. (Dinner is no longer on the table.)
   b. Dinner *has been* on the table for two hours. (Dinner is still on the table.)

3. a. A monument *will be erected* at the site of the battle when the general *returns*. (After the general gets back the monument will be built.)
   b. A monument *will have been erected* at the site of the battle when the general *returns*. (A monument will already have been built by the time the general gets back.)

4. a. She *has had* no luck in finding her ring. (She is still trying to find her ring.)
   b. She *had* no luck finding her ring. (In the past her search was unsuccessful, but whether she is still looking remains uncertain.)

5. a. Jenny *had driven* a delivery truck on weekends. (Jenny used to drive a truck.)
   b. Jenny *has been driving* a delivery truck on weekends. (Jenny still drives a truck.)

Shifting verb tenses

Stay alert for inconsistencies in sentences containing more than one verb:

> SHIFT: They *biked* (past) to the top of the mountain and then *come* (present) back down in time to eat lunch.

The sentence begins in the past tense but improperly shifts to the present.

> CONSISTENT: They *biked* (past) to the top of the mountain and then *came* (past) back down in time to eat lunch.

> SHIFT: By 4 o'clock all the bushes *had been pruned* (past perfect) and the grass *was* (past) watered.
> CONSISTENT: By 4 o'clock all the bushes *had been pruned* (past perfect) and the grass *had been* (past perfect) *watered*.

Consistency doesn't require every verb in a sentence to be in the same tense—far from it. But the verbs must convey the relative time that events occurred, as in:

> Henry *lost* (past) a twenty-dollar bill that *has* now *been found* (present perfect).

This sentence uses two different tenses because it's about two events that occurred at different times—namely, Henry's loss and the finding of the money.

Here's another example:

> Mike and Hessie *had dated* (past perfect) for six months before they *told* (past) their parents.

Because Mike and Hessie dated for half a year before telling their parents, the past perfect tense is needed to show the sequence of events.

More verb tense guidelines

You'll never go wrong if you remember three additional guidelines for using verb tenses:

• Use the present tense for true statements.

> Thanksgiving *falls* (present) on November 23rd this year.

In fact, use the present tense for true statements regardless of the tense of other verbs in the sentence:

> Tanisha *had been taught* (past perfect) that triangles *contain* (present) 180 degrees.

> When a sentence or clause starts with *if*, use the past perfect tense instead of *would have* to express the earlier of two actions.

• When a sentence or clause starts with *if*, use the past perfect tense instead of *would have* to express the earlier of two actions.

If Lenny *had driven* (not *would have driven*) more slowly, he would have made the curve easily.
The ceremony would have been better if Kirk *had been* (past perfect) the speaker.

• Get into the habit of adjusting participles according to the tense of the main verb (for details, turn to the discussion of participles, page 63). When a participle, which usually ends with *–ing*, indicates an action that occurred before the action named by the main verb, add *having*. Then revise the participle to the present perfect or past perfect tense.

> ORIGINAL: *Working* (participle) hard on the essay, Joan hated to reduce the number of words. (Because Joan worked hard on the essay before she got around to revising it, the participle needs to be changed.)
> REVISION: *Having worked* hard on the essay, Joan hated to reduce the number of words.
> ORIGINAL: *Walking* (participle) in the woods, Jan spotted a deer. (Because Jan was walking in the woods at the same time as she saw a deer, no change is needed.)

Checkpoint 5. VERB TENSE

Some underlined verbs in the following sentences are incorrect. Cross out the incorrect verbs and write the correct ones in the spaces provided. Some sentences contain no error.

1. <u>Coming</u> to the finals in the tournament, the team resolved to go home with the championship. _____

2. The garage mechanic thinks that at the time of the accident Mrs. Murphy <u>has owned</u> the car for only a week.

   _____

3. For anyone with enough brains to have thought about it, now <u>is</u> the time to work out the solution. _____

4. Don tells the class repeatedly that at one time New York <u>was</u> the capital of the United States. _____

5. If the wagon train <u>would have reached</u> Salt Creek in time, the massacre would have been prevented. _____

6. The aircraft controller <u>expects</u> to have spotted the plane on radar before dusk last night. _____

7. The family already <u>finished</u> dinner when the doorbell rang. _____

8. First he built a fire, then dragged a log over to use as a seat, and finally <u>collected</u> enough wood to burn all night. _____

9. Rose kept the promise she <u>has given</u> to Charles last year in India. _____

10. When he talks with Horatio, Hamlet <u>began</u> to suspect foul play in the kingdom.
_____

11. As they drove to Vermont, they <u>had stopped</u> for lunch at Burger King. _____

12. The trooper pulled him over and <u>gives</u> him a speeding ticket. _____

13. <u>Working</u> all year to improve her writing style, Debbie finally got a story published in the paper. _____

14. Matilda had taken an SAT course for six months before she <u>learns</u> how to solve that kind of problem. _____

15. That night at the show we met many people we <u>saw</u> that afternoon. _____

16. The current governor <u>lived</u> in the mansion at the present time. _____

17. <u>Reading</u> *War and Peace*, I know that Pierre falls in love with Natasha. _____

18. After the drought hit eastern Africa, the Somalis <u>began</u> to suffer. _____

19. Spring <u>came</u> before summer. _____

20. Greta does so well in her practice runs that she <u>had decided</u> to train for the New York Marathon. _____

Answers on page 51

Verb forms

You already know that verbs in the present tense regularly end in *–s* or *–es* (*runs/rushes*), and past tense verbs regularly end in *–d* or *–ed* (*smoked/shouted*). Which ending to use is generally governed by who is performing the action. If the performer(s) of the action is *I* or *we* (first person), you use one form; if the action is performed by *you* (second person) or *he, she,* or *they* (third person), you use another form. The form is also determined by the number (singular or plural) of the subject. The following chart shows various verb forms in the present, past, and perfect tenses.

	Singular	**Plural**
First person		
Present tense	I scream	we scream
	I wash	we wash
	I eat	we eat
Past tense	I screamed	we screamed
	I washed	we washed
	I ate	we ate
Present perfect/	I have/had screamed	we have/had screamed
past perfect tense	I have/had washed	we have/had washed
	I have/had eaten	we have/had eaten
Second person		
Present tense	you scream	you scream
	you wash	you wash
	you eat	you eat
Past tense	you screamed	you screamed
	you washed	you washed
	you ate	you ate
Present perfect/	you have/had screamed	you have/had screamed
past perfect tense	you have/had washed	you have/had washed
	you have/had eaten	you have/had eaten
Third person		
Present tense	he/she/it screams	they scream
	he/she/it washes	they wash
	he/she/it eats	they eat
Past tense	he/she/it screamed	they screamed
	he she/it washed	they washed
	he/she/it ate	they ate
Present perfect/	he/she/it has/had screamed	we have/had screamed
past perfect tense	he/she/it has/had washed	we have/had washed
	he/she/it has/had eaten	we have/had eaten

Most verbs change very little between tenses or when shifting between singular and plural. Usually an *–s* or *–es* is added when the verb changes from present to past in the third person. An *–ed* is added in shifts from present to past in the second person, and so on. Such changes follow a pretty regular pattern. But some verbs—called **irregular verbs**—refuse to conform. They change in ways that defy logic and include such common verbs as *sleep/slept, ride/rode, swim/swam, is/was, are/were, go/went, catch/caught,* and so on. Native speakers of English learn to use irregular verb forms as they learn to talk, although some verbs like *lie/lay* (to recline) and *lie/laid* (to place) remain a lifelong mystery for some.

English contains hundreds of irregular verbs. Here are a few dozen:

IRREGULAR VERBS

Present Tense	Past Tense	Perfect Tense (Add *have, has,* or *had*)
awake	awoke	awakened
bear	bore	borne
beat	beat	beaten
begin	began	begun
bid (to command)	bade	bidden
bite	bit	bitten
break	broke	broken
bring	brought	brought
burn	burnt or burned	burnt or burned
burst	burst	burst
catch	caught	caught
choose	chose	chosen
come	came	come
creep	crept *or* creeped	crept *or* creeped
dive	dived *or* dove	dived
dream	dreamt *or* dreamed	dreamt *or* dreamed
drink	drank	drunk
dwell	dwelt *or* dwelled	dwelt *or* dwelled
eat	ate	eaten
flee	fled	fled
fling	flung	flung
freeze	froze	frozen
go	went	gone
hide	hid	hidden
lay (to put or place)	laid	laid
lead	led	led
lend	lent	lent
lie (to recline)	lay	lain
lie (to tell an untruth)	lied	lied
ring	rang	rung
rise	rose	risen
shine	shone *or* shined	shone
shrink	shrank *or* shrunk	shrunk *or* shrunken
sing	sang	sung
sink	sank	sunk
slay	slew	slain
speak	spoke	spoken

spit	spit *or* spat	spit *or* spat
spring	sprang	sprung
steal	stole	stolen
strive	strove *or* strived	striven *or* strived
swear	swore	sworn
swim	swam	swum
tear	tore	torn
tread	trod	trod *or* trodden
wake	woke *or* waked	waked *or* woken
wear	wore	worn
write	wrote	written

Checkpoint 6.   VERB FORMS

Fill in the blanks with the correct verb form. If in doubt, refer to the list of irregular verbs above.

1. eat   They haven't _____ out in months.

2. caught   The umpire said that Reggie had _____ the ball before it touched the ground.

3. swim   They _____ across the lake in less than an hour.

4. drink   All the soda had been _____ by the end of the dance.

5. go   Charlotte had already _____ home by the time Peter arrived.

6. lay   After the burial, his widow _____ a wreath on his gravesite.

7. shine   The sun _____ all day.

8. shrink   When he put on the sweatshirt, he noticed that it had _____.

9. sing   The four of them have already _____ two songs.

10. slay   In the story the king was relieved when Theseus _____ the Minotaur.

11. steal   They concluded that the computer had been _____ over the weekend.

12. strive   All summer the crew _____ to finish the job in time.

13. awake   The sound of the smoke alarm had _____ the whole family.

14. wear   By Sunday the visitors had _____ out their welcome.

15. break   Dawn had just _____, and the floor was cold under my feet.

16. dive   No sooner had the submarine _____ than the destroyer appeared on the horizon.

17. creep   Last night the cat burglar _____ up the fire escape.

18. fling   After flunking the test, Zack _____ his math book out the window.

19. swear   Although they been _____ to secrecy, someone leaked the news to the press.

20. lead   John Wesley Powell _____ the expedition down the Green River in 1869.

Answers on page 52

The Infinitive

The basic form of all verbs is the **infinitive**, consisting of the verb and the word *to*, as in *to fly, to wander,* and *to twitter.* You can usually recognize an infinitive by putting the word *to* in front of it. If the *to* fits, chances are you've got an infinitive. If the combination makes no sense, as in *to carried, to shrunk,* and *to eating,* you can bet that the verb is in some other form.

Surprisingly, the infinitive form of a verb sometimes functions as a noun:

To shop (infinitive) is the purpose of Annie's existence.

Here the infinitive is the subject of the sentence. Infinitives can also function as adjectives and adverbs, too, but we'll get into that later.

The Subjunctive

Technically, the **subjunctive** is not a separate verb form. Rather, it's called a *mood.* Regardless of the label, though, you should know how it works because verbs change when sentences are cast in the subjunctive. The subjunctive is used to express a condition contrary to fact, usually in sentences beginning with *if, as if,* or *as though*:

If I were (not *was*) rich, I'd buy myself a sailboat. (The sentence is contrary to fact because I am not rich.)

Use the subjunctive, too, in statements expressing a wish:

I wish I were (not *was*) wealthy enough to buy a sailboat.

In each instance, the singular verb *was* has been changed to *were,* as though the subject were (not was) plural.

The subjunctive is also used to convey a sense of doubt:

If only the bus were (not *was*) uncrowded, we could find a seat.

Finally, the subjunctive is used to make a recommendation, a request, or a demand:

The lawyer insisted that her client be (not *should be*) released on bail.

An Encouraging Word to the Reader from the Author

> Having read this far, you've passed through a dense thicket of information about grammar. If some of it is confusing or even impenetrable, take heart. The truth is that it's less complicated than it may seem. So don't give up. The chapters ahead are designed to help to clear up what may now be a total muddle in your mind.

Subject-Verb Agreement

SUBJECTS and verbs must agree. That is, they must make a match, like a nut and a bolt. A mismatch occurs when a singular subject is used with a plural verb, or vice versa. That's why phrases like *the books was* and *the book were* are nonstandard usages. You should also know that this rule applies not only to sentence subjects and verbs—a topic discussed in detail on pages 57–59—but to all pairs of nouns and verbs, wherever they appear in a sentence.

Matching a subject and a verb poses few problems when the two are close or next to each other in a sentence. But, inconveniently, certain language constructions can obscure the connection and raise questions about their relationship:

Q. What happens when a clause or phrase falls between the subject and the verb?

A. Ignore the intervening words. Most of the time they have no bearing on the relationship between the subject and verb.

> MISMATCHED: *Delivery* (singular subject) of today's newspapers and magazines *have been delayed* (plural verb).

The prepositional phrase *of today's newspapers and magazines* blurs the relationship between subject and verb. The plural noun *magazines* has misled the speaker into using a plural verb.

> MATCHED: *Delivery* of today's newspapers and magazines *has been delayed*.

Also keep in mind also that common intervening words and phrases such as *in addition to, along with, as well as,* and *including* do not affect the number of the noun or the verb:

> *One* (singular subject) of his paintings, along with several sketches, *is* (singular verb) on display in the library.

Q. What should be done when the subject is composed of more than one noun or pronoun?

A. Nouns joined by *and* are called ***compound subjects*** and need plural verbs.

> The *picture and text* (compound subject) *go* (plural verb) inside this box.
> Several *locust trees and a green mailbox* (compound subject) *stand* (plural verb) outside the house.

Compound subjects thought of as a unit need singular verbs.

> *Green eggs and ham* (compound subject) *is* (singular verb) Reggie's favorite breakfast.
>
> Their *pride and joy* (compound subject), Samantha, *was* (singular verb) born on Christmas Day.

Singular nouns joined by *or* or *nor* need singular verbs.

> A Coke *or* a Pepsi *is* what I thirst for.

When the subject consists of a singular noun and a plural noun joined by *or* or *nor*, the number of the verb is determined by the noun closer to the verb.

> A subject made up of singular and plural nouns joined by *or* or *nor* requires a verb that agrees with the closer noun.

> Either *a pineapple* (singular noun) or *some oranges* (plural noun) *are* (plural verb) on the table.
>
> Neither the *linemen* (plural noun) nor the *quarterback* (singular noun) *was* (singular verb) aware of the tricky play.

When a subject contains a pronoun that differs in person from a noun or another pronoun, the verb agrees with the closer subject word.

> Neither Meredith nor *you are* expected to finish the job.
>
> Either he or *I am planning* to work late on Saturday.

When the subject is singular and the predicate noun is plural, or vice versa, the number of the verb is determined by the subject.

> The *bulk* of Wilkinson's work *is* two novels and a collection of poems.
>
> *Two novels and a collection of poems are* the bulk of Wilkinson's work.

Q. How do you handle subject words that may be either singular or plural?

A. It depends on how they are used. When a collective noun is used in its singular sense, use a singular verb. Likewise, when a collective noun is used in its plural sense, use a plural verb (see page 4 for details on collective nouns).

> The *majority* (singular) *favors* (singular) a formal senior prom.
>
> The *majority* (plural) *have* (plural) their tickets for the boat ride.

Q. What if subject words are singular but sound plural?

A. The names of books, countries, organizations, certain diseases, course titles, and other singular nouns may sound like plurals because they end in "s," but they usually require a singular verb.

> The *news is* good.
>
> *Measles is* going around the school.
>
> The *World Series is* played in October.

Q. What about subjects that consist of indefinite pronouns?

A. Indefinite pronouns like *everyone, both,* and *any* pose a special problem because a correct match depends on the sense of the sentence (for details, see page 10).

> *Some* of the collection *is* valuable. (*Some* is singular because it refers to collection, a singular noun.)
> *Some* of the bracelets *are* fake. (*Some* is plural because it refers to bracelets, a plural noun.)
> *None* of the ice cream *is* left.
> *None* of the people *are* going to be left behind.

Q. How do you handle sentences in which the verb precedes the subject?

A. No differently. Treat the subject and verb as though they came in the usual order—subject before verb.

> MISMATCHED: Here *comes* (singular verb) my *brother and sister* (plural subject).
> MATCHED: Here *come* (plural verb) my brother and sister.

Errors in subject-verb agreement often occur when the writer or speaker loses track of the subject of the sentence. Once the subject is nailed down, however, everything else, including the verb, usually falls into place. So, the key to agreement between subject and verb is no secret: **Identify the subject and keep your eye on it.** If finding the subject perplexes you in any way, you should study "*To find the 'bare bones' of a sentence*" (page 62), the surefire technique for finding the subject of any sentence.

Checkpoint 7. SUBJECT-VERB AGREEMENT

In some of the sentences below, nouns and verbs do not agree. Locate the error and write the corrected version in the space provided. Some sentences may be correct.

1. Brian's talent in acting and singing, two of the most important criteria for getting parts in plays, almost assure Brian that he'll have a role in this spring's musical.

   _____

2. The original play, which tells the story of thirteen young actors who aspire to succeed in show business careers, were one of history's most popular Broadway productions.

   _____

3. At the end of their first year in New York, the close-knit group, regardless of whether they earned stage parts, begin to split up.

   _____

4. On second thought, either Brian or you is going to be the male lead in the play.

   _____

5. Jane and Melissa, who starred in the show last spring, have decided not to try out this year.

   _____

6. There is many younger kids who will be glad to know that everybody has an equal chance to get a role in the production.

   _____

7. This year's admission proceeds from the play is going toward rebuilding the school's gazebo, burned down by vandals last summer.

   _____

8. The school paper reports that a committee of students and teachers are going to decide who get a role in the play.

   _____

9. Before the administration laid them off, neither the director nor the producer were told that their jobs were in danger.

   _____

10. Many teachers and parents claim that new policies in the drama department has had an adverse effect on morale.

    _____

11. Reading play reviews printed in the newspaper is a desirable thing to do by everyone who expect to develop a deep understanding of theater arts.

    _____

12. Plays, produced both on Broadway and in regional theaters, have always been one of Brian's passions.

    _____

13. Arthur Miller, along with his contemporary Tennessee Williams, are among the most impressive playwrights.

    _____

14. Katie Green, one of the best pianists in the school, and her brother Gene, who also plays extremely well, has been invited to provide musical accompaniment.

    _____

15. Nancy Atkins, along with her friend Sluggo, expect to be in charge of sets.

    _____

16. A number of innovative ideas for using the school's new lighting and sound systems have created enormous enthusiasm for the show.

    _____

17. Here's the costumes that were used last year.

    _____

18. The school board's insistence on high production standards are putting pressure on the stage crew and the production staff.

_____

19. It's so bad that members of the school band, in spite of how they all feel about the issue, wants to participate.

_____

20. According to school policy, there is to be two security guards stationed in the auditorium during each performance.

_____

Answers on page 53

THE ADJECTIVE

> Many adjectives are fickle. Sometimes they're adjectives, and at other times they're nouns.

ADJECTIVES are describers. They are the words that describe colors, sizes, and shapes, as well as the look and condition of things, feelings, and other qualities of every imaginable sort. Grammatically speaking, adjectives **MODIFY** nouns, which means they describe or limit them, turning, say, an *ordinary* day into one that is *sunny, boring, momentous, thrilling, wretched, frantic,* or *memorable.* They turn nights *dark* or *starry,* turn friends *loyal* or *hostile,* make food *nutritious* or *greasy.* How many adjectives exist no one can tell, but they give users of English unlimited opportunities for describing people, places, experiences, and things.

Not every adjective is so obviously an adjective as words such as *big* or *buxom* or *blissful.* Some adjectives also function as nouns. Take *baseball,* for instance. In the sentence Baseball rocks, *baseball* is a noun, but in The baseball game ended with a home run, *baseball* is an adjective modifying *game.* Incidentally, there are countless nouns, from *absolute* to *zigzag,* that can also serve as adjectives.

Some words neither look nor feel like adjectives. Yet, they belong to the adjective family because in their fashion they act more or less like adjectives. The articles *the, a,* and *an,* for instance, tell you whether a noun is specific (*the train, the olive, the principle*) or nonspecific (*a train, an olive, a principle*). Likewise, such words as *this, that, those,* and *these,* along with other types of pronouns—*his, her, our, their, my, your*—and words like *some, many, much,* and *few,* act like adjectives because they modify nouns, as in:

> *This* faded shirt is mine. (The word *this* identifies the shirt: It's not any scruffy old shirt, it's *this* one.)
> *Our* trip took four hours. (The word *our* identifies whose trip it was.)

Compound Adjectives

Although single-word adjectives are most common, *compound* adjectives—usually pairs of words such as: *world-famous, so-called, short-term, well-known, poorly organized*—show up frequently in speech and writing. In fact, three, four, five, or even more words can be strung together to make compound adjectives such as *off-the-wall* and *never-to-be-forgotten.* Notice that *hyphens* separate the words in compound adjectives. Don't jump to the conclusion, however, that every compound adjective needs a hyphen. The fact is that compound adjectives that come before the noun they modify usually contain hyphens, and those that follow usually don't:

> Arnold Schwarzenegger is a *world-famous* actor/governor.
> Actor/Governor Arnold Schwarzenegger is *world famous*.

Adjective Phrases and Clauses

We've seen that nouns and articles assume the role of adjectives. The same goes for phrases and clauses. Take, for example:

> The snow on the grass melted.

The noun *snow* is described, or modified, by the phrase *on the grass*, which describes the particular snow that melted. It wasn't the snow on the roof or the snow in Buffalo that melted, but the snow on the grass. Thus, the phrase *on the grass* acts like an adjective.

In the same manner, the italicized phrases in the following sentences serve as stand-ins for adjectives by modifying the underlined nouns.

> Look at Cyrano, the <u>man</u> *with the six-inch nose.*
> The *funniest* <u>jokes</u> *ever told* was the topic of my term paper.
> The gas <u>pumps</u> *marked "self-serve"* need to be replaced.
> A <u>deer</u> *hit by a car* lay on the road.

If phrases can serve as substitute adjectives, logic dictates that clauses can, too. Indeed, you'd be hard pressed to find many prose passages that don't contain adjective clauses—clauses that typically begin with the relative pronouns *that, which, who, whose,* or *whom* (go back to page 16 for a quick review of relative pronouns). Notice how the italicized clauses in the sentences below modify the underlined nouns:

> The <u>recording</u>, *which sold more than two million copies*, made Bruce Springsteen a household name.
> The <u>children</u> *who need a time-out* should go right to the flagpole.
> This is the <u>scene</u> *that always makes me cry*.
> <u>Most</u> of the battalion, *many of whom came from the Iowa National Guard*, decided to reenlist.

Comparing with Adjectives

The world is full of people described by the adjective *smart*. But some people are smarter than others, and someone is the smartest of them all—maybe you! In other words, there are degrees of smartness that can be compared with each other.

A unique feature of adjectives is that they come in different forms that allow you to make such comparisons. **Degrees of comparison** are indicated by endings, usually *–er* and *–est*, as in *smarter* and *smartest*, but also by the use of *more/most* and *less/least*, as in *more brilliant, most talented, less gifted,* and *least competent*.

English offers three degrees of comparison: ***positive, comparative***, and ***superlative***.

Positive	Comparative	Superlative
tall	taller	tallest
dark	darker	darkest
ugly	uglier	ugliest
handsome	handsomer *or* more handsome	handsomest *or* most handsome
cool	cooler	coolest
graceful	more graceful	most graceful
prepared	less prepared	least prepared
able	abler *or* more able	ablest *or* most able

As you can tell from this list, you form adjectives in the comparative degree by adding *-er* or putting *more* (or *less*) in front of the positive form. And to form adjectives in the superlative degree, you add *-est* or *most* (or *least*) in front of the positive form. But, as always, there are exceptions, among them: *good/better/best; well/better/best, bad/worse/worst, little/less/least, much/more/most,* and *many/more/most.*

You might also have gathered that *-er/-est* endings apply mainly to one-syllable words (*late/ later/latest*). The *more-most/less-least* pattern relates to words of two or more syllables (*more famous, most nauseous, less skillful, least beautiful*). Some two-syllable words follow the guidelines for words of one syllable (*pretty/ prettier/ prettiest*), although you can also say *more pretty* or *most pretty.*

Here are some additional facts to know about making comparisons:

- Three-syllable adjectives and all adjectives ending in *-ly* use the *more/most* or *less/least* combination (*most luxurious, less comfortable*).

- The comparative degree is used to compare two things.

> Use adjectives in the *comparative degree* to compare **two** things.
>
> Use adjectives in the *superlative degree* to compare **three or more** things.

This test was *harder* than that one. (Two tests are being compared.)
My *younger* sister takes dancing lessons. (The speaker has two sisters.)

- The superlative degree should be used to compare three or more things.

This is the *hardest* test we've had all year. (They've had at least three tests.)
Maria's *youngest* sister takes dancing lessons. (Maria has at least three sisters.)

Don't use *more, most, less,* and *least* in the same phrase with adjectives in the comparative or superlative degrees. For example, avoid phrases like *more friendlier, less prouder, most sweetest,* and *least safest.* Because such phrases make double comparisons, they contain redundancies.

Also, stay alert for several dozen *absolute* adjectives—adjectives whose meaning keeps them from being used to make comparisons. For instance, if you are *dead* or *pregnant*, that's it! You can't be "deader" or "deadest," or "more pregnant" than someone else. The same holds true for such common adjectives as *complete, final, square, full, superior, basic, empty, ultimate, fatal, perfect*, and *extreme*. Also, beware of *unique*, a particular troublemaker. By definition, *unique* means one of a kind. Therefore, it makes no sense to say "more" or "most unique."

Finally, be mindful of the difference between the adjectives *less* and *fewer*. Use *less* to refer to singular nouns: *less rain, less cocoa, less fighting*. Use *fewer* for plurals: *fewer people, fewer tickets, fewer voyages*. Put another way, reserve *fewer* for things that can be counted: *fewer children, fewer dollars, fewer cans of beans*. And save *less* to refer to nouns that can't or aren't likely to be counted: *less salt, less air*, and *less hostility*. There are exceptions, of course, like *less money*.

Checkpoint 8. COMPARATIVE DEGREE

Find the errors in comparative degree in the following sentences. Write the correct usage in the spaces provided. Some sentences may be correct.

1. Ross is a lot more rich than his brother.

   _____

2. Although Stephen King and Tom Clancy write thrilling books, King is the best storyteller.

   _____

3. Of all the colleges Bill visited, Pomona stood out as the most unique one.

   _____

4. This is by far the greater tuna-noodle casserole that I have ever eaten.

   _____

5. Sarah is about the forgetfulest person I've ever met.

   _____

6. Of all of Shakespeare's plays, *Hamlet* is the more popular.

   _____

7. Jim couldn't tell who is most stubborn—his sister or his brother.

   _____

8. Both situations were terrible, but Ron first tried to fix the worst of the two.

   _____

9. The climbers would be smart to take the less harder route to the summit.

   _____

10. After weighing the three fish he caught, Phil decided to throw the lightest one back.

_____

11. Lynne's victory was more sweeter because her opponent had beaten her last year.

_____

12. Bill's idea was profounder than Al's.

_____

13. Both I-95 and the parkway will take you to New Haven, but the latter is the fastest route.

_____

14. Because they received the new flu vaccine, the people are immuner than they were last year.

_____

15. That was the most unkindest remark I ever heard.

_____

16. Trust became a bigger issue than either taxes or crime in the election campaign.

_____

17. Because of the weather, Frankie's team played less games than last year.

_____

18. Because she felt unsure about her performance, the result was more nicer.

_____

19. Which is longest—the Mississippi River or the Colorado?

_____

20. In the autumn, Vermont has prettier colors than most other states.

_____

Answers on page 54

THE ADVERB

Adverbs answer such questions as How? When? Where? How much? In what way? In what manner?

The **ADVERB** is first cousin to the adjective. Both words describe—or modify—other words. Adjectives modify nouns; adverbs modify verbs. By modifying verbs, adverbs tell *how, why, when, where, how much, in what way,* or *to what degree* an action occurred. They answer such questions as *How did the action occur? When did it take place? Where did it happen?* and so on.

Dad snored *loudly*.

Here, the adverb *loudly* describes *how* Dad snored: He snored loudly.

Mom *immediately* poked him in the ribs.

Here, the adverb *immediately* tells *when* Mom did something about it: She poked him *right away. (Right away,* by the way, is an **adverbial phrase**—a phrase that functions like an adverb.)

Adverbs not only modify verbs, but also adjectives and other adverbs. Regardless of which words they modify, however, they always answer the same sorts of questions: How? When? Where? How much? In what way? In what manner?

Dad is *completely* unaware of the sounds he makes.

Here, *completely* is an adverb modifying the adjective *unaware.* It tells *to what degree* Dad is aware of his nocturnal snorts and wheezes. In a word, Dad is oblivious.

All through the night, he sleeps *remarkably soundly.*

This sentence contains two adverbs—*soundly* modifying the verb *sleeps,* and *remarkably,* which modifies *soundly,* an adverb that intensifies the depth of Dad's sleep: Dad doesn't just sleep soundly; he sleeps *remarkably* soundly.

Many adverbs come directly from adjectives. Add an *-ly* to an adjective and *voila!* you've got an adverb, as in *slow/slowly, late/lately, regular/regularly, indiscriminate/indiscriminately.* In fact, an *-ly* ending frequently says "Hey, this word is an adverb." But don't bet the farm on it, because plenty of adjectives also end with *-ly* (*lonely, sickly, daily, lovely*), and adverbs themselves come in all sorts of guises, among them:

How?	When?	Where?	How much?	In what way?
bravely	recently	here	exhaustively	extensively
glumly	soon	there	relentlessly	by all means
well	now	nowhere	often	in some respects
without a doubt	off and on	in town	heart and soul	sincerely

Adverbial phrases serve the same purpose as single-word adverbs: They modify verbs, adjectives, and other adverbs:

> Timothy *is* (verb), ***without a doubt*** (adverbial phrase), the world's worst waiter.
> Not only is he *gruff* (adjective) ***beyond belief*** (adverbial phrase), but he can't remember what people order.
> He treats customers so *discourteously* (adverb) ***to begin with*** (adverbial phrase) that they flee the restaurant without eating.

Adverbial clauses also function like adverbs, modifying verbs, adjectives, and adverbs. The italicized adverbial clauses in these sentences modify the underlined verbs:

> ***Unless the mail comes before noon,*** you <u>will miss</u> the deadline.
> <u>Watch out</u> when you give the news to Gertie *because she is short tempered.*
> Hank, *even though he's old enough to drive,* <u>prefers to ride</u> a bicycle.

Placing adverbs in sentences

Recognizing an adverb when you meet one can help you analyze sentences, but placing it properly into a sentence is far more useful. In fact, where you put an adverb can steer the meaning and intent of a sentence in different directions. For instance, in the following pair of sentences, the placement of the adverb could make a huge difference to a boy named Mike and a girl named Sharon:

> Mike *only* loves Sharon.

Here the adverb *only* modifies the verb *loves*. The position of *only* is appropriate if Mike feels nothing but love for Sharon—no admiration, no awe, no respect, nor any other emotion. But if Mike has but one love in his life, and she is Sharon, then *only* is misplaced. Properly placed, *only* should come either before or after *Sharon*:

> Mike loves *only* Sharon.
> or
> Mike loves Sharon *only*.

Now Sharon knows where she stands with Mike, and together maybe they'll live happily ever after.

Splitting Infinitives

In everyday speech and writing, splitting the two parts of an infinitive with an adverb is a common practice. But it's not good form, especially when the split is unnecessary, because either way the meaning of the sentence is the same:

> SPLIT: It felt creepy *to,* after all this time, *visit* my elementary school.
> UNSPLIT: It felt creepy after all this time *to visit* my elementary school.
> SPLIT: The nurses were trained *to* silently *enter*.
> UNSPLIT: The nurses were trained *to enter* silently.

Even though some guardians of pure English object to splitting infinitives, doing so may occasionally be the most accurate way to express an idea, as in:

> The hikers neglected to thoroughly clean up the campsite.

A version with the adverb inserted before the infinitive fails to deliver the same message:

> The hikers neglected thoroughly to clean up the campsite.

And were you to put the adverb after the infinitive—well, you'd mangle the language but good:

> The hikers neglected to clean up thoroughly the campsite.

Making comparisons with adverbs

Adverbs follow the same pattern as adjectives when they are used to make comparisons. When you compare two qualities, for instance, add an -*er* or use *more* before the adverb. To compare three or more things, add -*est* or use *most* before the adverb.

Which form to use depends largely on syllable count. One-syllable adverbs use -*er* and -*est*:

> Mitzi drives *fast*.
> Mitch drives *faster*.
> Mike drives *fastest* of all.

Adverbs of two or more syllables, including all adverbs with -*ly* endings, use *more* or *most*:

> Mitzi eats *quickly*.
> Mitch eats *more quickly*.
> Mike eats *most quickly*.

Adverbs vs. Adjectives

Most of the time, choosing between an adverb or an adjective is a simple matter. But occasionally it can pose a problem, even when the words are seemingly simple, such as when choosing between *good* and *well*.

A few pages back you learned that adjectives describe, or modify, nouns and pronouns. In the phrase "good book," for example, the adjective *good* modifies *book*. That's easy enough. But *good*, along with some other adjectives, may cause trouble when used after a verb, as in *talks good, drives good, writes good*—all nonstandard phrases.

Yet, *good* is perfectly acceptable after some verbs, called **linking verbs,** such as *look, smell, taste, feel, appear, stay, seem, remain, grow, become*, and all forms of *to be*. Therefore, such phrases as *sounds good, feels good*, and *smells good* are perfectly correct.

The guidelines for using adjectives are generally straightforward. But grammar, being grammar, occasionally throws you curveballs. Here is one of them: Linking verbs are sometimes used as active verbs. For example, *look* is a linking verb when it refers to someone's health or appearance, as in *He looks good in that hat*. But *look* becomes an active verb when it refers to the act of looking, as in *Margie looked sadly at her sick cat*. In such cases, an adverb (*sadly*) is correct, whereas an adjective (*sad*) is not.

To determine whether the verb is a linking verb or an active verb, substitute a form of *to be* in its place. If the sentence retains its basic meaning, the verb is probably a linking verb. For instance:

> Claude *climbs* a ladder well./Claude *is* a ladder well.

Because the second sentence makes no sense, *climbs* is clearly not a linking verb.

> The salad *tastes* spicy. /The salad *is* spicy.

Because the two sentences have essentially the same meaning, *tastes* is a linking verb. Therefore, *tastes* may not be followed by an adverb such as *well, sweetly, weirdly*, and so on. Instead, use whatever adjective suits you: *good, sweet, weird, bland, spoiled*, etc.

Checkpoint 9. USING ADVERBS

Check each sentence for proper placement and use of adverbs. If you find an error, write a correct version of the sentence in the space provided. Some sentences may be correct.

1. The trekkers felt bitterly that they had been abandoned by their guide.

   _____

2. Rover smelled badly after swimming in the swamp.

   _____

3. Of the two sisters, Janie swims most quickly but Marnie dives best.

   _____

4. Lauren felt anxious before her college interview.

   _____

5. No problem, I can do both jobs as easy as pie.

   _____

6. Amy sounded sincere when she apologized to Alberto.

   _____

7. Be sure to proceed slow through the construction zone.

   _____

8. The generalissimo looked down cynical on the people gathered in the plaza below.

   _____

9. This soup tastes badly. Give me another kind, please.

   _____

10. Of all the songs in the show, I more fully enjoyed "The Stomp."

    _____

11. The coach talked slow about the team's decline during the second half.

    _____

12. José always feels good after a long workout and a hot shower.

    _____

13. At graduation, he mounted the stage happy to pick up his diploma.

    _____

14. I expected to early get up this morning, but I lolled around in bed until noon.

    _____

15. The water in the pool felt coldly this morning.

    _____

16. Diana learned to play the piano good by taking lessons from Mr. Mittler.

    _____

17. Has he told you lately that he loves you truly?

    _____

18. Jack chose a comfortable place to lie down and slept more comfortable than he did the night before.

    _____

19. When the kitten decided to finally eat, it scampered over to the saucer of milk.

    _____

20. They felt their way uncertainly along the walls of the dark cave.

    _____

Answers on page 55

THE PREPOSITION

A **PREPOSITION** is defined as a word (or sometimes a phrase) that can connect a noun or pronoun to some other piece of a sentence. That's a pretty fuzzy definition, isn't it?

So, let's try to do better. How about this: In your mind's eye, picture a flying airplane and a puffy cloud. The plane can fly *to* the cloud, *through* the cloud, *above* the cloud, *under* the cloud, and so forth. All the words in italics—*to*, *through*, *above*, and *under*—are prepositions, serving to show the relative position of one object, the plane, to another, the cloud. (Notice the word *position* within the word pre*position*.) English offers dozens of other prepositions that more or less refer to location, among them: *at, off, between, among, over, beside, near, onto, out, past, toward, with, within, behind,* and *across.*

Another group of prepositions enables you to express the relative time when events took place, among them: *before, after, during, since, until.*

Still other prepositions serve to connect and compare objects and ideas, as in:

He walks *like* a duck, *unlike* Jim, who walks *like* a chicken.
No one is as good *as* you at throwing horseshoes.
Except *for* Marion, no one at the party wanted to be there.
Because of you, my life is now worthwhile.

You won't find prepositions wandering around on the loose. They are always attached to nouns or pronouns in what are known as ***prepositional phrases***: *to* the country, *over* him, *after* the ball, *in accordance with* her wishes. Grammatically speaking, the noun or pronoun in a prepositional phrase is called the ***object of the preposition***, which means, in terms of pronouns at least, that you must use the objective case. (Remember that pronouns fall mainly into two cases—the nominative and the objective? Turn to page 6 to refresh your memory.) Therefore, *between* (preposition) you and *I* (*I* is a nominative case pronoun) is incorrect. Instead use *between* you and *me* (*me* is a pronoun in the objective case).

> A pronoun serving as the object of a preposition must be in the objective case. Therefore, say *between you and me,* not *between you and I.*

NONSTANDARD: The toll collector argued *with* Harry and *I.*
STANDARD: The toll collector argued *with* Harry and *me.*

Take note of these four additional issues involving prepositions:

• **When to use *like* and when to use *as***

Like is a preposition used for making comparisons. Because *like* introduces a prepositional phrase, it must be followed by a noun or pronoun, as in

Barney looks *like* my dog.
My dog looks *like* me.

(*Like* can also be a verb, a noun, an adjective, or an adverb—but that's a matter that needn't concern us now.)

As—along with its chums *as if* and *as though*—is a **conjunction** (a discussion of conjunctions comes up next.) *As* introduces clauses and is followed by a verb, as in

Alice does *as* her father says.
Do *as* I say, not *as* I do.

When you are uncertain whether to use *like* or *as*, look for a verb. If a verb follows, you'll know that *as* is the word to use. For instance:

Every day the child acts more *like* her mother (no verb).
He acts *as if* he *had seen* (verb) Elvis alive.

In comparisons the verb may sometimes be left out to avoid wordiness. So stay alert for usages in which the verb is optional, as in:

Melissa loves the city as much *as* I (do).

- **When to use *between;* when to use *among***

Use *between* to refer to anything split into two or divided by two, such as the trail mix that Barbie split *between* Ken and herself. Use *among* for a division by more than two, say, the seven famished hikers who divided a bag of Doritos *among* themselves. Also:

> *Among* the three of us, we ought to figure out the solution.
> We should probably choose *between* Sam's and Kathy's answers.

- **Ending a sentence with a preposition**

English teachers have fought hard to keep students from ending sentences with prepositions. It's a losing battle, however, because the rule often forces you to use odd-sounding language, as in:

> After the test, we had many things *about* which to talk.

You'd probably raise some eyebrows on the school bus if you talked like that. In the 21st century, it's far more natural to say

> After the test, we had many things to talk *about*.

Yet, you should respect the restriction against sentence-ending prepositions whenever possible. A reasonable rule of thumb to follow is to avoid sentence-ending prepositions, unless by so doing you'll end up sounding phony or pompous.

- **The idiomatic use of prepositions**

Many words go hand in hand with certain prepositions. That's why *wait for the bus* is standard English, whereas *wait on the bus* is not. Yet, you can *wait for a table* or *wait on a table*, depending on whether you intend to eat lunch or serve it. In short, there is no consistent logic why certain words go with certain prepositions. Customary English idiom simply obliges you to choose your prepositions with care.

> NONSTANDARD: Maude stepped *in* a puddle.
> STANDARD: Maude stepped *into* a puddle.
> NONSTANDARD: I sympathize *on* your loss.
> STANDARD: I sympathize *with* your loss.

Keep in mind, among many others:

agree *to* (a thing), agree *with* (a person)
angry *at* (a thing), angry *with* (a person)
compare *to* (for illustration), compare *with* (to examine qualities)
concern *in* (be interested), concern *for* (troubled), concern *with* (involved)
concur *in* (an opinion), concur *with* (a person)
differ *from* (things), differ *with* (a person)

Checkpoint 10. PREPOSITIONS AND PREPOSITIONAL PHRASES

In the spaces below write a short sentence that includes the preposition in parentheses. In each, underline the prepositional phrase and circle the object of the preposition.

1. (in) _____

2. (about) _____

3. (into) _____

4. (toward) _____

5. (besides) _____

6. (contrary to) _____

7. (aside from) _____

8. (in lieu of) _____

9. (during the course of) _____

10. (inasmuch as) _____

Answers on page 56

THE CONJUNCTION

CONJUNCTIONS work hard but earn little credit. They are the glue that ties words, phrases, and clauses together. And the conjunction that does more gluing than any other is the word *and*, as in ham *and* eggs, Romeo *and* Juliet, and yesterday *and* today. Notice that the previous sentence began with this very hardworking conjunction. In formal speech and writing, it's best to avoid starting a sentence with *and* or its close companion *but*, but in more casual communication it's done all the time. But don't do it too often, because it can get monotonous.

Both *and* and *but* belong to a group of seven **_coordinating conjunctions_**. The others are *or*, *yet*, *for*, *nor*, and *so*, easily remembered using the acronymn BOYFANS [C. Edward Good, *A Grammar Book for You and I . . .Oops, Me!*, Capital Books, 2002, p. 150]. Coordinating conjunctions get their name from their function—joining equivalent words, phrases, and clauses.

> Please pick up some bread *or* rolls (two nouns) for dinner.
> So close, *yet* so far (two phrases).
> I love you, *but* you don't love me (two clauses).

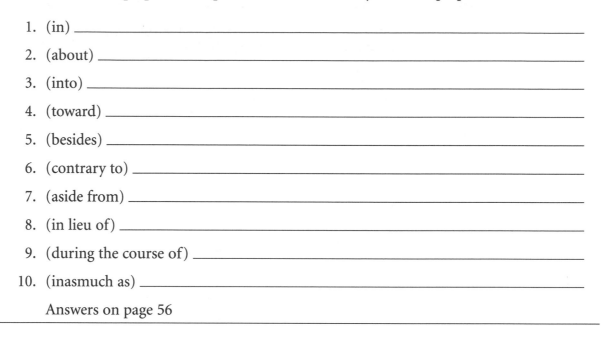

A coordinating conjunction that links two or more independent clauses results in a compound sentence.

A coordinating conjunction that links two or more clauses results in a **_compound sentence_** consisting of coordinated ideas of more-or-less equal rank (the next chapter explains the ins and outs of *compound* and other types of sentences). If the ideas in a compound sentence seem unrelated or are otherwise mismatched, the choice of conjunction could be at fault, but more than likely the ideas themselves may be at odds with each other:

My sister got married *and* she wolfed down a peanut butter and jelly sandwich.

In spite of rumors to the contrary, getting married and gobbling up a PBJ sandwich are not equivalent or connected actions, so unless the sentence was meant as a joke, a revision is in order.

How to fix the incongruity shouldn't be a problem, provided you employ another kind of conjunction, called a **subordinating conjunction**, which allows you to link two seemingly unrelated ideas in a single sentence.

> *After* getting married, my sister wolfed down a peanut butter and jelly sandwich.

By using the subordinating conjunction *after*, the sentence now makes slightly more sense, however surreal.

For another example, say that you wanted to convey what seem like two unrelated facts: 1) Jody rushed to school, and 2) Jody put on mascara.

> Subordinating conjunctions help you to link two disparate ideas in a single sentence.

The link between these two statements can be quickly clarified with a subordinating conjunction. Let's use *while*:

> *While* she rushed to school, Jody put on mascara.

Or the sentence might have been stated:

> *While* she put on mascara, Jody rushed to school.

In each sentence the less important idea—that is, the *subordinate* idea—is contained in the subordinate clause, that is, the part of the sentence that starts with the subordinating conjunction.

Some other common subordinating conjunctions are *although, as if, as though, because, before, if, in order to, since, so that, that, though, unless, until, when, whenever, where, whereas, wherever,* and *whether.* It's useful to keep in mind that subordinate clauses, also called **dependent clauses,** cannot stand alone as complete sentences. In other words, they depend grammatically on **independent clauses** . . . but let's leave the nitty-gritty of clauses alone for now. Details are on deck.

A third type of conjunction, called a **correlative conjunction,** comes in pairs: *neither-nor, either-or, whether-or not, both-and, not only-but also.* Some pairs are almost inseparable. You'll rarely find *either* without *or* or *neither* without *nor.*

> I'll *either* go for a walk *or* go to sleep when I get home.
> *Neither* rain *nor* sleet will keep me from seeing you tonight.
> Lucy excels in school *not only* as a student *but also***** as an athlete.

*In this sentence, *also* is optional.

Because correlative conjunctions can't swap partners, avoid *either-nor* and *neither-or* combinations.

Checkpoint 11. CONJUNCTIONS

Underline the conjunctions in the sentences below. Then name the type of conjunction it is by writing (COO for "coordinating," SUB for "subordinating," and COR for "correlative" in the space that follows. Some sentences may contain no conjunctions.

1. Without a doubt, the bike we saw was neither new nor in good condition.

---

2. Still and all, I think we should buy it, fix it up, and sell it for a profit.

   _____

3. Although it's expensive, there is a strong market out there for used bikes.

   _____

4. Not only can we make lots of money, but we will learn about the business.

   _____

5. We haven't got all the skills we need, so it's a little risky.

   _____

6. But since you have the tools and I have the space for a bike repair shop, we can be equal partners.

   _____

7. We have no experience, yet I think we ought to try.

   _____

8. So that we can avoid conflict, we should decide ahead of time who has the final say in making important decisions.

   _____

9. Whatever happens, though, we must be prepared for failure because most small businesses fold within a year.

   _____

10. Whether or not we end up doing this, the thought of starting a business is exciting but a little intimidating.

    _____

Answers on page 56

ANSWER KEY

Page 9, Personal Pronouns

1. me   Because "my sister" and the speaker received the action (they were taken to the show), use the *object* pronoun.

2. her, him   Object pronouns are needed because the pair (*her* and *him*) were being acted upon; they were being seen.

3. me   Because the speaker received the action (they were being asked), use the object pronoun.

4. me   The phrase *you and me* is the object of the preposition *between*.

5. him   The pronoun *him* is the object of the preposition *for*.

6. he   The phrase *Roxanne and he* is the subject of the sentence. Therefore, use the subject pronoun *he*.

7. I   The pronoun *I* is part of the subject of the sentence.

8. me   The phrase *me and my sister* is the object of the preposition *between*.

9. we   Choose the pronoun that would be used if the final verb had been included (*harder than <u>we</u> laughed*).

10. we   *We* is the subject of the sentence.

Page 11, Pronoun Shift and Pronoun Agreement

1. . . . his term paper   The antecedent *everyone* is singular; the pronoun *their* is plural.

2. . . . one collects   The switch from *one* to *she* is a shift in pronoun person. (This is not an error in informal writing and speech.)

3. . . . its collection   The antecedent *library* is singular; the pronoun *their* is plural.

4. . . . owns her own car   The antecedent *Each* is singular; the pronoun *their* is plural.

5. No error

6. . . . you should   The switch from *you* to *one* is a shift in pronoun person. (This is not an error in informal writing and speech.)

7. . . . himself   The antecedent *individual* is singular; the pronoun *themselves* is plural.

8. . . . its rider   The antecedent *each horse* is singular; the pronoun *their* is plural.

9. . . . its first match   The antecedent *team* is singular; the pronoun *their* is plural.

10. . . . one can't, one should   The switch from *one* to *you* is a change in person; also, the antecedent *one* is singular; the pronoun *they* is plural.

Page 13, Pronoun References

These are only suggestions. Your sentence may eliminate pronoun reference problems just as effectively as these.

1. When we teenagers loiter outside the theater on Friday night, the manager gives us a hard time.

2. I took the test and handed it in after collecting my pencils and pens.

3. The root of their problem is that Barbara told Ken that she wanted only a short wedding trip to Florida.

4. Bob had only an hour to get to the airport, and his father told him so.

5. During her tenure in office, Mrs. Clinton traveled more than any other secretary of state.

6. Henry disapproved of war, but he drove his ambulance to the front lines anyway.

7. After the campus tour, Mike said to Todd, "I think I'll be happy going to Auburn."

8. Peggy hit a truck, but her car wasn't even dented.

9. Within the last month, Andy's older brother Pete made his parents very happy by finding a new job and marrying Felicia. But he also broke his leg while skiing.

10. She wore her new black leather jacket to school.

Page 19, Pronoun Problems

1.	. . . and *I*	Reflexive pronouns may not be used as the subject of a sentence.
2.	. . . *whom* I like	Use *whom* when it functions as the object of the verb.
3.	. . . *you* should	Sentences cast in the second person should remain so throughout.
4.	. . . Stacy and *me*	Use the objective case when the pronoun is the object of a preposition.
5.	. . . scared *them* . . . *their*	Plural pronouns are needed for plural antecedents.
6.	. . . *which* once	Use *which* to refer to nonessential information in a relative clause.
7.	When *I* . . .	Reflexive pronouns may not be used as the subject of a sentence or a clause.
8.	. . . *one* practices *one's* or . . . *you* must . . .	Sentences cast in the third person should remain so throughout. Informally, a switch from "one" to "he/she practices" and "his/her instrument" is acceptable. Another possibility: Cast the whole sentence into second person (*you . . . your*).
9.	*He and I*	Use subject pronouns in the subject of a sentence.
10.	. . . *his* seat belt	Use singular pronouns to refer to singular antecedents.
11.	To *whom* . . .	Use *whom* in a prepositional phrase.
12.	. . . *they* were done	Plural pronouns are needed for plural antecedents.
13.	No error	

14. . . . *his* reservation	Use singular pronouns to refer to singular antecedents.
15. . . . person *who*	Use *who* to refer to people.
. . . *his* own	Use singular pronouns to refer to singular antecedents.
16. . . . and *me,*	Use the objective case when a pronoun is the object of a
. . . *us* girls	preposition and when a pronoun is the object of the verb.
17. *This* includes	Use singular pronouns to refer to singular antecedents.
. . . asking *occupants*	Pronouns require specific antecedents.
18. . . . *who* give	Use *who* to refer to people.
19. . . . and *him*	Use an object pronoun when it functions as the object of the verb.
20. . . . *they* had . . . *on them*	Plural pronouns are needed for plural antecedents.

Page 24, Verb Tense

1. Having come	A participle describing an action that occurred before the action of the main verb must include *having* plus the present or past perfect form of the verb.
2. had owned	The past perfect tense refers to actions completed in the past before some other past action.
3. No error	
4. had been	The past perfect tense refers to actions completed in the past before some other past action.
5. had reached	When a sentence or clause starts with *if,* use the past perfect tense to express the earlier of two actions.
6. had expected	The past perfect tense refers to actions completed in the past before some other past action.
7. had finished	The past perfect tense refers to actions completed in the past before some other past action.
8. No error	
9. had given	The past perfect tense refers to actions completed in the past before some other past action.
10. begins	The same tense is used to describe events occurring at the same time.
11. stopped	The same tense is used to describe events occurring at the same time.

12. gave	Sentences cast in one tense should remain in that tense unless a shift in time has occurred.
13. Having worked	A participle describing an action that occurred before the action of the main verb must include *having* plus the present or past perfect form of the verb.
14. learned	Past tense verbs refer to action completed in the past.
15. had seen	The past perfect tense refers to actions completed in the past before some other past action.
16. lives	Present tense refers to actions and conditions currently in progress.
17. Having read	A participle describing an action that occurred before the action of the main verb must include *having* plus the present or past perfect form of the verb.
18. No error	
19. comes	Use present tense to express common truths.
20. has decided	The present perfect tense refers to actions occurring at no particular time in the past and that may still be in progress.

Page 28, Verb Forms

1. eaten
2. caught
3. swam
4. drunk
5. gone
6. laid
7. shone or shined
8. shrunk
9. sung
10. slew
11. stolen
12. strove or strived
13. awakened
14. worn

15. broken

16. dived

17. crept

18. flung

19. sworn

20. led

Page 32, Subject-Verb Agreement

1. talent . . . assures

2. play . . . was

3. group . . . began

4. No error

5. No error

6. are . . . kids

7. proceeds . . . are

8. committee . . . is, who gets

9. neither . . . was

10. policies . . . have had

11. everyone . . . expects

12. No error

13. Miller . . . is

14. Katie and Gene . . . have been invited

15. Nancy Atkins . . . expects

16. number . . . has created

17. Here are the costumes

18. insistence . . . is

19. members . . . want

20. are to be . . . guards

Page 37, Comparative Degree

1. . . . a lot richer — *More rich* may be acceptable in some contexts, but ordinarily add *-er* to one-syllable adjectives in the comparative degree.

2. . . . the better — Use adjectives in the comparative degree when comparing two things or people.

3. unique *or use* most unusual — *Unique* is an absolute adjective that cannot be used in making comparisons.

4. . . . greatest — Use the superlative degree to compare more than two things.

5. . . . most forgetful — Use *more/most* with three-syllable adjectives.

6. . . . most popular — Use the superlative degree to compare more than two things.

7. . . . more stubborn — Use adjectives in the comparative degree when comparing two things.

8. . . . the worse — Use adjectives in the comparative degree when comparing two things.

9. . . . less hard — Avoid making redundant double comparisons.

10. No error

11. . . . was sweeter — Avoid making redundant double comparisons.

12. . . . more profound — Use *more/most* with most two-syllable adjectives.

13. . . . the faster — Use adjectives in the comparative degree when comparing two things.

14. . . . more immune — With many two-syllable adjectives, use *more/most.*

15. . . . most unkind — Avoid making redundant double comparisons.

16. No error

17. . . . fewer games — Use *fewer* when comparing countable things.

18. . . . was nicer — Avoid making redundant double comparisons.

19. . . . is longer — Use adjectives in the comparative degree when comparing two things.

20. No error

Page 42, Using Adverbs

1. . . . felt bitter — *Felt* is a linking verb and must be followed by an adjective instead of an adverb.

2. . . . smelled bad — *Smelled* is a linking verb and must be followed by an adjective instead of an adverb.

3. . . . more quickly, . . . dives better — Use words in the comparative degree when comparing two things.

4. No error

5. . . . as easily as — In spite of how silly it sounds to say it, "as easily as pie" is grammatically correct because "do" is an active verb that should be modified by an adverb. But everyday English idiom makes "as easy as pie" perfectly acceptable.

6. No error

7. . . . proceed slowly — Because *proceed* is an active verb, it is modified by an adverb.

8. . . . looked . . . cynically — In context, *looked* is an active verb and, therefore, must be modified by an adverb.

9. . . . tastes bad — *Tastes* is a linking verb and must be followed by an adjective.

10. . . . most fully — Use the superlative degree (*most*) when comparing more than two things.

11. . . . talked slowly — Because *talked* is an active verb, it is modified by an adverb.

12. No error

13. . . . stage happily — Because *mounted* is an active verb, it is modified by an adverb.

14. . . . to get up early — Splitting the infinitive leads to an awkward expression.

15. . . . felt cold — In context, *felt* is a linking verb and must be followed by an adjective.

16. . . . piano well — Because *play* is an active verb, it is modified by an adverb.

17. No error

18. . . . slept more comfortably — Because *play* is an active verb, it is modified by an adverb.

19. . . . finally decided to eat — The split infinitive is unnecessary.

20. No error

Page 46, Prepositions and Prepositional Phrases

Your sentences will no doubt be different from these, but each one should illustrate the proper use of a preposition.

1. A theme *in* the poem "Richard Cory" is envy.

2. The poem is *about* a man whom others admire from a distance.

3. The poet doesn't go *into* the details of Cory's life.

4. Cory's attitude *toward* the people is distant and aloof.

5. *Besides* wealth, Cory had good looks and good breeding.

6. But *contrary to* the people's perception, Cory was a troubled man.

7. *Aside from* his appearance, Cory was a mystery to them.

8. *In lieu of* getting to know him, people held him up as an icon.

9. *During the course of* the poem, the reader cannot suspect its shocking ending.

10. *Inasmuch as* you may someday read the poem, I won't tell you how it ends.

Page 47, Conjunctions

1. neither . . . nor (COR)

2. and (COO), and (COO)

3. Although (SUB)

4. Not only . . . but (COR)

5. so (SUB)

6. But (COO), since (SUB), and (COO)

7. yet (COO)

8. So that (SUB)

9. Whatever (SUB) because (SUB)

10. Whether (SUB) or not (COR), but (COR)

Chapter 2

Sentences

> **A Note to the Reader**
>
> You are about to plunge into a chapter on the grammar of sentences, a subject that requires you to absorb many facts, rules, and, of course, numerous exceptions to the rules. So, please take your time. Don't let it weigh you down. Read a couple of pages, then read them again. Underline key ideas, take notes. Circle anything that puzzles you and return to it later for further study.
>
> Here's another idea: Skim the chapter to see what it contains. Then go on to the grammar questions in Part 2 of this book. Come back to this chapter whenever you need help in solving a particular problem or want to clarify a point of grammar. In other words, use these pages as a handy resource, a place to visit again and again for answers to your questions.

SENTENCE BASICS

A **SENTENCE** is a group of words that begins with a capital letter and concludes with an end mark of punctuation, usually a period. Most of the time, it also conveys a more or less complete thought. That's a handy description of a sentence, but honestly, it doesn't tell the whole story. There is much more to know about a creature that takes innumerable forms and shapes and can perform an endless variety of functions. A simple definition just won't do.

For one thing, when talking about sentences, you're obliged to use grammatical terminology. In fact, it's almost impossible to say something intelligent about sentences without referring to **nouns, verbs, prepositions**, and the other parts of speech introduced in Chapter 1.

With that in mind, let's begin with a surprising fact: Did you know that the longest sentence in the world will never be written? That's because a sentence can go on indefinitely. The shortest sentence, on the other hand, is probably a single letter—the answer to a question such as, "Is your name spelled with a *J* or a *G*?" Some might argue that a letter of the alphabet doesn't qualify as a sentence because sentences must consist of two parts, a **SUBJECT** and a **PREDICATE**. They may have a point.

> A sentence must have at least a subject and a predicate verb. Without both parts, an utterance is technically not a sentence.

There's no doubt, though, that the simplest **subject** of a sentence is a noun or pronoun, and the simplest **predicate** is a verb.

Ophelia (*subject*) wept (*verb*).
She (*subject*) wailed (*verb*).
Push (*verb*)! (In this sentence the subject *you* is implied. Spelled out, the sentence is You push!)

It goes without saying that sentences are rarely as short and simple as these examples. In fact, a sentence subject can contain any number of words that modify the noun or pronoun, as, for example, in *poor, broken-hearted, miserable, troubled, pitiful, pathetic Ophelia*. Furthermore, a string of nouns or pronouns can also make up the subject, as in

Snow, sleet, and freezing rain (subject) poured down on the city.
He and she (subject) are engaged to be married.

Phrases that contain neither nouns nor pronouns can also be the subject of a sentence. A verb, for example, when it functions as a noun, as in:

To eat (subject consisting of the infinitive of a verb) like a pig is the sole purpose of Matt's existence.

To identify the grammatical subject of a sentence, look first for the verb. Then ask who or what is performing the action described by the verb, and chances are you'll have found the subject.

Jack ran away with Jill. Who ran? Jack did. Therefore, *Jack* is the subject.
The *mail* arrived late this afternoon. What arrived late? The *mail*.
There were *cars* parked illegally. What was parked? *Cars*.

The subject usually comes before the verb, but not always, as in There in the middle of the room stood *Papa*. Who stood? *Papa*.

Although this method of finding the subject works much of the time, some sentences refuse to yield their subjects so easily. Then you need to employ additional steps, detailed on page 62.

Predicates are easy to identify because they consist of everything in a sentence that isn't the subject. They can be just a single verb, or a verb accompanied by any number of additional words (italicized in the following sentence) that tell you something about the subject. Predicates can ramble off in all different directions, giving you more details than you need or maybe even want to know.

Ophelia (subject) *wept* (verb) *without stopping for two hours this afternoon, then all through dinner and into the evening until her boyfriend Hamlet sent her an e-mail to apologize for thoughtlessly calling her a moron.*

Regardless of its length or complexity, a sentence must have at least a subject and a predicate verb. Without a subject and verb, you might have an utterance of some kind—even one that communicates a profound thought—but technically, it's not a sentence.

The following are examples of non-sentences:

NO SUBJECT:	Reminded me of the troubles they had building the Panama Canal.
NO VERB:	A ship by the name of HMS *Georgia* with three smokestacks and a weight of 20,000 tons.
NO SUBJECT AND NO VERB:	Too cold, overcooked, and tasteless.

With the addition of the missing ingredient, each of these nonsentences becomes a fully formed complete sentence:

A *video* (subject) on YouTube reminded me of the troubles they had building the Panama Canal.

A ship by the name of HMS *Georgia* with three smokestacks and a weight of 20,000 tons *docked* (verb) at Pier 44 last night.

Chef Marcus (subject) *served* (verb) vegetable soup that was too cold, overcooked, and tasteless.

Objects—Direct and Indirect

The predicates of some sentences contain **objects**—nouns that name the things being acted upon. Objects, in other words, don't perform actions, but rather have actions done to them. Let's say, for instance,

Gloria kissed Mike.

Gloria is the subject, the one doing the kissing. *Kissed* is an action verb, and *Mike* is the object of the verb because he was lucky enough to receive Gloria's kiss. Mike, the recipient of the action, is the **direct object**.

Let's now assume that after being kissed, Mike returned Gloria's affection:

Mike gave Gloria a hug.

Mike is the subject of the sentence. It's true that Gloria received the hug, but in this sentence she has been turned into the **indirect object**. The *direct object* is *hug*, the thing that Mike physically gave.

Confusing? Well, maybe, but look at it this way:

Mike gave a hug to Gloria.

An *indirect object* is the thing or person for whom or to whom something is given—in this case, Gloria. The *direct object* is the thing actually given—the hug.

The following sentence illustrates the point in another way:

Mike bought Gloria a card for Valentine's Day.

Here, *card* is the thing that Mike bought, making it the direct object. *Gloria*, as the secondary receiver of the action, is the indirect object.

Between you and I, most people get along in the world without ever distinguishing between direct and indirect objects. To speak and write correctly, however, it helps to know about *objects*—not only objects of the verb, but also objects of prepositions. *Otherwise, you might not have noticed the grammatical blunder in the first phrase of this paragraph.*

CLAUSES

A *CLAUSE* is part of a sentence that contains a subject and a verb. By that definition, a *clause* sounds strangely like a sentence, and to a point, it *is* a sentence—but even though some clauses are complete sentences, others are not. Those that are full-fledged sentences go by the name of *independent*, or *main*, *clauses*, which can stand alone, strong and grammatically perfect. The others are called *dependent clauses* because they depend for their meaning and grammatical validity on independent clauses. Without an independent clause, they would be *sentence fragments*—that is, incomplete sentences.

> Some clauses are complete sentences; others are not.

To illustrate, here is a complete, independent sentence with its subject and verb italicized:

Hank chewed a wad of bubble gum.

Now, let's add a dependent clause:

Because he was nervous, Hank chewed a wad of bubble gum.

The new clause contains a subject (*he*) and a verb (*was*), but by themselves they don't make a sentence. The clause *Because he was nervous* is a fragment, a piece of a sentence. On its own, it lacks grammatical status, which can be achieved only by attaching it to an independent clause.

Dependent clauses serve various functions. They can serve as nouns, as adjectives, and even as adverbs. When they act like nouns, they are called *noun clauses*; when they act like adjectives, they go by the name *adjective clauses*, and so on.

Noun clauses often begin with words such as *that, which, who, whom, when,* and *whatever.* They can be the subject of a sentence, the object of a preposition, or the object of a verb, among other things.

> Using different types of clauses can help you develop a more interesting style of writing and speaking.

Whoever chews gum regularly can develop strong jaw muscles (*whoever chews gum regularly* is the subject).
Over time, Hank discovered *that he was a gum addict* (*that he was a gum addict* is the object of the verb *discovered*).

Adjective clauses often begin with the relative pronouns *who, whom, whose, which,* or *that.* Like single-word adjectives, they modify nouns and pronouns.

The bag *that held Hank's gum supply* was plastic.

The clause *that held Hank's gum supply* modifies the noun *bag.*

Hank had paid the woman *who sells bags full of gum* two dollars for it.

The clause *who sells bags full of gum* modifies *woman.*
Adverbial clauses start with such words as *although, because, while, since, as, as though, unless, so that,* and many other subordinating conjunctions. They modify verbs, adjectives, and adverbs.

If Hank had known the effects of gum, he would not have started chewing.

The clause *if Hank had known the effects of gum* modifies the verb *would not have started.*
Frankly, knowing the names and characteristics of various types of clauses won't take you far in this world. What's important is knowing that a variety of clauses can help you develop a more interesting and varied style in speech and writing.

TYPES OF SENTENCES

Although every sentence has a main clause, not every sentence has a dependent clause. **Simple sentences**, for example, have only one clause containing a subject and a verb. Even if you add modifiers and objects galore, it remains a *simple* sentence. Take the following two sentences. In spite of the difference in their length, both are *simple* sentences:

> Berkeley admitted Sarah.

> Situated on the eastern side of San Francisco Bay, Berkeley, the University of California's flagship institution, admitted Sarah as a freshman starting next semester, not only to the delight of Sarah herself but to the satisfaction of her family, teachers, and friends.

Leave aside the jumble of miscellaneous information crammed into the second sentence. In the end, you're still left with a simple declarative sentence—*Berkeley admitted Sara.*

Compound sentences are made up of at least two simple sentences joined by a conjunction, such as *and, but, so*, or any of the other conjuctions discussed in Chapter 1:

> Berkeley admitted Sarah, and she was delighted.

What is noteworthy about compound sentences is that they give more or less equal emphasis to the information in each clause. In everyday conversation it's common for people to use fairly lengthy compound sentences, as in:

> In school yesterday, a water main broke, and we could not take showers in gym, and there was no water to drink, and the toilets could not be flushed, so the principal decided that the situation was unhealthy, and she consulted with the superintendent, and the school was closed before lunch.

This sentence tells a story without breaking a single rule of grammar. But it's stylistically flawed, because each idea appears in an independent clause, suggesting that no one idea ranks above any other in importance. Clauses of equal rank and structure are called **coordinate clauses**.

If storytellers want to highlight some details more than others, they would do well to use **complex sentences**—that is, sentences that contain both a main clause and one or more subordinate clauses:

> *When Berkeley admitted her,* Sarah was delighted. (Subordinate clause italicized.)

Here, the cause-and-effect relationship between the two ideas is made clear. This process is called **subordination**, a simple act of giving prominence to ideas in the main clause and letting secondary ideas slide into the background.

The structure of some sentences can be still more elaborate. For instance, a sentence that combines elements of both compound and complex sentences is called a **compound-complex** sentence. To illustrate:

> *Sarah was not in the top quarter of her class,* but Berkeley admitted her as a freshman anyway, and she was delighted.

SENTENCE PROBLEMS

Nonsentences

Partial sentences, called **sentence fragments**, often look remarkably like complete sentences. But looks can be deceptive.

The bike that Martha often borrowed.

This fragment appears to have all the characteristics of a sentence: It starts with a capital letter and ends with a period. It conveys a complete thought (*Martha often borrowed the bike* is a complete thought), and it seems to contain a subject (*Martha*) and a verb (*borrowed*). What makes it a fragment, though, is that *Martha* isn't the subject. Rather, *bike* is the subject, and the trouble is that *bike* and the verb *borrowed* don't fit together. A bike, after all, is an inanimate object and can't do any borrowing—not in this world, in any case. Clearly, Martha did the borrowing, but the noun *Martha* cannot be the subject of the sentence because it is part of the subordinate clause, *that Martha borrowed*. Therefore, *bike* needs a verb of its own.

The bike that Martha often borrowed was stolen.

> You'll never find the subject of a sentence in a prepositional phrase or a dependent clause.

With the addition of *was stolen*, the sentence is now complete.

Sentence fragments often occur when writers fail to distinguish between dependent and independent clauses, when they confuse phrases and clauses, or when they attempt to use verbals as verbs. (See page 63.) To determine whether a sentence is complete, uncover its bare bones. That is, take it apart by eliminating dependent clauses, phrases, and verbals. If what remains does not have a subject and a verb, it's probably a fragment.

To identify the subject of long sentences may take some doing, but the "bare bones" strategy usually works. Using this approach, you'll strip away everything in a sentence but its subject and verb, a task that may be easier said than done. It's not very formidable, though, if you remember that the grammatical subject can never be in a prepositional phrase, in a dependent clause, or in a phrase that interrupts the flow of the sentence.

To find the "bare bones" of a sentence:

<u>First step</u>: Look for prepositional phrases, such as *up the wall, around the corner, to the beach, over the counter,* and cross them out. For example, if you were to eliminate all the prepositional phrases in these sentences, only the subject and the verb—the "bare bones"—will remain.

COMPLETE SENTENCE: In the middle of the night, Priscilla slept.
BARE BONES: Priscilla slept.
COMPLETE SENTENCE: Several of the sentences are in the book.
BARE BONES: Several are.
COMPLETE SENTENCE: One of Frieda's friends is in need of help.
BARE BONES: One is.

<u>Second step</u>: Locate all the dependent clauses—those parts of sentences that contain a noun and a verb but don't qualify as complete sentences because they begin with words and phrases like *although, as, as though, because, before, even though, if, in spite of, regardless of, since, so that, unless, whenever, whether,* and *while*. Other dependent clauses are statements (not questions) that start with *when, where, which, who,* and *what*.

After deleting the dependent clauses in the sentences below, only the main clause will remain. That's where to find the bare bones of each sentence.

COMPLETE SENTENCE: Because she missed the bus, Marnie wept.
BARE BONES: Marnie wept.
COMPLETE SENTENCE: While Willie waited for the bus, he studied vocabulary.
BARE BONES: He studied.
COMPLETE SENTENCE: Andy helps out whenever he has the time.
BARE BONES: Andy helps out.

<u>Third step</u>: Look for and delete interrupters—those parts of sentences that impede the smooth flow of the main idea. Interrupters may be just one word (*however, nevertheless*) or dozens. They're often set off by commas.

COMPLETE SENTENCE: Ellen, regardless of the look on her face, rejoiced.
BARE BONES: Ellen rejoiced.
COMPLETE SENTENCE: The boat, a sleek white catamaran, sank.
BARE BONES: The boat sank.
COMPLETE SENTENCE: Marty, who got ticketed for doing 60 in a
30 MPH zone, paid the fine.
BARE BONES: Marty paid.

The process of identifying the bare bones of a sentence can be more complex than suggested by these examples. But by carefully peeling away sentence parts that cannot contain the subject or verb, you'll eventually lay bare the subject and verb.

Verbals

What may further complicate a search for subject and verb is that subjects sometimes look suspiciously like verbs. These so-called **verbals** come in two main forms: **infinitives** and **gerunds**.

- Infinitives. To read books makes life worth living. Here, the infinitive phrase *to read* plays the part of a noun and is the subject of the sentence.
- Gerunds. *Reading* books makes life worth living. Here, the gerund *Reading* (the *-ing* form of the verb *to read*) is the subject.

Another type of verbal is the **participle**, also called a **participial phrase**. Instead of acting like a noun, participles play the part of adjectives, modifying the subject.

Having read all day, Hilary was ready to live it up at night.

Here, the participle *Having read* modifies Hilary, the subject of the sentence. Likewise,

Turning over in his sleep, Jake fell out of bed.

Again, the function of the participial phrase is to describe, or modify, the subject.

Dangling Participles

Hurrying to his chem lab, the bell rang.

The participle in this sentence is *Hurrying to his chem lab*. If you look closely at the meaning, however, the sentence says that the bell rang as it hurried to chem lab—not a likely scenario. To fix this so-called "***dangling participle***," the object being modified (in this case the person rushing to lab) must be included in the main clause.

> Hurrying to his chem lab, Simon heard the bell ring.

The grammatical subject, *Simon*, is now properly modified by the participle *hurrying to chem lab.*

Run-on Sentences

A **run-on sentence** consists of two independent clauses with nothing but a blank space—not a conjunction, not a mark of punctuation—between them:

> Birthstones are supposed to bring good luck mine has never brought me any.

> "Run-ons" are two or more complete sentences with no punctuation between them.

To fill the gap between *luck* and *mine*, turn the run-on into a compound sentence by inserting the coordinating conjunction *but.*

> Birthstones are supposed to bring good luck, *but* mine has never brought me any.

Note the comma. It's been added because compound sentences require a comma between their clauses unless the clauses are very short, as in:

> Carla drove but I walked.

Another solution might have been to write two separate sentences:

> Birthstones are supposed to bring good luck. Mine has never brought me any.

Or you could have used a semicolon, which, in effect, functions like a period.

> Birthstones are supposed to bring good luck; mine has never brought me any.

Notice that the initial letter of the second sentence is not capitalized. (See page 83 for more on the proper use of semicolons.)

Comma Splices

A variation on the run-on sentence is the comma splice, in which a comma instead of a period or semicolon is used to join, or splice, two independent sentences.

> Othello was fooled by a disloyal friend, he should have known better.

Replace the comma with a period and start a new sentence with *He*. Or, use a semicolon:

> Othello was fooled by a disloyal friend; he should have known better.

Checkpoint 12. CORRECT SENTENCES

Look for sentence fragments, run-ons, and comma splices. Use the spaces to identify the error and write a correct sentence. Some items may contain no error.

1. Although Elizabeth is stressed out about her sore back.

   _____

2. Jim asked for an extension on the assignment, the teacher agreed.

   _____

3. My grandmother is 86 years old therefore she walks very slowly.

   _____

4. Many other examples that I could choose to show who I am, many of them not vivid images of memorable moments but everyday aspects of my life.

   _____

5. I wake up, having slept for the four shortest hours of my life, I force open my eyes and I crawl to the shower then my brain begins to function.

   _____

6. For me to believe that the crucial time has arrived when I will leave the protective world of high school and enter college.

   _____

7. The large brown garage door creaks open slowly, out into the morning sunshine a rider on a road bike emerges.

   _____

8. What are the rules that we all must follow what might happen if we break them.

   _____

9. A biologist working in the field of genetic engineering and involved in the controversy surrounding human cloning.

   _____

10. Use the space below to tell one story about yourself to provide the admissions committee, either directly or indirectly, with an insight into the kind of person you are.

   _____

Answers on page 88

Faulty Parallel Structure

Parallel structure keeps equivalent ideas in the same grammatical form. Consider this sentence that lists the contents of a student's locker:

> The locker held a down jacket, aromatic sweatpants, three sneakers, two left-handed gloves, an unused tuna sandwich, a broken ski pole, a hockey puck, six overdue library books, a disposable camera, and a hiking boot.

Every item listed is an object, each expressed in the same grammatical form: a noun preceded by one or two adjectives. When the student wrote a list of his favorite pastimes, though, the sentence lost its parallelism:

> I like skiing, hiking, to take pictures, and running.

The message is clear, but the phrase "to take pictures" is not parallel with the other phrases. To revise it, write "taking pictures":

I like skiing, hiking, taking pictures, and running.

Ideas in a series should be grammatically parallel, even when the series consists of only two items.

When you structure the pieces of a sentence in parallel form, you put yourself in the company of world-class stylists. Abraham Lincoln, for one, used parallelism at Gettysburg: "We cannot dedicate, we cannot consecrate, we cannot hallow this ground. . . ." And later, ". . . that government of the people, by the people, and for the people shall not perish from the earth." John F. Kennedy used parallelism in his inaugural speech: "Let every nation know, whether it wishes us good or ill, that we shall pay any price, bear any burden, meet any hardship, support any friend, oppose any foe to assure the survival and the success of liberty."

To apply the essential principles of parallel construction to your prose:

- Express all ideas in a series in the same grammatical form, even when the series consists of only two items:

Express parallel ideas in the same grammatical form.

Her parents objected to the loud music she played and to the late hours she kept.

Here, parallelism is achieved with prepositional phrases, *to the loud music* and *to the late hours*. Each phrase is followed by the pronoun *she* and the past tense of a verb.

After graduation she promised to turn the volume down and to come home earlier.

Each parallel idea consists of an infinitive followed by a noun and an adverb.

- Use grammatical equivalents to make comparisons and contrasts. When comparing two ideas, for example, express both ideas in phrases, or pair an idea stated in a clause with a second idea also stated in a clause.

FAULTY: They are worried more about public opinion than for what the effect of the proposal may be.

The prepositional phrase *about public opinion* may not be paired with the clause *what the effect of the proposal may be.*

PARALLEL: They are worried more about public opinion than about the effect of the proposal.

Parallelism is achieved by pairing two prepositional phrases.

FAULTY: Going out to eat no longer thrills me as much as to cook at home.

The gerund *going out* should not be paired with the infinitive *to cook.*

PARALLEL: Going out to eat no longer thrills me as much as cooking at home.

Parallelism is achieved by pairing two gerunds, *going* and *cooking.*

- Stay alert for pairs of words that signal the need for parallelism, such as *either/or, neither/nor, whether/or, both/and,* and *not only/but also.*

Alice will attend *neither* NYU *or* Columbia.

Revise by changing *neither* to *either*, or changing *or* to *nor*. Remember to keep the pair of words close to each other in the sentence. If they are too far apart, your sentence may be hard to follow:

Jake *both* started on the basketball and the volleyball teams.

The signal word *both* is too far removed from the parallel phrase, *basketball and volleyball teams*. Its placement misleads the reader into thinking that the verb *started* is one of the parallel ideas. Correctly worded, the sentence reads:

Jake started on *both* the basketball and the volleyball teams.

- When an article, preposition, or a conjunction appears before the first in a series of parallel items, repeat the word before the others in the series.

    UNCLEAR: Our mechanic did a better job on my car than his.

Did two mechanics work on the same car or did one mechanic work on two different cars? To clear up the ambiguity, repeat the preposition *on*, as in:

    CLEAR: Our mechanic did a better job on my car than *on* his.

Sometimes repeating both a preposition and an article is necessary:

    UNCLEAR: Before signing the contract, Tiffany spoke with the president and treasurer of the company.

Did Tiffany speak with one person or with two? Repeating *with the* helps to clarify the meaning:

    CLEAR: Before signing the contract, Tiffany spoke *with* the president and *with the* treasurer of the company.

- Make sure that parallel ideas are logical equivalents.

    ABSURD: Terry is six feet tall, kind, and a Texan.

Physical features, traits of character, and place of origin are not logically coordinated.

    LESS ABSURD: Terry, a six-foot Texan, is kind.

Still not terribly logical, but at least the revision emphasizes only one of Terry's qualities—his kindness.

    ILLOGICAL: San Diego's *harbor* is reported to be more polluted than *any city*.

This sentence is meant to compare pollution in the San Diego harbor with pollution in the harbors of other cities, but it fails to achieve its goal. Instead, it illogically compares San Diego's harbor with a city.

    LOGICAL: San Diego's *harbor* is reported to be more polluted than the *harbor of any other city*.
    ILLOGICAL: Unlike most *cars* on the street, *Ellie* has her Subaru washed almost every week.

This sentence is intended to compare Ellie's car with other cars on the street, but it manages only to compare Ellie with the other cars, an illogical comparison.

    LOGICAL: Ellie's *Subaru*, unlike *most cars* on the street, is washed almost every week.

Checkpoint 13. PARALLEL STRUCTURE

Seek out flaws in parallel structure in the sentences that follow. Write a corrected version of the offending word or phrase in the space provided.

1. Steve likes canoeing, biking, to read good books, and writing.

   _____

2. Smoking should be prohibited in public places because it harms people's health, deprives nonsmokers of clean air, and an offensive, smelly habit.

   _____

3. To endure extreme cold, you need to be well trained in survival tactics as well as in excellent physical condition.

   _____

4. As an actor, Arnold Schwarzenegger is admired more for his body instead of portraying characters.

   _____

5. The accountant found that business was bad during the third quarter, just like Tony.

   _____

6. Matthew enrolled in painting, harmony, music appreciation, and to study art history.

   _____

7. On our first day we visited Fisherman's Wharf, the Golden Gate, and rode the cable cars.

   _____

8. The lawyer insisted that her job took more hours than a teacher.

   _____

9. In the speech, the senator accused his colleague of being an ignoramus and too dense to know what was at stake in the legislation.

   _____

10. It has been said that walking is better for you than to jog the same distance.

   _____

Answers on page 89

Active and Passive Sentences

We've already seen that active verbs differ from being verbs. Because active verbs (*leap, launch, laugh*) show movement, they re-create life. Even active verbs that name sedentary activities as *thinking, writing,* and *sleeping* pulse with greater energy than such passive verbs as *is, were,* and *has been.*

In like manner, active sentences—those structured in the **active voice**—place emphasis on actions and who performed them:

> Bruce *slept* through a performance of *Our Town.*
> Diana *applauded* wildly at the end of the play.

Is there any doubt in these sentences about who did what?

A passive sentence, one in the **passive voice**, on the other hand, puts its emphasis on the receiver of the action or on the action itself. What's more, the performer of the action may be left out altogether:

> Six weeks were spent preparing for the play.

Who prepared for the play? From this sentence it's impossible to tell.

> A new painting was hung in the gallery.

Similarly, in this sentence whoever hung the painting gets no recognition. To give credit to the performer of the action, the sentences might read:

> Six weeks were spent preparing for the play by the acting group.
> A new painting was hung in the gallery by Carmine.

These versions contain more information than the originals, but each still emphasizes the action instead of the performer of the action. To turn them into sentences in the active voice, make the actor the subject of the sentence and place it before the verb:

> The *acting group* prepared for the play for six weeks.
> *Carmine* hung a new painting in the gallery.

Sometimes, of course, passive construction makes a good deal of sense:

> The hospital was built in 2005.

What's important here is the construction date of the hospital, not who poured the foundation and constructed the building.

In general, however, good writers prefer to use the active voice because most events in life don't just occur by themselves. Somebody *does* something; a person or thing *acts.* Hamburgers don't just get eaten; people cook and then devour them. Marriages don't just happen; couples deliberately go out and get hitched. Goals don't score, salmon don't get caught, wallets don't get lost all by themselves. Because people do these things, writers take advantage of readers' natural curiosity about others and strive to put the performer of the action into the grammatical subject of sentences. By doing so, they eliminate passive verbs and pep up their prose.

> To pep up your prose, use the active, rather than the passive, voice.

Checkpoint 14. PASSIVE CONSTRUCTION

Put the following sentences into the active voice:

1. The backyard was covered by dead leaves.

2. The crisis in the Mideast was discussed by us.

3. Friday's quiz was failed because I had been at play rehearsal every night that week.

4. Portland was flown to at the start of our weeklong vacation in Oregon.

5. The great white whale was pursued by Captain Ahab and his crew.

6. The newspaper is fetched by Fido every morning.

7. The decision to go to war was made by the president and his advisers.

8. Dinner was taken out by more than twenty customers on Friday night.

9. Five of Shakespeare's plays were seen by our group in three days.

10. Normally, the brain is called on by the body before you do something physical.

Answers on page 89

SENTENCE STRUCTURE

Most sentences used in everyday speech and writing start with the grammatical subject followed by the verb, as in:

Cats (subject) *fall* (verb) asleep in about three seconds.
They (subject) *sleep* (verb) best after eating and cleaning themselves.
I (subject) *wish* (verb) to be a cat in my next life.

Seasoned writers, however, try to vary the structure of their sentences. Instead of leading off with the subject every time, they may begin with a prepositional phrase, an adverb, an adjective, or some other grammatical unit.

> Good writers try to vary the structure of their sentences.

The following pairs of sentences show how a subject can be shifted from its customary position:

> **BEFORE THE SHIFT:** Mike Bennett is one of the most hardworking officers in the Boston Police Department.
> **AFTER THE SHIFT:** Of all the officers in the Boston Police Department, Mike Bennett is one of the hardest workers.

With the insertion of a pair of prepositional phrases, the subject (*Mike Bennett*) and verb (*is*) have been been moved farther along in the sentence.

> **BEFORE:** Mike goes to work each day with great enthusiasm.
> **AFTER:** Enthusiastically, Mike goes to work each day.

Obviously, the revised sentence begins with an adverb.

> **BEFORE:** Many of his fellow officers are less excited about police work than Mike.
> **AFTER:** Yet, many of his fellow officers are less excited about police work than Mike.

Well, here the subject (*many*) is stated after an opening conjunction.

> **BEFORE:** Mike has tried to win the respect of the people in the area he patrols, although not every resident has learned to trust him.
> **AFTER:** Although not every resident has learned to trust him, Mike has tried to win the respect of the people in the area he patrols.

After starting with a dependent clause, the writer names the subject, *Mike*, and then adds the rest of the sentence.

> **BEFORE:** Mike introduced the idea of holding monthly block parties to reduce crime and help the residents get to know each other.
> **AFTER:** To reduce crime and help the residents get to know each other, Mike introduced the idea of holding monthly block parties.

To revise this sentence the writer begins with a verbal, in this case, the infinitive form of the verb *to reduce.*

> **BEFORE:** Three hundred people attended the first party, hoping that it would help to unite their neighborhood.
> **AFTER:** Hoping that it would help to unite their neighborhood, three hundred people attended the first party.

Aiming to vary sentences openings, the writer starts this sentence with a participle.

> BEFORE: The police department was impressed by Mike's effort and awarded him a medal for humanitarianism.
> AFTER: Impressed by Mike's effort, the police department awarded him a medal for humanitarianism.

Determined to try something different, the writer begins this sentence with an adjective that happens to sound like a verb because of its *-ed* ending.

Still another variation is the sentence constructed from matched ideas set in juxtaposition:

> It wasn't that the spirit of a community caught their imagination, it was their imagination that created a community spirit.

The power of such sentences lies in the balance of parallel clauses. Each clause could stand alone, but together they express the idea more vigorously.

Sentences can be classified not only by their structure but also according to their main purpose. **Declarative sentences** predominate in most speech and writing. (Just to refresh your memory, a *declarative* sentence, such as the one you are now reading, simply makes a statement.) But to ask a question, you'd use an **interrogative sentence**, and to make requests or give a command you employ **imperative sentences**. (Hold my hand when we cross the street.) Finally, **exclamatory sentences** serve to express sudden strong emotions (What nonsense that is!). On occasion you can drive home a point with a single exlamatory word. (Excellent!)

Varying Sentences—A Summary

Use a variety of sentence types: *simple, compound,* and *complex.*

Create variety by starting sentences with:

- A prepositional phrase: *From the start, In the first place, At the outset*
- Adverbs and adverbial phrases: *Originally, At first, Initially*
- Dependent clauses: *When you start with this, Because the opening is*
- Conjunctions: *And, But, Not only, Either, So, Yet*
- Adjectives and adjective phrases: *Fresh from, Introduced with, Headed by*
- Verbal infinitives: *To launch, To take the first step, To get going*
- Participles: *Leading off, Starting up, Commencing with*

Checkpoint 15. SENTENCE STRUCTURE

Rewrite each sentence below according to the instructions given. Try to preserve the original meanings.

1. Mr. Finn assigned a huge amount of homework to his students over the weekend. (*Begin with a prepositional phrase.*)

---

2. Many nations pollute the world's oceans, dumping garbage, sewage, and other hazardous waste products into the sea.
   (*Begin with a participle.*)

   _____

3. Toxic materials end up in fish, lobsters, clams, and other sea life, and the toxins enter our bodies when we eat seafood.
   (*Begin with a subordinate clause.*)

   _____

4. An increase in natural disasters has been experienced by our planet during the last half century.
   (*Change to active voice.*)

   _____

5. The increase has occurred because people in greater numbers now occupy areas prone to natural disasters, according to the evidence.
   (*Begin with adverb or adverbial phrase.*)

   _____

6. As the population has grown, more people have settled on floodplains, along the seacoast, and cities have been built on subterranean fault lines.
   (*Revise problems in parallel structure.*)

   _____

7. Community groups have increased college scholarship awards, they hope to motivate young people to study harder in school.
   (*Eliminate the comma splice and begin with an infinitive phrase.*)

   _____

8. The American Dream, a popular concept in American culture, with different meanings for different people.
   (*Write a complete sentence.*)

   _____

9. An ideal dream in the movies, on television, and in countless books means finding a good job getting married, having a couple of kids, and owning a home.
   (*Begin with an adjective or adjective clause.*)

   _____

10. Typical homes in the community have a white picket fence and a two-car garage. (*Begin with an adverb.*)

Suggested answers on page 90

SENTENCE EXPRESSION AND STYLE

Having ventured 74 pages into the world of grammar, you deserve a pat on the back for your determination to write and speak correctly. As admirable as your commitment may be, however, you should know that perfect grammar can take you only so far. The use of standard English suggests a certain level of schooling and a degree of sophistication. Yet, grammatically perfect language can still be dull, repetitious, wordy, awkwardly expressed, and stylistically flawed in any number of ways. Correct sentences don't necessarily mean that they are good sentences, only that they contain no grammatical mistakes. Recognizing that skill in language consists of more than just knowing and applying grammatical rules, the College Board, the ACT, and others have included test questions on style and expression. They believe that clear, cogent, idiomatic, and graceful expression goes hand in hand with correct grammar, and that to test one without the other begets an incomplete picture of a student's English skills.

The pages that follow discuss sentences that are grammatically correct but stylistically flawed. Some are long-winded; or their word order—known as **syntax**—is not only ungraceful but downright jarring, like the wrong note in a familiar melody. Other sentences may lack clarity or suffer from faulty **diction**. They contain a poor choice of words or they violate standard English *idiom* by combining words or phrases that shouldn't be seen together. In general, they are characterized by the catchall phrase *poorly written*.

Awkwardness

> Awkward writing is hard to define, but you know it when you hear it.

The adjective *awkward* covers a great many writing weaknesses, including poor grammar and flawed sentence structure. Most often, though, awkwardness occurs when the words sound odd or off kilter. Awkwardness is difficult to define, but you know it when you hear it. Your ear tells you that a phrase or sentence is clunky. No specific rules can explain its defects. It just doesn't sound right.

AWKWARD: Rather than walk, Mr. Perkins drove his SUV to mail his letter owing to the knowledge that the post office closed at 4:30.

The phrase *owing to the knowledge* is grammatical but awkward. Here's a less clumsy version of the sentence:

> Rather than walk, Mr. Perkins drove his SUV to mail his letter because he knew that the post office closed at 4:30.

> AWKWARD: Even though factual contents were there, the film about Charles Lindbergh's solo flight to Paris seemed like fiction.

The first clause of the sentence is grammatically correct but its words are cumbersome. Plain, idiomatic language would help:

> Although it was factual, the film about Charles Lindbergh's solo flight to Paris seemed like fiction.

Faulty Idiom

An **idiom** usually consists of a group of words that seems absurd if taken literally. When you "have a ball," the experience has nothing to do with a spherical object used in basketball or ping-pong. The expression "that's cool" doesn't refer to temperature, and to "bite the bullet" is unrelated to guns. And so on. Such idioms often puzzle speakers of other languages, but to native speakers of English they are as natural as breathing.

Idioms cannot be rationally explained. We say "three-foot ruler" when we mean "three-feet." A building "burns *down*," a piece of paper "burns *up*," and a pot of stew just "*burns.*" Both *flammable* and *inflammable* mean the same thing—easily set afire. When you don't understand something, you might say it's "*over my head*," an expression that also means deep in debt. We accept these and many other linguistic quirks because they are simply part of our language. Likewise, native speakers of English say *go to the movies* and *arrive at the movies*. For someone just learning English, though, "arrive *to* the movies" would make perfect sense. But we don't say it because it's not idiomatic English.

With respect to grammar tests, however, the word *idiom* has another meaning. It refers primarily to **idiomatic usage**—that is, to the selection and sequence of words used to convey a meaning. The italicized words in the following sentence are examples of faulty idiom:

> The general was unwilling to pay the *price for victory*.
> Nancy has a negative *opinion toward* me.
> *In regards* to her future, Tina said she'd go to college.

The meaning of each sentence is clear, but the italicized sections don't conform to standard English usage. Revised, the sentences would read:

> The general was unwilling to pay the *price of victory*.
> Nancy has a negative *opinion of* me.
> *With regard* to her future, Tina said she'd go to college.

To identify faulty idiom you must, to a certain extent, follow your instincts and your ear for language. There are no specific guidelines to help untangle problems in idiom. An awkward-sounding word or phrase may be the only evidence.

> The First Amendment is invoked *in those times* when journalists are asked to disclose their sources.

The phrase *in those times* is awkward. Replace *in* with *at*, a preposition that often refers to time—*at* four o'clock, *at* the turn of the century. Or better still, discard the phrase entirely:

> The First Amendment is invoked when journalists are asked to disclose their sources.

Another example:

> A knight was faithful to his king, to his church, and to his lady, and he would gladly die in the name of them.

The phrase *in the name of them* is grammatical but unidiomatic.

> A knight was faithful to his king, to his church, and to his lady, and he would gladly die in their name.

Although errors in English idiom often pertain to the faulty use of prepositions, you're just as likely to find problematic verbs, adverbs, and other parts of speech.

A particular problem related to idiom is the **double negative**. English is a quirky language in some respects because it allows you to use two negative words in a sentence to say something positive, as in

> The halftime performance of the marching band was *not* at all *bad*.

Combining the negative word *not* and the negative word *bad* pays a compliment (however mild) to the marching band.

On the other hand, double negatives meant to express negativity violate standard English usage. Therefore, you mustn't use modifiers such as *never, no,* and *not* with other negative words such as *none, neither, no one, nobody,* and *nothing.*

> DOUBLE NEGATIVE: The kids are not doing nothing during the winter vacation.
> REVISED: The kids are not doing anything during the winter vacation.

Because the adverbs *hardly, scarcely,* and *barely* also qualify as negative words, they should not be combined with other negatives. Instead, replace a negative word with a positive one, as in

> DOUBLE NEGATIVE: There are *hardly* no chocolate doughnuts left on the tray.
> REVISED: There are *hardly any* chocolate doughnuts left on the tray.

Grammar Basics

Checkpoint 16. IDIOM

Identify the errors in English idiom in the following sentences. Write revised versions in the spaces provided. Some sentences may contain no error.

1. To die at battle for their religion was considered an honor.

   _____

2. After the ceremony, the newlyweds ascended up the stairs.

   _____

3. I hope that the admissions office will comply to my request for an extension.

   _____

4. Paleontologists say that bronze was used by hardly no primitive people before the advent of iron and tin.

   _____

5. Because of his preoccupation in classical music, Justin bought a subscription to Symphony Hall concerts.

   _____

6. Most rock climbers are lured by either danger and love of adventure.

   _____

7. When Lucy returned home, she felt as though she'd never been away.

   _____

8. The posse went in pursuit after the horse thieves.

   _____

9. The new security system uses electronic eye scans in the identifying of employees.

   _____

10. Work-study programs offer opportunities to both students and the business community.

    _____

11. No new plans were developed in respect to the environment.

    _____

12. Columbus sailed west in search for a way to the Indies.

    _____

13. The wounded marine could not endure that kind of a pain without passing out.

    _____

14. The children were waiting on the bus to arrive.

    _____

15. Generic drugs are not nearly as expensive than brand-name drugs.

    _____

16. Billy Collins is regarded to be one of the most popular contemporary American poets.

    _____

17. To support themselves, artists must often make a choice between teaching and not doing nothing except trying to earn money by creating art full time.

    _____

18. Most people who travel at Thanksgiving prefer driving more than flying.

    _____

19. Because the boat's engine had failed, the sailor was never far away from harm during the storm.

    _____

20. Although Jackie's term paper was neither well written or fully researched, its grade was A+.

    _____

Answers on page 90

Faulty Diction

Faulty diction means faulty word choice. It occurs when *good* is used instead of *well* after a certain verb, or when *where* is used instead of *when,* as in "the time *where* he took the bus to Jersey." The English language offers many other opportunities to choose incorrect words, as discussed in Chapter 1.

Problems in word choice usually occur when writers ignore word connotations, fail to draw fine distinctions between synonyms, or simply don't know the precise meaning of words. For example:

The poem contains *illusions* to Greek mythology.

This sentence contains an error in diction because the writer meant *allusions.*

The boys ran *a fowl* of the law when they shoplifted the DVD.

Here the writer confused *a fowl* (a chicken or duck) with the word *afoul.*

Another quality common to firefighters is their *reliability* on their fellow firefighters.

The writer probably intended to use *reliance* but put down *reliability* instead.

You may recall that the pronoun *that* can be used to refer to people as well as to animals and nonliving things:

> Pedestrians *that* jaywalk put their lives at risk.
> *Saving Private Ryan* is the name of the film *that* caused a great deal of controversy when it was shown on network television.

Sometimes, the choice of words is a toss-up. It's fine to say, Those are the geese *who* are damaging the grass, but it's also acceptable to say, Those are the geese *that* are damaging the grass.

Wordiness and Redundancies

Sentences need revision when they contain words and phrases that either add no meaning or reiterate what has already been stated. For example:

> A necessary requirement for applying to many colleges is the autobiographical essay.
> An important essential ingredient of a hamburger is meat.
> Have you read *Lust for Life,* the biography of the life of Vincent Van Gogh?

Each of these sentences contains a needless word or phrase. In the first, omit *necessary* because *necessary* by definition implies *requirement.* The phrase *necessary requirement,* therefore, is redundant. In the next sentence, an ingredient described as *essential* must by definition be *important,* so delete the word *important.* And in the last sentence, the phrase *of the life* should be removed because a biography cannot be anything other than the story of someone's life.

> To write effective sentences, omit needless words.

Sentences cluttered with unnecessary words are less effective than tightly written sentences in which every word counts. While paring sentences to the bone, try the following techniques:

1. Look for redundancies.

   > Sal carried a fake, forged ID card.

   The words *fake* and *forged* have essentially the same meaning. To eliminate the redundancy, remove one of the words.

   > Sal carried a fake ID card.

2. Shorten or eliminate unnecessary clauses.

   > At the party there were forty guests who got dressed up in Halloween costumes.

   Rewriting this sentence can reduce it by half.

   > Forty costumed guests attended the Halloween party.

3. Recast phrases as single words or eliminate them altogether.

   > She wore a smile on her face.

   Because smiles are worn nowhere else but on one's face, the phrase *on her face* can be deleted without changing the meaning of the sentence.

   > She wore a smile.

4. Omit needless words.

> He rapidly descended down the steps.

This sentence can be improved by editing out the redundancy in the phrase *descended down* (by definition *descended* indicates downward motion) and by choosing more concise words.

> He sprinted down the steps.

The word *sprinted* cogently captures the sense of a rapid descent.

Here are two more examples:

> WORDY: During the months of July and August last summer, I had a wonderful summer vacation.

Because July and August are the names of summer months, jettison the needless words:

> TIGHT: Last July and August I had a wonderful vacation.

> WORDY: As you continue down the road a little farther, you will be pleased and delighted with the beautiful and gorgeous views of the scenery that you'll be seeing.

The sentence is heavy with redundancies. Lighten its load by turning the initial clause into a phrase and eliminating redundant ideas:

> TIGHT: Continuing down this road, you'll be delighted with the beautiful scenery.

Checkpoint 17. WORDINESS

Revise the following sentences for economy of expression.

1. She constantly irritates and bothers me all the time.

   _____

2. He spoke to me concerning the matter of my future.

   _____

3. Is it a true fact that the ozone layer is being depleted?

   _____

4. I thought that if I didn't take chemistry that I couldn't go to a good college.

   _____

5. Consequently, as a result of the election, the state will have its first female governor.

   _____

6. My father's habitual custom is to watch the sun set in the West.

   _____

7. Harold picked up a brush at the age of ten years old and hasn't stopped painting since.

   _____

8. Research shows that avid sports fans not only suffer fewer depressions, but they are also generally healthier, too, than those not interested in sports.

   _____

9. His field of work is that of a chemist.

   _____

10. For the second time, the cough recurred again.

    Answers on page 91

SENTENCE MECHANICS: PUNCTUATION AND CAPITALIZATION

Punctuation

Cracking the punctuation code is not all that difficult. Perhaps the trickiest thing about punctuation rules is knowing where and when to apply them. The following guidelines should help:

Apostrophes

Apostrophes are used in only three places:

1. In contractions, such as *won't, it's, could've,* and *where's,* apostrophes mark the spot where one or more letters have been omitted. You can also re-create the pronunciation of spoken words by using apostrophes in place of dropped letters. For instance, *goin',* *ma'm,* or *ma'am* and *o',* as in t*op o' the mornin'.*
2. In plurals of letters, signs, or numbers, as in *A's* and *B's,* the *1960's,* and *10's* and *20's.* This custom is changing, however, and many experts now simplify matters by writing *1960s, Ps* and *Qs,* and so forth.
3. In *possessive nouns* such as the *student's class, women's room,* and in indefinite pronouns such as *anybody's guess.* When the noun is plural and ends in *s,* put the apostrophe after the *s,* as in *leaves' color* and *horses' stable.*

   In a series of nouns showing joint possession, only the last noun receives the apostrophe, as in *Susan and George's house.* If Susan and George had separate houses, the phrase would read *Susan's and George's houses.*

   A few possessive forms use both an apostrophe and *of,* as in *a friend of the family's;* a few others that specify time, space, value, or quantity also require apostrophes, as in an *hour's time, a dollar's worth,* and *at my wit's end.*

Commas

Commas are meant to prevent confusion and misunderstanding. They divide sentences into parts, clarifying meaning by separating groups of words into discrete units. They often signal a pause that helps readers understand text. In some situations a comma is optional. When given the choice, leave it out unless its inclusion would prevent ambiguity.

1. Use a comma to signal a pause, as in:

    > NO PAUSE: After brushing his teeth gleamed.
    > PAUSE: After brushing, his teeth gleamed.

    A comma is needed here to separate a phrase and a clause, although that sort of separation is not always essential, as in On the desk a letter from the admissions office lay waiting.

    Commas are needed after some introductory words and in various forms of address:

    > *Well,* you can open it whenever it's convenient.
    > The letter will be waiting for you at home, *Jimmy*.

2. Use commas to set off words that *interrupt the flow* of a sentence. For example, commas are required when conjunctive adverbs are inserted between the subject and verb:

    > Carolyn, *regrettably*, was omitted from the roster.
    > Jennie, *on the other hand,* was included.

    Commas are also needed when a subordinate clause containing information not essential to the main clause is embedded in the main clause:

    > The lost hikers, *who had come from New Jersey,* found shelter in a cave.
    > The three bikers, *whose map of the course was out of date,* arrived two hours after the winner of the race.

    Commas are needed to set off **appositives**—phrases that describe nouns or pronouns, as in:

    > Samantha Higgins, *the defense counsel,* strode into the courtroom.
    > The judge, *Mr. Peterson,* arrived late.

    Single-word appositives may or may not require commas. It depends on the meaning.

    > Jill's brother, *Pete,* lives in Newark.

    In this case, Jill has one brother whose name is Pete. But if Jill has more than one brother, and one of them is Pete, the sentence would be written this way:

    > Jill's brother Pete lives in Newark.

3. A comma is often needed to separate the independent clauses of a compound sentence:

    > The competition is stiff, but it won't keep Miriam from winning.
    > Stacey better call her mom on Mother's Day, or she'll be in big trouble.

    If clauses are very short, however, omit the comma, as in He ate a snack and then he fell asleep.

4. Use commas in a series:

> Rosie's car needs *new tires, a battery, a muffler, and an oil change.*
>
> It was amazing that Marv could sit through the *long, boring, infantile, and ridiculous* lecture.

> Before the last item in a series, a comma is optional. It can't hurt to put it in, however.

Some writers prefer to skip the comma before the last item in a series, but just in case clarity may suffer, it can't hurt to put it in.

5. Commas separate parts of addresses, dates, and place names:

> Who lives at 627 West 115th Street, New York, NY?
> Richard was born on May 27, 1990, the same day as Irene.
> Dave has lived in Madison, Wisconsin; Seattle, Washington; and Eugene, Oregon.

Note that, because each item in the last example already contains a comma, semicolons are needed to avoid confusion.

6. When writing dialogue, use commas to separate quotations from attributions:

> John said, "Close the window."
> "I want it open," protested Ben.

Semicolons

Semicolons are handy when you have written two sentences that are so closely tied to each other that separating them would diminish their integrity. The semicolon, in effect, shortens the pause that ordinarily occurs at the juncture of two separate sentences:

> Jake never stays out this late; his mother worried.
> The momentum was building; she couldn't be stopped now.

One word of caution: Semicolons are substitutes for periods, not for commas. Therefore, use them only to separate independent clauses.

> Semicolons are substitutes for periods, not for commas.

> INCORRECT: On the test Lucy got a 90; which raised her final average.

The clause *which raised her final average* is not an independent clause.

> CORRECT: On the test Lucy got a 90; this grade raised her final average.

Or use them to avoid confusion in a series in which one or more items contains a comma, as in:

> On his trek, Norwood met Allen, a carpenter from Maine; Dr. Jones, a pediatrician from St. Louis; Jonathan, an airline pilot; and me, of course.

Colons

A *colon* calls attention to the words that follow it. It is useful to introduce a list, add an appositive, or, in certain contexts, introduce a quotation. To illustrate:

> In his work, Whitney uses at least five kinds of saws: table saw, radial-arm saw, keyhole saw, coping saw, and jigsaw.

> During vacation Marty must have set two world's records: sleeping 15 hours out of every 24, and consuming more than two pounds of pretzels a day.

> Think about what Polonius says: "Above all, to thine own self be true."

Use a colon between two sentences if the second sentence explains or summarizes the first. Although no rule says that you must capitalize the second sentence, many writers prefer to do so.

> My gym class feels like outer space: It goes on forever.

It's a mistake to use a colon after an incomplete sentence, as in

> Three common types of hardwood trees are: maple, oak, and ash.
> Lucy's courseload consists of: English, math, chemistry, and social studies.
> The paint comes in unusual colors such as: sky-blue pink and strawberry green.

The colons in these examples spoil the unity of what would otherwise be perfectly good sentences.

Dashes

Nothing attracts attention like a *dash*. A dash makes readers pay attention because it marks an abrupt change in thought. A dash is used mostly to define or explain a word or idea:

> Halfway through the speech he lost sight of his purpose—to inform the audience about risky investments.

By using a pair of dashes, you can insert parenthetical material into a sentence or include a sudden change in thought:

> The state finally agreed to install a traffic light—why did it take them so long?—at the intersection of Route 35 and Bedford Road.

Single dashes can combine closely related ideas:

> The state finally agreed to install a traffic light at the intersection of Route 35 and Bedford Road—Hallelujah!

But beware. Many editors and teachers claim that dashes don't belong in formal prose, so if you insist on using them, do so sparingly and only when you are convinced that they will most effectively express your ideas.

Quotation marks

Quotation marks usually surround direct quotations, as in:

> Rita said to Bob, "I'm nuts about you."

But they don't apply to *indirect quotations*—quotations that convey the sense of what was said without using the actual words. For example:

> INCORRECT: Bob told Rita "that he would marry her someday."
> CORRECT: Bob told Rita that he would marry her someday.

Quotation marks can also be used to call attention to certain technical or unusual words and phrases, as in

> Serena quickly established a reputation as a "counter-blogger."

Quotation marks enclose the titles of poems, stories, chapter headings, essays, magazine articles, and other short works. Longer works such as novels, plays, films, and magazine titles are underlined when they appear in handwritten essays and italicized when they appear in print.

Avoid using quotation marks to call attention to clichés, trite expressions, or slang terms. Rewrite instead, using fresh, original language.

Finally, quotation marks may enclose words that express the silent thoughts of a character, as in:

> Carlos glanced at his watch. "I'm going to be late," he thought.

When a narrative includes both silent thoughts and spoken words, steer clear of this technique to avoid confusion.

In American English, periods and commas are placed inside closed quotation marks. Put question marks and exclamation points outside the quotation marks unless they are part of the quote itself.

> "When will the seminar start?" asked Regis.
> Do you understand the meaning of the term "Age of Anxiety"?

Question marks

A direct question should be followed by question mark.

> How do you get to Lexington Avenue from here?

If the question is worded as a request, however, a question mark usually follows, but not always, as in:

> Would you please close the window.

Note that no question mark should appear after an indirect question—that is, after a report that a question has been asked.

> She asked me what time it was.

Exclamation points

Exclamation points are terrific for conveying strong feelings. But think of them as a form of shouting, and because readers don't want to be shouted at, use exclamation points sparingly. Good writers, knowing that overuse of exclamation points dilutes the effect of each one, rely on words, not marks of punctuation, to pump up their prose.

> **"Run!" yelled the crowd as the sprinters neared the finish line.**

If an exclamation point is part of a quotation, as above, the quotation mark follows the exclamation point, but if the strong emotion belongs to the writer, the exclamation point goes outside the quotation mark.

> **As the tsunami approached, we were told, "Relax, it's only a wave"!**

Capitalization

Although capitalization isn't totally standardized, it's not a free-for-all either. Guidelines are so numerous that even experienced professional writers often consult their dictionaries just to be sure.

1. Capitalize first words of sentences, direct quotations, and lines of poetry (most of the time). This *may* include sentences that follow colons, as in He had all the symptoms of love: He could think of nothing but Cheryl all day long. On the other hand, never capitalize a sentence that follows a semicolon.
2. Capitalize proper nouns and adjectives derived from proper nouns: *Victoria, Victorian; Shakespeare, Shakespearean; France, French dressing* (but not *french fries*, which has become a generic term).
3. Capitalize place names: *North America, Lake Moosilauke, Yosemite National Park, Gobi Desert, Mount Rushmore, Panama Canal, the Arctic Ocean, Times Square, Route 66.* Don't capitalize *north, east, south,* and *west* unless you are referring to a particular region of the country, as in They went camping in the *West.* Nor should you capitalize a common noun that is not part of the actual place name: Capitalize *Panama Canal,* but not *the canal across Panama; Moline,* but not *the city of Moline.*
4. Capitalize languages, races, nationalities, religions, and their adjectival forms *the Hungarian language, Inuit, Catholicism, Argentinian, Hispanic, Islam, Muslim.*
5. Capitalize organizations, institutions, and brand names: *United Nations, Pittsburgh Pirates, Library of Congress, Automobile Club of America, Amtrak, Southwest Airlines, the Internet, Toyota.* Don't, however, capitalize the common noun associated with the brand name, as in *Crest toothpaste or Starbucks coffee.*
6. Capitalize titles of people that indicate rank, office, or profession, when they are used with the person's name: *Congressman Kelly, Doctor Dolittle, Coach McConnell, Judge Judy, Lieutenant Lawlor.* Also, the titles of high officials when they are used in place of the official's name, as in the *Secretary General, the Prime Minister, the Secretary of the Treasury.* Don't capitalize titles when referring generically to the position: *the superintendent of schools, the assistant librarian, the clerk of the highway department.*
7. Capitalize family relationships, but only when they are used with a person's name, as in *Uncle Wesley, Grandma Jones, Cousin Dave.*

8. Capitalize titles of books, plays, stories, articles, poems, songs, and other creative works, as in *The Grapes of Wrath, Hamlet,* "*An Occurrence at Owl Creek Bridge,*" "*The World Around Us,*" "*Ode on a Grecian Urn,*" "*Box of Rain.*" Note that articles, conjunctions, and prepositions of less than five letters are not capitalized unless they appear as the last or the first words in the title.

9. Capitalize names that refer to the Deity and the titles of religious tracts, as in *God, the Gospel, the Torah, the Koran, the Lord, the Prophet.* Also pronouns referring to *Him* or *Her.*

10. Capitalize historical names, events, documents, and periods, as in *Battle of Gettysburg, Alien and Sedition Acts, War of 1812, Bill of Rights, Middle Ages.*

11. Capitalize days of the week, months, and holidays, as in *Monday, May, Mother's Day.* The seasons are not capitalized unless given an identity such as *Old Man Winter.*

12. Capitalize the names of specific courses and schools, as in *History 101, Forensic Science, Brookvale High School, Columbia College.* Although course names are capitalized, subjects are not. Therefore, you study *history* in *American History 101* and learn *forensics* in *Forensic Science.* Similarly, you attend *high school* at *Brookvale High School* and go to *college* at *Columbia.*

Checkpoint 18. CAPITALIZATION

Add capital letters where they are needed in the following sentences.

1. on labor day bennington county's fire department plans to hold a turkey shoot on the field at miller's pond.

2. the judge gave district attorney lipman a book entitled *the rules of evidence* and instructed her to read it before she ever dared set foot in the court of appeals of the ninth circuit again.

3. the secretary of state greeted the president of austria at the ronald reagan airport in washington, d.c.

4. the shackleton expedition nearly met its doom on georgia island in antarctica.

5. for christmas he got a black & decker table saw from the sears store next to the old bedford courthouse.

6. according to georgetown's high school principal, eugene griffiths, georgetown high school attracts students from the whole west coast. at georgetown students may major in drawing and painting, design, graphics, or sculpture. mr griffiths said, "i attended a similar high school in new england just after the vietnam war."

7. we expect to celebrate new year's eve again this year by renting a movie of an old broadway musical and by settling down in front of the dvd player with some pepsi and a box of oreos.

8. after traveling all the way to the pacific, the corps of discovery rode down the missouri river going east on their way back to st. louis.

9. This irish linen tablecloth was bought at k-mart in the emeryville mall off powell street.

10. on our way to the west we stopped at yellowstone national park in the northwest corner of the state of wyoming.

Answers on page 91

ANSWER KEY

Page 64, Correct Sentences

Although your sentences may differ from these, be sure you have correctly identified one or more errors.

1. *Sentence fragment.* Elizabeth is stressed out about her sore back.

2. *Comma splice.* Jim asked for an extension on the assignment, and the teacher agreed.

3. *Run-on sentence.* My grandmother is 86 years old and, therefore, walks very slowly.

4. *Sentence fragment.* Although there are many other examples that I could choose to show who I am, many of them are not vivid images of memorable moments but everyday aspects of my life.

5. *Comma splice and run-on sentence.* I wake up, having slept for the four shortest hours of my life. I force open my eyes, and I crawl to the shower. Then my brain begins to function.

6. *Sentence fragment.* It's hard for me to believe that the crucial time has arrived when I will leave the protective world of high school and enter college.

7. *Comma splice.* The large brown garage door creaks open slowly. Out into the morning sunshine a rider on a road bike emerges.

8. *Run-on sentence.* What are the rules that we all must follow? What might happen if we break them?

9. *Sentence fragment.* Louise is a biologist working in the field of genetic engineering and involved in the controversy surrounding human cloning.

10. No error

Page 68, Parallel Structure

Although your answers may be slightly different from these, they should demonstrate your grasp of parallel structure.

1. Steve likes canoeing, biking, reading good books, and writing.

2. Smoking should be prohibited in public places because it harms people's health, deprives nonsmokers of clean air, and is an offensive, smelly habit.

3. To endure extreme cold, you need to be well trained in survival tactics and be in excellent physical condition.

4. As an actor, Arnold Schwarzenegger is admired more for his body than for his portrayal of characters.

5. Like Tony, the accountant found that business was bad during the third quarter.

6. Matthew enrolled to study painting, harmony, music appreciation, and art history.

7. On our first day we rode the cable cars and visited Fisherman's Wharf and the Golden Gate.

8. The lawyer insisted that her job took more hours than a teacher's job.

9. In the speech, the senator accused his colleague of being an ignoramus, too dense to know what was at stake in the legislation.

10. It has been said that walking is better for you than jogging the same distance.

Page 70, Passive Construction

Your sentences may differ from these, but be sure you've used the active voice.

1. Dead leaves covered the backyard.

2. We discussed the crisis in the Mideast.

3. I failed Friday's quiz because I had rehearsed for the play every night that week.

4. We flew to Portland to begin our weeklong vacation in Oregon.

5. Captain Ahab and his crew pursued the great white whale.

6. Fido fetches the newspaper every morning.

7. The president and his advisers decided to go to war.

8. On Friday night, more than twenty customers took out dinners.

9. In three days our group saw five Shakespearean plays.

10. Before you do something physical, the body normally calls on the brain.

Page 72, Sentence Structure

Your sentences may differ from these.

1. Over the weekend, Mr. Finn assigned a huge amount of homework to his students.

2. Dumping garbage, sewage, and other hazardous waste products into the sea, many nations pollute the world's oceans.

3. Because they end up in fish, lobsters, clams, and other sea life, toxic materials enter our bodies when we eat seafood.

4. Our planet has experienced a sharp increase in natural disasters during the last half century.

5. Evidently, the increase has occurred because people in greater numbers now occupy areas prone to natural disasters.

6. As the population has grown, more people have settled on floodplains, along the sea-coast, and in cities built on subterranean fault lines.

7. To motivate young people to study harder in school, community groups have increased college scholarship awards.

8. The American Dream, a popular concept in American culture, has different meanings for different people.

9. Idealized by the movies, television, and countless books, the dream consists of finding a good job, getting married, having a couple of kids, and owning a home.

10. Typically, homes in the community have a white picket fence and a two-car garage.

Page 77, Idiom

1. in battle
2. ascended the stairs
3. comply with
4. hardly any
5. preoccupation with
6. either danger or love
7. Correct
8. in pursuit of
9. to identify employees
10. Correct
11. with respect to

12. in search of a way

13. that kind of pain

14. for the bus

15. as expensive as

16. regarded as one

17. not doing anything

18. driving to flying

19. far from harm

20. neither well written nor fully researched

Page 80, Wordiness

Answers may vary.

1. She constantly bothers me.

2. He spoke to me about my future.

3. Is it true that the ozone layer is being depleted?

4. I thought that without chemistry I couldn't go to a good college.

5. The voters elected the state's first female governor.

6. My father habitually watches the sun set.

7. Harold hasn't stopped painting since picking up a brush at age ten.

8. Research shows that avid sports fans suffer fewer depressions and are generally healthier than those not interested in sports.

9. He is a chemist.

10. The cough recurred twice.

Page 87, Capitalization

1. On Labor Day Bennington County's fire department plans to hold a turkey shoot on the field at Miller's Pond.

2. The judge gave District Attorney Lipman a book entitled *The Rules of Evidence* and instructed her to read it before she ever dared set foot in the Court of Appeals of the Ninth Circuit again.

3. The Secretary of State greeted the President of Austria at the Ronald Reagan Airport in Washington, D.C.

4. The Shackleton expedition nearly met its doom on Georgia Island in Antarctica.

5. For Christmas he got a Black & Decker table saw from the Sears store next to the old Bedford Courthouse.

6. According to Georgetown's high school principal, Eugene Griffiths, Georgetown High School attracts students from the whole West Coast. At Georgetown students may major in drawing and painting, design, graphics, or sculpture. Mr. Griffiths said, "I attended a similar high school in New England just after the Vietnam War."

7. We expect to celebrate New Year's Eve again this year by renting a movie of an old Broadway musical and by settling down in front of the DVD player with some Pepsi and a box of Oreos.

8. After traveling all the way to the Pacific, the Corps of Discovery rode down the Missouri River going east on their way back to St. Louis.

9. This Irish linen tablecloth was bought at K-mart in the Emeryville Mall off Powell Street.

10. On our way to the West, we stopped at Yellowstone National Park in the northwest corner of the state of Wyoming.

Part II
Grammar Tests

Chapter 3

Grammar Pitfalls

This chapter describes twenty-four problems in grammar and usage—two dozen linguistic pitfalls that show up repeatedly on the SAT, the ACT, and other standardized tests. Regardless of which test you take, you can count on being asked one or more times about the points of grammar illustrated by the first ten pitfalls. After that, there's less likelihood of a question, but not that much less. The way to prepare yourself, therefore, is to become familiar with all two dozen pitfalls and learn what to do about them.

List of 24 Grammatical Pitfalls

1. Using an incompatible subject and verb
2. Shifting verb tenses
3. Using an incorrect verb form
4. Disregarding parallel structure
5. Using faulty diction
6. Using a mismatched pronoun and antecedent
7. Making an ambiguous pronoun reference
8. Making a faulty comparison
9. Connecting sentences with commas
10. Using unrelated sentence parts
11. Misusing semicolons and commas
12. Misplacing modifiers
13. Dangling participles
14. Writing incomplete and run-on sentences
15. Shifting pronoun person
16. Choosing the wrong pronoun
17. Misusing coordinate and/or subordinate clauses
18. Wordiness
19. Using faulty idioms
20. Misusing adjectives and adverbs
21. Mixed sentence construction
22. Shifting noun and pronoun numbers
23. Using awkward language
24. Shifting from active to passive sentence construction

Frankly, if you can identify all twenty-four errors right off the bat and can explain which rule of grammar they've broken, you probably don't need this book. Life is too short to waste time studying principles of grammar and usage that you've already mastered. So, instead of studying these pages, take your dog for a stroll or go see a movie. Or better yet, tutor a friend who can't tell a pronoun from a preposition.

Instructions:

Look for faulty grammar in each of the sentences and paragraphs labeled "INCORRECT." Before reading the explanation, try to spot the error and decide how to fix it.

Pitfall 1: **Using an incompatible subject and verb**

INCORRECT: Tony's talent in chess and weight lifting prove his mental and physical strength.

Explanation: The word *talent*, the subject of the sentence, is a singular noun. The verb *prove* is plural. Therefore, the subject and verb fail to agree. Correct the error by changing *talent* to *talents* or *prove* to *proves.*

CORRECTED: Tony's *talent* (singular noun) in chess and weight lifting *proves* (singular verb) his mental and physical strength.

or

Tony's *talents* (plural noun) in chess and weight lifting *prove* (plural verb) his mental and physical strength.

For details on **subject-verb agreement**, turn to page 30.

Pitfall 2: **Shifting verb tenses**

INCORRECT: On Interstate 80, a trooper pulls me over and gave me a speeding ticket.

Explanation: The verb *pulls* is in the present tense, but the verb *gave* shifts the action to the past tense. Correct the inconsistency either by changing *pulls* to *pulled* or *gave* to *gives.*

CORRECTED: On Interstate 80, a trooper *pulled* (past tense) me over and *gave* (past tense) me a speeding ticket.

or

On Interstate 80, a trooper *pulls* (present tense) me over and *gives* (present tense) me a speeding ticket.

For details on **shifting verb tenses**, turn to page 23.

Pitfall 3: **Using an incorrect verb form**

INCORRECT: After dinner, Katie cleared the table and blowed out the candles.

Explanation: The past tense of the verb *to blow* is *blew*. Therefore, the sentence includes an incorrect verb form. Correct the error by changing *blowed* to *blew.*

CORRECTED: After dinner, Katie cleared the table and *blew* out the candles.

For details on **faulty verb forms**, turn to page 25.

<u>Pitfall 4</u>: **Disregarding parallel structure**

> INCORRECT: Many sports fans think that pro athletes are spoiled, selfish, and they earn too much money.

Explanation: Items in a series should be stated in the same grammatical form. That is, the way each item is phrased should be parallel to all the others. The words *spoiled* and *selfish* are adjectives, but *they earn too much money* is a clause. Correct the error by changing the clause to an adjective.

> CORRECTED: Many sports fans think that pro athletes are spoiled, selfish, and overpaid.

For details on **faulty parallelism**, turn to page 65.

<u>Pitfall 5</u>: **Using the wrong word, a.k.a. faulty diction**

[handwritten: which refers to things]

> INCORRECT: The doctor first treated the passengers which were most severely injured in the crash.

Explanation: The relative pronouns *who* and *that* are used to refer to people; *which* refers to other things.

> CORRECTED: The doctor first treated the passengers *who* (or *that*) were most severely injured in the crash.

[handwritten: who, that refers to people]

For details on **relative pronouns**, turn to page 16.

<u>Pitfall 6</u>: **Using a mismatched pronoun and antecedent** *[handwritten: singular]*

> INCORRECT: Budget cuts are forcing the library to reduce their hours.
> *[handwritten: its]*

Explanation: The plural pronoun *their* improperly refers to the singular noun *library*. Because pronouns and their antecedents must agree in number, change *their* to *its* or *library* to *libraries*.

> CORRECTED: Budget cuts are forcing the *library* (singular) to reduce *its* (singular) hours.
>
> or
>
> Budget cuts are forcing *libraries* (plural) to reduce *their* (plural) hours.

For details on **pronoun-antecedent agreement**, turn to page 10.

<u>Pitfall 7</u>: **Making an ambiguous pronoun reference**

> INCORRECT: The friendship between Joan and Jane fell apart after she went away to college.

Explanation: The pronoun *she* appears to refer to either *Joan* or *Jane*. Because the reference is unclear, replace *she* with the name of one of the women.

> CORRECTED: The friendship between Joan and Jane fell apart after *Joan* (or *Jane*) went away to college.

For details on **faulty pronoun references** turn to page 12.

<u>Pitfall 8</u>: **Making a faulty comparison**

    INCORRECT: Rosie's score on the SAT was better than Charlie.

Explanation: This sentence means to compare Rosie's score on the SAT with Charlie's score. Instead it compares Rosie's score with Charlie himself, a nonsensical comparison. Correct the error by making a reference to Charlie's score or by writing a completely new sentence.

    CORRECTED: Rosie's score on the SAT was better than Charlie's score.

or:

    Rosie scored higher on the SAT than Charlie.

For details on **faulty comparisons** turn to page 35.

<u>Pitfall 9</u>: **Connecting sentences with commas**

    INCORRECT: The concert on Saturday night was terrific, we got home very late.

Explanation: This construction is made up of two independent sentences joined, or "spliced," by a comma. Correct the error by using a period and capital letter between the sentences, or replace the comma with a semicolon.

    CORRECTED: The concert on Saturday night was terrific. We got home very late.

or

    ✳ The concert on Saturday night was terrific; we got home very late.

For details on **comma splices** turn to page 64.

<u>Pitfall 10</u>: **Using unrelated sentence parts**

    INCORRECT: Eli Whitney invented the cotton gin, and who did so during the final years of the 18th century.

Explanation: The first clause of the sentence states a fact about *Eli Whitney*, the grammatical subject. The second clause, beginning with *and*, adds a piece of relevant information but its construction is not grammatically related to the first clause. The phrase *and who did so* is meaningless and out of place in the context. Correct the error by revising the sentence.

    CORRECTED: Eli Whitney invented the cotton gin during the final years of the 18th century.

For details on **mismatched sentence parts**, turn to page 61.

✳ <u>Pitfall 11</u>: **Misusing semicolons and commas**

    1. INCORRECT: Lucy wrote a children's story; which her little sister adored.

Explanation: This construction uses a semicolon instead of a comma to separate an independent clause (*Lucy wrote a children's story*) and a dependent clause (*which her little sister adored*). Because a semicolon serves the same function as a period—to separate two grammatically independent sentences—it may not be used as a comma substitute.

    CORRECTED: Lucy wrote a children's story; her little sister adored it.

2. INCORRECT: Mr. and Mrs. Bennett sent their son to grammar camp last summer and that's why Newt is so adept at using commas.

Explanation: A compound sentence consisting of a pair of brief, closely related clauses doesn't require a comma before the conjunction (*and, but, or, for*, and so on). When the clauses are long and have different grammatical subjects, however, insert a comma before the conjunction.

CORRECTED: Mr. and Mrs. Bennett sent their son to grammar camp last summer, and that's why Newt is so adept at using commas.

For details on **semicolon and comma errors**, turn to page 82. Also see **sentence structure**, page 70.

Pitfall 12: **Misplacing modifiers**

INCORRECT: The house stood on the corner which was painted red.

Explanation: The words *which was painted red* are meant to describe the house but appear instead to describe the *corner*. The description, called a *modifier* because it changes (i.e., *modifies*) our image of the house, is too far removed from *house*, the noun it intends to modify. To correct the error move *house* and its modifier closer to each other.

CORRECTED: The house, which was painted red, stood on the corner.

For details on **misplaced modifiers**, turn to page 35.

Pitfall 13: **Dangling participles, a.k.a. dangling modifiers**

INCORRECT: Running to biology class, the bell rang before Jake arrived.

Explanation: A *participle* is a verb form ending in *-ing* in the present tense and is used to modify a noun or pronoun. Here, the participle *running* is meant to modify *Jake*, but it modifies *bell* instead, an error that conjures a bizarre image of a bell sprinting down the corridor. Correct the error by moving *Jake* closer to the participle.

CORRECTED: Running to biology class, Jake heard the bell ring before he arrived.

For details on **dangling modifiers**, turn to page 63.

Pitfall 14: **Writing an incomplete sentence**

— Fragment

INCORRECT: Sergeant York, a hero of World War I and the subject of a popular movie that starred Gary Cooper.

Explanation: This string of words is meant to be a complete sentence, but it is only a sentence fragment because it lacks a verb that goes with the grammatical subject, *Sergeant York*. Correct the error by deleting the comma and adding *was* or some other appropriate verb after the word *York*.

CORRECTED: Sergeant York was a hero of World War I and the subject of a popular movie that starred Gary Cooper.

For details on **sentence fragments**, turn to page 62.

Grammar Tests

Pitfall 14 (cont.): **Running sentences together**

> INCORRECT: Maria aspires to be a ballerina she practices dancing five hours a day.

Explanation: This construction is made up of two independent clauses that lack the punctuation needed to signal where the first clause ends and the second begins. Correct the error by separating *ballerina* and *she*. Use a semicolon or a period and capital letter.

> CORRECTED: Maria aspires to be a ballerina; she practices dancing five hours a day.

or

> Maria aspires to be a ballerina. She practices dancing five hours a day.

Another solution: Subordinate one clause to the other, thereby creating a single sentence:

> Because Maria aspires to be a ballerina, she practices dancing five hours a day.

For details on **run-on sentences**, turn to page 64.

Pitfall 15: **Shifting pronoun person**

> INCORRECT: If you apply to the state university, I should hear from the admissions office within a month.

Explanation: The sentence starts out using the second-person pronoun *you*, but then shifts into the first person with the pronoun *I*. Because the use of pronouns should be consistent throughout a sentence, change *I* to *you*.

> CORRECTED: If *you* apply to the state university, you should hear from the admissions office within a month.

For details on **shifts in pronoun person**, turn to page 9.

Pitfall 16: **Choosing the wrong pronoun**

> INCORRECT: Between you and I, the food at the party was awful.

Explanation: The pronoun *I* is in the nominative case and may be used only in the grammatical subject of a sentence. A pronoun in a phrase that begins with a preposition (*e.g.*, *between*), on the other hand, must be in the objective case. Correct the error by changing *I* to *me*.

> CORRECTED: Between you and me, the food at the party was awful.

For details on **the case of pronouns**, turn to page 6.

Pitfall 17: **Misusing coordinate and/or subordinate clauses**

> INCORRECT: During rush hour a truck full of tomatoes turned over on the highway, but it caused a huge traffic jam.

Explanation: This sentence consists of two coordinate clauses joined by *but*. The word *but* is a poor choice because it ordinarily introduces a contrast or contradictory idea (e.g., He's not a genius *but* a buffoon). Therefore, the coordinating conjunction *and* should replace *but*.

> CORRECTED: During rush hour a truck full of tomatoes turned over on the highway, and it caused a huge traffic jam.

Another solution: Turn one of the coordinate clauses into a subordinate clause, thereby tightening the sentence, as in:

> When a truck full of tomatoes turned over on the highway during rush hour, it caused a huge traffic jam.

For details on **faulty coordination and subordination**, turn to page 46.

For details on **faulty coordination and subordination**, turn to page 46.

Pitfall 18: **Wordiness**

> INCORRECT: Due to the fact that the building is scheduled to be built in the near future, we will revert back to Plan B in the event of a strike.

Explanation: This sentence is wordy. (Technically, wordiness is not a grammatical flaw, but the excess verbiage clearly relates to correct and effective English usage.) *Due to the fact that* can easily be reduced to one word: *Because*. Similarly, *in the near future* can be expressed as *soon*, and *in the event of* can be reduced to *if*. Also, the phrase *revert back* is redundant, because by definition *revert* means *to go back*.

> CORRECTED: Because the building is scheduled to go up soon, Plan B will take effect if a strike occurs.

(*Note*: This version is but one of many possibilities.)
For details on **wordiness**, turn to page 79.

Pitfall 19: **Using faulty idioms**

> INCORRECT: Listening at the radio kept Jimmy from falling asleep while driving.

Explanation: The word *idiom* refers to idiomatic usage—that is, to the selection and sequence of words. In the given sentence, the use of *at* fails to conform to standard English usage. Correct the error by substituting *to* for *at*.

> CORRECTED: Listening *to* the radio kept Jimmy from falling asleep while driving.

For details on **faulty idioms**, turn to page 75.

Pitfall 20: **Misusing adjectives and adverbs**

> INCORRECT: Her father spoke sharp to Terry when she arrived home two hours late.

Explanation: Because adverbs, not adjectives, modify verbs, the adjective *sharp* is misused. You can tell by asking the question, *How* did her father speak to Terry? The answer: He spoke *sharply*. The adverb *sharply*, therefore, modifies the verb *spoke*. Correct the error by substituting *sharply* for *sharp*.

> CORRECTED: Her father spoke *sharply* to Terry when she arrived home two hours late.

For details on **choosing adjectives and adverbs**, turn to page 41.

Pitfall 21: **Mixed sentence construction**

> INCORRECT: Lilah's ambition is to be a lawyer and intends to go to law school after college.

Explanation: Mixed sentence construction suggests that the writer, in finishing a sentence, ignored how it had begun. Here, the grammatical subject of the sentence, *ambition*, goes with the verb *is*. But the subject seems to have been forgotten in the second part of the sentence, because the verb *intends* stands without an appropriate subject. Correct the oversight with a compound sentence containing two subjects and two verbs, for example: Lilah's ambition is to be a lawyer, and she intends to go to law school after college. For an even better sentence, subordinate one of the clauses:

> CORRECTED: Lilah, who aspires to be a lawyer (subordinate clause), intends to go to law school after college.

For details on **mixed construction**, turn to page 61.

Pitfall 22: **Shifting noun and pronoun numbers**

> INCORRECT: Reading to children every day encourages them to grow up as a literate, book-loving adult.

Explanation: The noun *children* and the pronoun *them* are plural. But the noun *adult*, which refers to both *children* and *them*, is singular. Because both nouns and the pronoun should be consistent in number, delete the *a* and change *adult* to *adults*.

> CORRECTED: Reading to children every day encourages them to grow up as literate, book-loving adults.

For details on **shifts between noun and pronoun numbers**, turn to page 10.

Pitfall 23: **Using awkward language**

> INCORRECT: Although its being informative, the film ignored the basic causes of alcohol abuse.

Explanation: An awkwardly worded sentence can be grammatically sound but still in need of repair. Revise the awkward phrase *Although its being informative* to convey the same meaning in standard English.

> CORRECTED: Despite its informative content, the film ignored the basic causes of alcohol abuse. (Note: This version is but one of many possibilities.)

For details on **awkwardness and standard syntax**, turn to page 74.

Pitfall 24: **Shifting from active to passive sentence construction**

> INCORRECT: Cindy yearns to go to an out-of-state private college, but the tuition is unable to be afforded by her family.

Explanation: The first clause is written in the active voice because *Cindy*, its grammatical subject, performs the action, *yearns*. The second clause is in the passive voice, however, because its subject, *tuition*, is not the performer of the action. Technically, the sentence is correct, but the shift from active to passive voice is a stylistic weakness that buries *family*, the performer of the action, in a prepositional phrase. Keep the spotlight on *family* by making it the subject.

> CORRECTED: Cindy yearns to go to an out-of-state private college, but her family can't afford the tuition.

For details on **active and passive construction**, turn to page 69.

Chapter 4

SAT Grammar Questions

The SAT is a test of reading, math, and writing. It takes three hours and 45 minutes to complete. Only one part of the exam—the hour-long Writing Test—includes questions on English grammar. The first 25 minutes of the Writing Test are given to essay writing. The remaining 35 minutes consist of multiple-choice questions on English grammar and usage.

The grammar section contains three types of questions:

Improving Sentences:	25 questions that ask you to correct poorly written sentences
Identifying Sentence Errors:	18 questions that ask you to find grammar and usage errors in a given set of sentences
Improving Paragraphs:	Six questions that ask you to make corrections in a first draft of a student-written essay

The questions are offered in two parts. The first part, lasting 25 minutes, includes all three types of questions, 35 questions in all. The second part—10 minutes long—is made up of 14 additional Improving Sentence questions.

Of the three types of questions, Identifying Sentence Errors questions are the briefest—rarely more than two or three lines. Most students answer them more quickly and easily than the others. The Improving Sentences questions take a little longer because they require more reading, and the Improving Paragraph questions take longer still because they refer to problems embedded in the text of an essay that you are given to read. Strictly speaking, the Improving Paragraph questions don't ask about grammar. Rather, they deal mostly with issues of essay writing—style, organization, paragraph development, and so forth. Every so often a question of grammar is thrown into the mix. That happens so rarely that this chapter discusses only those issues of grammar found in the first two types of questions. For matters raised by the Improving Paragraph questions, turn to Chapter 7.

Questions on the SAT will ask you to identify common sentence errors and to improve the expression of a variety of sentences. You won't be tested on parts of speech or grammatical terminology. In effect, the questions deal with everyday problems in grammar and usage—those described in Chapter 3, "Grammar Pitfalls."

Answering the Questions

There's no need to rush through the questions on the SAT. The test has been carefully calibrated to coincide with the time allotted, provided you work steadily. You'll earn one point for each correct answer and lose a quarter of a point (.25) for each wrong answer. An item left blank will neither add to nor take away from your score. A machine will score your responses to the 49 questions and will report a subscore on a scale of 20–80.

Subtracting credit for wrong answers on multiple-choice questions is meant to discourage blind guessing. Therefore, if you don't have a clue about how to answer a question, leave it blank—but it pays to guess if you can confidently eliminate one of the five choices. The odds are one in four that you'll be right. Not terrific odds, but suppose that on four questions you eliminate one wrong choice and you guess four times. If you guess right just once, you'll earn one point and lose three-quarters of a point, a net gain of one quarter point. If you leave all four blank, you will gain nothing. Yes, it's a gamble, because you could make four incorrect guesses, but the chances of losing every time are only one in four. And you could get lucky and hit two, three, or even four correct answers.

When a question gives you trouble, and you can't decide among, say, three choices, common wisdom says that you should go with your first impulse. Testing experts and psychologists agree that there's a better than average chance of success if you trust your intuition. However, there are no guarantees, and because the mind works in so many strange ways, relying on your initial choice may not always work for you. If you come to a question that baffles you, don't agonize over it. Just go to the next one, and go back later if time permits.

> If a question stumps you, guess at the answer if you can eliminate at least one choice.

Another piece of folk wisdom about guessing is that if one answer is longer than the others, that may be your best choice. That's not information you should depend on. In fact, since economy of expression is a virtue in writing, a shorter choice may more often be the best answer. The truth of the matter is that you can't depend on tricks or gimmicks on the SAT.

Improving Sentences Questions

In this section of the test you are asked to recognize errors in standard English, as well as problems in style and expression. In each question, part of a sentence—or sometimes the whole sentence—is underlined. You are given five versions of the underlined words. Your task is to choose the best one. Because Choice A always repeats the original underlined segment, select A only if you think no change is needed. A word of caution: Never choose an alternative that substantially changes the meaning of the original sentence, even if its grammar and style are perfect.

Sample Questions

1. <u>Studying and taking practice tests</u> helps students raise their SAT scores.
   - (A) Studying and taking practice tests
   - (B) Studying and practicing tests
   - (C) Studying, along with taking practice tests,
   - (D) By studying and practicing tests,
   - (E) Due to studying and practicing tests

Explanation: A basic rule of English grammar is that the subject of a sentence must agree in number with its verb. That is, a singular subject must have a singular verb, and a plural subject must be accompanied by a plural verb. The sample sentence has a compound subject (*studying <u>and</u> taking*), made up of two different and distinct activities. In effect, it is a plural subject. The correct verb, therefore, is *help*. But you can't change *helps* to *help* because *helps* is not underlined. Instead, you must search the choices for a singular subject, one that goes with the singular verb *helps*. Only C contains a singular subject (*Studying*). Therefore, C is the correct answer.

To answer this question you need to know the grammatical rules governing noun-verb agreement, including the one that says the insertion of phrases beginning with such words as *along with*, *in addition to*, and *with* have no influence on the number (singular or plural) of the verb.

(*For more details on subject-verb agreement turn to Chapter 1, page 30.*)

2. Many students insist that the schoolwork in junior year is far harder <u>than senior year.</u>
   - (A) than senior year
   - (B) than the schoolwork in senior year
   - (C) than senior year's schoolwork
   - (D) in comparison to senior year
   - (E) compared to schoolwork in senior year

Explanation: The original sentence illogically compares *schoolwork* and *senior year*. Because the writer clearly intended to compare schoolwork in junior year with schoolwork in senior year, Choice A cannot be correct.

Choice B makes the comparison clear. Expressing the comparison with phrases in parallel form (i.e., *schoolwork in junior year* and *schoolwork in senior year*) conveys the meaning that the writer intended. B, therefore, is the correct answer.

Choice C, although grammatically correct, is stylistically weak because the phrase *schoolwork in junior year* is not parallel in form to *senior year's schoolwork*.

Choice D is wrong because it makes an awkwardly worded and unnecessary comparison. The word *harder* indicates that a comparison is being made. To add the phrase *in comparison*, therefore, is redundant.

Choice E is wrong for the same reason as D.

To answer this question correctly you need to know that comparisons should be stated in parallel grammatical form.

(*For more details on parallelism, turn to Chapter 2, page 65.*)

3. The SAT Writing Test has the effect <u>to make</u> teachers and students think more about the need to know grammar basics.
   (A) to make
   (B) to force
   (C) in making
   (D) of making
   (E) by making

    Explanation: In the given sentence, the verb *make* is used in its infinitive form. Infinitives are most often used as nouns, as in "*To take* this test is fun," but also as adjectives ("You have the skill *to improve*,") and as adverbs ("Study *to do* better."). Analyzing the grammatical uses of infinitives, however, isn't the most likely path to the correct answer. Rather, in this and in other Improving Sentences questions, you may need to rely on your sense of standard English idiom to determine the right answer. Only D expresses the idea in standard English.

How to Find Answers to Improving Sentences Questions

- Read the entire sentence, paying close attention to its meaning.
- Be aware that any errors will exist *only* in the underscored segment of the sentence.
- Try to *hear* the sentence in your head.
- Try to determine whether a problem exists.
- Search for wordiness and awkward expression in the underscored segment of the sentence.
- Read the choices, but ignore Choice A, which is identical to the underscored segment of the original sentence.
- Eliminate all choices that contain obvious errors.
- Review the remaining choices for flaws in grammar and usage. (See Chapter 1 *for details about precisely what to look for.*)
- Eliminate any choice that changes the meaning of the sentence.
- If no change is needed, mark A on your answer sheet.

Identifying Sentence Errors

These questions ask you to recognize errors in grammar and standard English usage. You aren't required to name or label the error, only to find it. Once you have located the error, if there is one, that's it. You've done your job.

    Only the underlined and lettered parts of each sentence may contain an error. Assume that the rest of the sentence is correct. No sentence contains more than one error. If a sentence contains no error, the correct choice is always E (No error).

Sample Questions

1. <u>At the conclusion</u> of the ceremony, the new members <u>sweared</u> that <u>they</u>
     (A)   (B)   (C)

     would never <u>reveal</u> the secret handshake. <u>No error</u>.
               (D)   (E)

Explanation: The correct answer to Question 1 is B because the past tense of the verb *swear* is *swore*. The verb *swear* doesn't adhere to the usual pattern of verbs—that is, creating the past tense by adding *-ed* to the present tense, as in *walk/walked* or *love/loved*. Rather, it follows a pattern of its own, just like other so-called irregular verbs, including *eat/eaten, ring/rung, sleep/slept,* and many more.

Knowing about irregular verbs could have led you to the right answer. Yet, had you never heard about such verbs, you still might have been drawn to Choice B by your innate sense of the way English sounds. In other words, your language "ear" may have told you that something was amiss. Nevertheless, even a good ear for language is not a reliable substitute for a thorough understanding of grammar and usage.

(*For more details on irregular verbs, see Chapter 1, page 26.*)

2. <u>With the development</u> of antitoxins and serums, <u>there</u> are hardly <u>no</u> cases
           (A)   (B)   (C)
     of smallpox or yellow fever <u>anywhere</u> in the world. <u>No error</u>
                        (D)   (E)

Explanation: The correct answer to Question 2 is C because the underlined word is a double negative. Both *hardly* and *no* are negative words. Therefore a phrase containing both words constitutes an error in standard English grammar.

(*For more on double negatives, turn to Chapter 2, page 76.*)

3. <u>Yesterday</u>, the guidance department announced the time of the
     (A)
     SAT and <u>sends</u> a letter to all students <u>that</u> wished <u>them</u> good
           (B)   (C)   (D)
     luck. <u>No error</u>.
          (E)

Explanation: The events described in the sentence took place in the past—yesterday, in fact. The verb *sends* is in the present tense. Because the sentence is meant to describe a past event, the verb should be in the past tense (*sent*). Therefore, B is the correct answer.

In colloquial speech, the present tense is sometimes used to talk about the past, as in: "So, yesterday they *board* the plane and *settle* into their seats, when suddenly the flight attendant *announces* . . . ," but it is rarely used in standard English. In any case, the verb tense throughout a sentence should be consistent.

How to Find Answers to Identifying Sentence Errors Questions

- Read the whole sentence.
- Try to *hear* the sentence in your head.
- Focus your attention on awkward–sounding words and phrases.
- Try to explain what the grammatical flaw might be. Review the remaining choices for flaws in grammar and usage. (*Likely errors are discussed fully in Chapter 5.*)
- If all the underscored words are correct, mark E on your answer sheet.

SAT QUESTIONS FOR PRACTICE

The remainder of this chapter consists of SAT practice questions. The two exercises, or "Checkpoints," are arranged in SAT format:

1. 11 questions on Improving Sentences
2. 18 questions on Identifying Sentence Errors
3. 14 more questions on Improving Sentences

Write your answers on the Model Answer Sheet accompanying each Checkpoint. Administer the questions to yourself as though you were actually taking the SAT. Find a quiet place at a table or desk. Remove all distractions, sharpen your pencil, read the directions, and go to work. Allow yourself 25 minutes to complete each exercise.

If you finish in less than 25 minutes, use the remaining time to review your answers. If you don't answer all the questions in the allotted time, you are probably working too slowly—more slowly, in fact, than you'd be expected to work during an SAT exam. With practice, however, you're likely to pick up your pace and answer all the questions before time is up.

After each exercise, use the answer key to check your responses, then read the answer explanations. Read the explanations for questions you missed, as well as for those you got. You may pick up some helpful pointers about grammar. In time, you'll also discern your strengths and weaknesses. Knowing where you erred will help you focus your studying as you prepare for the SAT.

Are you ready to begin? If so, go on to the next page. Good luck!

SAT CHECKPOINT 1
ANSWER SHEET
(Total time: 25 minutes)

Improving Sentences

1. Ⓐ Ⓑ Ⓒ Ⓓ Ⓔ   5. Ⓐ Ⓑ Ⓒ Ⓓ Ⓔ   9. Ⓐ Ⓑ Ⓒ Ⓓ Ⓔ

2. Ⓐ Ⓑ Ⓒ Ⓓ Ⓔ   6. Ⓐ Ⓑ Ⓒ Ⓓ Ⓔ   10. Ⓐ Ⓑ Ⓒ Ⓓ Ⓔ

3. Ⓐ Ⓑ Ⓒ Ⓓ Ⓔ   7. Ⓐ Ⓑ Ⓒ Ⓓ Ⓔ   11. Ⓐ Ⓑ Ⓒ Ⓓ Ⓔ

4. Ⓐ Ⓑ Ⓒ Ⓓ Ⓔ   8. Ⓐ Ⓑ Ⓒ Ⓓ Ⓔ

Identifying Sentence Errors

12. Ⓐ Ⓑ Ⓒ Ⓓ Ⓔ   18. Ⓐ Ⓑ Ⓒ Ⓓ Ⓔ   24. Ⓐ Ⓑ Ⓒ Ⓓ Ⓔ

13. Ⓐ Ⓑ Ⓒ Ⓓ Ⓔ   19. Ⓐ Ⓑ Ⓒ Ⓓ Ⓔ   25. Ⓐ Ⓑ Ⓒ Ⓓ Ⓔ

14. Ⓐ Ⓑ Ⓒ Ⓓ Ⓔ   20. Ⓐ Ⓑ Ⓒ Ⓓ Ⓔ   26. Ⓐ Ⓑ Ⓒ Ⓓ Ⓔ

15. Ⓐ Ⓑ Ⓒ Ⓓ Ⓔ   21. Ⓐ Ⓑ Ⓒ Ⓓ Ⓔ   27. Ⓐ Ⓑ Ⓒ Ⓓ Ⓔ

16. Ⓐ Ⓑ Ⓒ Ⓓ Ⓔ   22. Ⓐ Ⓑ Ⓒ Ⓓ Ⓔ   28. Ⓐ Ⓑ Ⓒ Ⓓ Ⓔ

17. Ⓐ Ⓑ Ⓒ Ⓓ Ⓔ   23. Ⓐ Ⓑ Ⓒ Ⓓ Ⓔ   29. Ⓐ Ⓑ Ⓒ Ⓓ Ⓔ

Improving Sentences

30. Ⓐ Ⓑ Ⓒ Ⓓ Ⓔ   35. Ⓐ Ⓑ Ⓒ Ⓓ Ⓔ   40. Ⓐ Ⓑ Ⓒ Ⓓ Ⓔ

31. Ⓐ Ⓑ Ⓒ Ⓓ Ⓔ   36. Ⓐ Ⓑ Ⓒ Ⓓ Ⓔ   41. Ⓐ Ⓑ Ⓒ Ⓓ Ⓔ

32. Ⓐ Ⓑ Ⓒ Ⓓ Ⓔ   37. Ⓐ Ⓑ Ⓒ Ⓓ Ⓔ   42. Ⓐ Ⓑ Ⓒ Ⓓ Ⓔ

33. Ⓐ Ⓑ Ⓒ Ⓓ Ⓔ   38. Ⓐ Ⓑ Ⓒ Ⓓ Ⓔ   43. Ⓐ Ⓑ Ⓒ Ⓓ Ⓔ

34. Ⓐ Ⓑ Ⓒ Ⓓ Ⓔ   39. Ⓐ Ⓑ Ⓒ Ⓓ Ⓔ

Cut along dotted line.

Grammar Tests: SAT

CHECKPOINT 1
Time: 25 minutes

IMPROVING SENTENCES

INSTRUCTIONS: The underlined sentences and sentence parts below may contain errors in standard English, including awkward or ambiguous expression, poor word choice, incorrect sentence structure, or faulty grammar and usage. Read each sentence carefully and identify which of the five versions most effectively and correctly expresses the meaning of the underlined material. Indicate your choice by filling in the corresponding space on the answer sheet. Because Choice A always repeats the original, choose A if none of the other choices improves the original sentence.

1. Tom, Derek, and Steve were eating lunch together <u>when, choking on a piece of raw carrot, he began to cough</u>.
   (A) when, choking on a piece of raw carrot, he began to cough.
   (B) and then he coughed after he choked on a piece of raw carrot
   (C) when Tom began to cough after choking on a piece of raw carrot
   (D) when Tom began coughing, being he choked on a piece of raw carrot
   (E) and, since Tom has choked on a piece of raw carrot, he began to cough

2. To be a world-class athlete in any sport, <u>one must be willing to sacrifice oneself completely</u> to a superhuman regimen of training, travel, and competition.
   (A) one must be willing to sacrifice oneself completely
   (B) a complete sacrifice of oneself
   (C) one must be willing to sacrifice themself completely
   (D) they must be willing to sacrifice themselves completely
   (E) one must be willing to sacrifice yourself completely

3. Daisy had just returned from her dental appointment <u>and then she found out</u> that her essay had won first prize.
   (A) and then she found out
   (B) and that was when it was told to her
   (C) when it was heard by her
   (D) and then they let her know
   (E) when she learned

4. Public transportation in the suburbs and outlying areas is generally not so convenient and reliable <u>as it is</u> in the city.
   (A) as it is
   (B) as they are
   (C) as those
   (D) as getting around
   (E) compared to

5. While passing by the firehouse, <u>the siren began to screech loud, which scared me</u>.
    (A) the siren began to screech loud, which scared me
    (B) the siren began screeching loudly, which scared me
    (C) the screech of the loud siren scared me
    (D) I was scared by the loud screech of the siren
    (E) I heard the siren screeching loudly and scaring me

6. Linguists have found that cursing <u>in English is no more common than other languages</u>.
    (A) in English is no more common than other languages
    (B) is no more common in English than cursing in other languages
    (C) is no more common in other languages than they are in English
    (D) compared to English is no more common in other languages
    (E) in comparison to English is no more common in other languages

7. Mattel has manufactured a doll that <u>cries, smiles, and it has a vocabulary of one hundred words</u>.
    (A) cries, smiles, and it has a vocabulary of one hundred words
    (B) cries, smiles, and speaks with a vocabulary of one hundred words
    (C) can cry, can smile, and it has a vocabulary or one hundred words
    (D) will cry and smile, although its vocabulary is one hundred words
    (E) is smiling, crying, and speaking a vocabulary of one hundred words

8. In most countries around the world, <u>they have laws that allow gay people to serve in the military</u>.
    (A) they have laws that allow gay people to serve in the military
    (B) they have a law allowing gay people to serve in the military
    (C) the laws that allow gay people to serve in the military
    (D) their laws allow gay people to serve in the military
    (E) the law allows gay people to serve in the military

9. October 15th will mark the second anniversary <u>of us coming to live in Oakland</u>.
    (A) of us coming to live in Oakland
    (B) of our coming to live in Oakland
    (C) of we arriving to live in Oakland
    (D) of we living in Oakland
    (E) of us moving to Oakland to live

10. Is it certain that the opening of the new mall, scheduled for this weekend, <u>would be</u> delayed at least a week?
    (A) would be
    (B) having been
    (C) will have been
    (D) will be
    (E) had been

11. The Southwest's center for art and music, <u>Santa Fe, an annual destination for thousands of visitors</u>.
    (A) Santa Fe, an annual destination for thousands of visitors
    (B) visitors by the thousands flock to Santa Fe annually
    (C) annually thousands of visitors flock to Santa Fe
    (D) thousands of visitors annually flock to Santa Fe
    (E) Santa Fe annually attracts thousands of visitors

IDENTIFYING SENTENCE ERRORS

INSTRUCTIONS: The underlined and lettered parts of each sentence below may contain an error in grammar, usage, word choice (diction), or expression (idiom). Read each sentence carefully and identify which item, if any, contains an error. Indicate your choice by filling in the corresponding space on the answer sheet. No sentence contains more than one error. Some sentences may contain no error. In that case, the correct choice will always be E (No error).

12. <u>To sing a song good,</u> <u>you</u> must focus your
         (A)   (B)
    attention <u>not only</u> on the music but <u>on</u> the words
           (C)   (D)
    <u>No error</u>.
      (E)

13. In <u>his</u> retirement, my grandfather is as active
      (A)
    as he had <u>been when</u> <u>he</u> worked in business, but
           (B)   (C)
    now, instead <u>of holding</u> a full-time job, he does
            (D)
    volunteer work. <u>No error</u>.
            (E)

14. <u>When I see</u> abstract or expressionistic art,
        (A)
    <u>the subject matter</u> and point of the paintings
         (B)
    <u>is</u> often <u>hard</u> for me to figure out. No error.
     (C)   (D)   (E)

15. The baseball fan <u>which</u> arrived <u>earliest</u> at the stadium
            (A)   (B)
    to buy World Series tickets camped <u>on the sidewalk</u>
                         (C)
    by the box office for two days <u>before</u> the first game.
                    (D)
    <u>No error</u>.
      (E)

16. The army regulation says <u>that</u>, if you are <u>of</u> a
$\qquad\qquad\qquad\qquad\quad$ (A) $\qquad\qquad\qquad$ (B)
higher rank than someone else, <u>you</u> have the
$\qquad\qquad\qquad\qquad\qquad\qquad\qquad$ (C)
authority to give <u>them</u> orders. <u>No error.</u>
$\qquad\qquad\qquad\quad$ (D) $\qquad\qquad\qquad$ (E)

17. <u>To grasp</u> the magnitude of the vandalism that
$\quad$ (A)
<u>has been</u> committed, imagine <u>every</u> square inch
$\quad$ (B) $\qquad\qquad\qquad\qquad$ (C)
of the Taj Mahal or St. Peter's Square <u>covered from</u>
$\qquad\qquad\qquad\qquad\qquad\qquad\qquad\qquad$ (D)
spray paint and graffiti. <u>No error.</u>
$\qquad\qquad\qquad\qquad\quad$ (E)

18. The emperor penguin is one of the <u>most unique</u>
$\qquad\qquad\qquad\qquad\qquad\qquad\qquad$ (A)
birds in the world because <u>instead</u> of flying it
$\qquad\qquad\qquad\qquad\qquad$ (B)
<u>walks and slides</u> around on <u>its</u> belly. <u>No error.</u>
$\quad$ (C) $\qquad\qquad\qquad$ (D) $\qquad\qquad$ (E)

19. Anne Frank's sensitivity and intelligence,

<u>in addition to</u> her courage during the <u>years-long</u> exile
$\qquad$ (A) $\qquad\qquad\qquad\qquad\qquad\qquad$ (B)
in the secret annex, <u>is</u> what appeal to <u>most readers</u>
$\qquad\qquad\qquad\qquad$ (C) $\qquad\qquad\qquad$ (D)
of her famous diary. <u>No error.</u>
$\qquad\qquad\qquad\qquad$ (E)

20. If one <u>were to write</u> a constructive letter to a senator
$\qquad\qquad$ (A)
or representative, <u>they</u> should <u>at least</u> be <u>assured of</u>
$\qquad\qquad\qquad$ (B) $\qquad\qquad$ (C) $\qquad\qquad$ (D)
a thank-you. <u>No error.</u>
$\qquad\qquad$ (E)

21. <u>Steps</u> <u>for painting</u> a room include removing
$\quad$ (A) $\qquad$ (B)
<u>all</u> the furniture, patching the walls with plaster,
(C)
choosing a color, and then <u>you apply</u> paint with
$\qquad\qquad\qquad\qquad\qquad$ (D)
a roller or brush. <u>No error.</u>
$\qquad\qquad\qquad$ (E)

22. History books for Bud and Louie <u>were</u> <u>being held</u> at
                         (A)   (B)
    the library desk just <u>like</u> Mr. Donaldson <u>had said</u> they
                   (C)   (D)
    would be. <u>No error</u>.
            (E)

23. The agency responsible <u>for investigating</u> airplane
                          (A)
    accidents <u>is</u> less concerned with the location of crashes
           (B)
    <u>than</u> <u>whether they were caused</u> by mechanical or human
    (C)   (D)
    error. <u>No error</u>.
          (E)

24. Bright colors <u>which</u> are used <u>to decorate</u> the lobby
            (A)   (B)
    of the building and <u>are</u> <u>abundantly used</u> in the
                 (C)   (D)
    hallways, elevators, and offices upstairs. <u>No error</u>.
                                 (E)

25. <u>Despite</u> their busy schedules, they drove
     (A)
    <u>all the way</u> to Albany together <u>to hear</u> a fascinating
      (B)   (C)
    lecture <u>on the status</u> of cloning research in Europe.
           (D)
    <u>No error</u>.
      (E)

26. The late entertainer Ray Charles <u>combined</u> a <u>wider</u>
                           (A)   (B)
    variety of singing and piano-playing techniques

    <u>than</u> <u>any</u> pop star. <u>No error</u>.
    (C) (D)   (E)

27. If the SUV driver <u>would have</u> checked her
                  (A)
    brakes before <u>entering</u> the intersection, the
             (B)
    vehicle <u>might</u> not <u>have smashed</u> into the pole.
         (C)   (D)
    <u>No error</u>.
      (E)

28. The chief announced that <u>his</u> firefighters will continue
                 (A)
    <u>their</u> battle against the fierce forest fire until they <u>brought</u>
     (B)   (C)
    <u>it</u> under control. <u>No error</u>.
    (D)   (E)

29. <u>As</u> the story continued, the doctor, <u>suffering from</u>
    (A)   (B)
    insomnia, stared out his window one night and <u>witnesses</u>
                                                   (C)
    a mugging <u>during which</u> a man was beaten up in the street.
               (D)
    <u>No error</u>.
       (E)

IMPROVING SENTENCES

30. It was virtually impossible for <u>Brandon and I, sitting near the rear of the auditorium, to</u>
    <u>hear Erica and he</u> on the stage.
    (A) Brandon and I, sitting near the rear of the auditorium, to hear Erica and he
    (B) Brandon and me, sitting near the rear of the auditorium, to hear Erica and he
    (C) Brandon and I, sitting near the rear of the auditorium, to hear Erica and him
    (D) Erica and he to be heard by Brandon and me, sitting near the rear of the auditorium
    (E) Brandon and me, sitting near the rear of the auditorium, to hear Erica and him

31. Dreena has seen more Tennessee Williams plays than anyone <u>I know because of being her</u>
    <u>favorite playwright</u>.
    (A) I know because of being her favorite playwright
    (B) I know; this has occurred as the result of Williams being her favorite playwright
    (C) I know because Williams is her favorite playwright
    (D) I know as a resulting consequence of Williams being her favorite playwright
    (E) I know since Williams is her most favorite as a playwright

32. Olympians are supposed to be more <u>than athletes, they are</u> also meant to be symbols of the
    greatness of the respective countries.
    (A) than athletes, they are
    (B) athletes and are
    (C) athletes; they are
    (D) athletes, whereas they are
    (E) athletes; being that they are

33. Kevin stepped up to the Starbucks counter <u>and bought a cup of coffee with Janine's money,</u>
    <u>which he drank quickly,</u> before going to school.
    (A) and bought a cup of coffee with Janine's money, which he drank quickly,
    (B) buying a cup of coffee. Janine's money was used, and he drank it quickly.
    (C) and using Janine's money and buying a cup of coffee that he drank quickly
    (D) and with Janine's money bought a cup of coffee that he quickly drank
    (E) and, using money from Janine, buys a cup of coffee which he quickly drinks

34. Some of the framers' most important values, from freedom of speech to the representative form of government, <u>coming from</u> ancient Greek culture.
    (A) coming from
    (B) they came from
    (C) came from
    (D) they have come from
    (E) which came from

35. After studying math all night, <u>receiving an F on the test was shocking to Sally</u>.
    (A) receiving an F on the test was shocking to Sally
    (B) Sally was shocked to receive an F on the test
    (C) shocking to Sally was the F she received on the test
    (D) the F on the test was shocking to Sally
    (E) Sally's receiving an F on the test was shocking

36. In 2009, the country celebrated the 200th anniversary of <u>the birth of Lincoln, the sixteenth president</u>.
    (A) the birth of Lincoln, the sixteenth president
    (B) Lincoln's birth, he was the sixteenth president
    (C) Lincoln's birthday; the sixteenth president
    (D) the sixteenth president's birthday—Lincoln
    (E) Lincoln's birth who was the sixteenth president

37. The job of <u>us peer counselors was to see that every freshman were included</u> in the survey.
    (A) us peer counselors was to see that every freshman were included
    (B) we peer counselors, was to assure that all freshman were included
    (C) we peer counselors was to include every freshman
    (D) us peer counselors was to include every freshman
    (E) we peer counselors were to be sure that no freshmen were omitted

38. After the earthquake, a Red Cross nurse led the effort to care for <u>the injured as well as comfort the dying</u>.
    (A) the injured as well as comfort the dying
    (B) the injured and also comforting the dying
    (C) injured, she also comforted the dying
    (D) injured as well as comforting the dying
    (E) injured. They comforted the dying, too.

39. Lola was backed by <u>her classmates, and this support enables</u> her to win the election.
    (A) her classmates, and this support enables
    (B) her classmates and this support enabled
    (C) her classmates, this support enabled
    (D) the support of her classmates, which enables
    (E) her classmates, whose support enabled

40. <u>No one but her and me know</u> where the key to the house is hidden.
    (A) No one but her and me know
    (B) No one but her and me knows
    (C) Nobody but she and me knows
    (D) Nobody but she and I knows
    (E) Nobody but her and I know

41. Thinking it over, <u>the solution to our problems are</u> more announcements and publicity.
    (A) the solution to our problems are
    (B) our problems can be solved by
    (C) our problems are to be solved with
    (D) I believe that the solution to our problems is
    (E) I think that the solution to our problems are

42. It is <u>more easier to get to Redding from here than from here to Red Bluff.</u>
    (A) more easier to get to Redding from here than from here to Red Bluff
    (B) more easier to get to Redding from here than to get to Red Bluff from here
    (C) more easy to get from here to Redding than Red Bluff from here
    (D) easier to get from here to Redding than from here to get to Red Bluff
    (E) easier to get to Redding than to Red Bluff from here

43. Behind the house there <u>is just one broken-down shed and one pile of rubble that</u> need to be carted away.
    (A) is just one broken-down shed and one pile of rubble that
    (B) was a broken-down shed and a pile of rubble which
    (C) stands a broken-down shed and a pile of rubble that
    (D) are a broken-down shed and a pile of rubble that
    (E) you will have found a broken-down shed and a pile of rubble which

ANSWER KEY

1. C	11. E	21. D	31. C	41. D
2. A	12. A	22. C	32. C	42. E
3. E	13. E	23. D	33. D	43. D
4. A	14. C	24. A	34. C	
5. D	15. A	25. E	35. B	
6. B	16. D	26. D	36. A	
7. B	17. D	27. A	37. D	
8. E	18. A	28. C	38. A	
9. B	19. C	29. C	39. E	
10. D	20. B	30. E	40. B	

ANSWER EXPLANATIONS

Improving Sentences

Although some items have multiple errors, in most cases only one error is noted.

1. **C** A. Pronoun reference. The pronoun *he* fails to refer to a specific noun or other pronoun.
   B. Same as A.
   D. Idiom error. In the context *being he choked* is not standard usage.
   E. Verb tense. The verb tense improperly shifts from the past (*were eating*) to present perfect (*has choked*).

2. **A** B. Sentence fragment. The construction lacks a verb.
   C. Word choice. The word *themself* is not standard English.
   D. Pronoun-antecedent agreement. *Athlete* is singular; *they* is plural.
   E. Shift in pronoun person. The pronouns shift from third person (*one*) to second person (*yourself*).

3. **E** A. Faulty coordination. The sentence emphasizes its two clauses equally, although the second one contains more important information than the first. Written as a complex sentence, the sentence would be more effective.
   B. Mixed construction. The sentence begins in the active voice, then shifts into the passive, leaving the reader to wonder who delivered the good news to Daisy.
   C. Shift in grammatical subject. The subject shifts from *Daisy* to *it*.
   D. Faulty pronoun reference. The pronoun *they* does not refer to any specific noun or other pronoun.

4. **A** B. Subject-verb agreement. *Transportation* is singular; *are* is plural.
   C. Pronoun-antecedent agreement. *Those* is plural; *transportation* in singular.
   D. Faulty comparison. *Transportation* is being compared to *getting around*, an illogical comparison.
   E. Incomplete comparison. Exactly what *transportation* is being compared to remains unclear.

5. **D** A. Word choice. An adverb (*loudly*), not an adjective (*loud*), is needed to modify the verb *screech*.
   B. Dangling participle. The phrase that begins *While passing* should modify *I* (the speaker), not *siren*.
   C. Dangling participle. The phrase that begins *While passing* should modify *I* (the speaker), not *screech*.
   E. Clumsy construction. The clause *I heard the siren . . . scaring me* is awkward.

6. **B**   A. Faulty comparison. *Cursing* may not be logically compared to *languages.*
C. Pronoun-antecedent agreement. *Cursing* is singular; *they are* is plural. Use *it is.*
D. Faulty comparison. *Cursing* may not logically be compared to *English.*
E. Faulty comparison. *Cursing* may not logically be compared to *English.*

7. **B**   A. Faulty parallelism. Coordinate elements in a sentence must be in parallel grammatical form.
C. Same as A.
D. Faulty subordination. The subordinate clause beginning with *although* is not logically related to the previous clause.
E. Idiom error. In standard idiom, one doesn't speak *vocabulary;* one uses vocabulary to speak.

8. **E**   A. Faulty pronoun reference. The pronoun *they* fails to refer to any specific noun or pronoun.
B. Same as A.
C. Sentence fragment. The construction lacks a main verb.
D. Faulty pronoun reference. The pronoun *their* fails to refer to any specific noun or pronoun.

9. **B**   A. Pronoun choice. Use a possessive pronoun (*our*) before a gerund (*coming*).
C. Pronoun choice. A pronoun in the objective case must be used after a preposition. Use *us.*
D. Same as C.
E. Wordiness. *Moving to* and *to live* are redundant.

10. **D**   A. Faulty verb tense. The verb shifts from present to future conditional.
B. Sentence fragment. The construction lacks a main verb.
C. Faulty verb tense. The verb shifts from present to future perfect.
E. Faulty verb tense. The verb shifts from present to past perfect.

11. **E**   A. Sentence fragment. The construction lacks a main verb.
B Misplaced modifier. The phrase *center for art and music* should modify *Santa Fe,* not *visitors.*
C. Misplaced modifier. The phrase *center for art and music* should modify *Santa Fe,* not *thousands.*
D. Misplaced modifier. The phrase *center for art and music* should modify *Santa Fe,* not *thousands.*

IDENTIFYING SENTENCE ERRORS

12. **A**   Word choice. Adverbs modify active verbs. Use *well*, not *good*, to modify the verb *to sing*.

13. **E**   No error.

14. **C**   Subject-verb agreement. The compound subject (*matter and point*) needs a plural verb: *are* instead of *is*.

15. **A**   Pronoun choice. Use *who* or *that* to refer to people, *which* to refer to other things.

16. **D**   Pronoun-antecedent agreement. The pronoun *them* is plural; the antecedent *someone else* is singular. Use *him* or *her*.

17. **D**   Idiom error. In standard English, the phrase is *covered by* or *covered with*.

18. **A**   Word choice. *Unique* means "one of a kind." Therefore, *most unique* is illogical. Use *most unusual* or another synonym instead of *unique*.

19. **C**   Subject-verb agreement. A compound subject (*sensitivity and intelligence*) requires a plural verb. Use *are* instead of *is*.

20. **B**   Pronoun-antecedent agreement. The pronoun *they* is plural; its antecedent *one* is singular. Use *he*, *she*, or better still, *one*.

21. **D**   Faulty parallelism. Coordinate elements in a sentence must be in the same grammatical form. Use *applying* instead of *you apply*.

22. **C**   Word choice. In this context, *like* is a preposition and may not be used as a conjunction to introduce a subordinate clause. Use *as*.

23. **D**   Faulty parallelism. Coordinate elements in a sentence must be in the same grammatical form. The phrase *location of crashes* is not parallel to the clause *whether they were caused*.

24. **A**   Sentence fragment. The construction lacks a main verb. Eliminate *which*.

25. **E**   No error.

26. **D**   Faulty comparison. *Other* should be included when comparing one thing with a group of which it is a member. Use *any other*.

27. **A**   Verb form. In an *if* clause, avoid using *would have* to express the earlier of two actions. Use the past perfect *had*.

28. **C**   Verb tense. Verbs improperly shift from the present to the past tense. Use *bring* or *have brought*.

29. **C**   Verb tense. Verb tense improperly shifts from the past to the present tense. Use *witnessed*.

IMPROVING SENTENCES

30. **E**   A. Faulty pronoun choice. The objective case pronoun *me* should be used instead of *I* in a prepositional phrase.

   B. Faulty pronoun choice. The objective case pronoun *him* should be used instead of *he* as the object of the verb *to hear*.

   C. Faulty pronoun choice. The objective case pronoun *me* should be used instead of *I* in a prepositional phrase.

   D. Faulty pronoun choice. The objective case pronoun *him* should be used instead of *he* in a prepositional phrase.

31. **C** A. Incomplete construction. The clause beginning with *because* lacks a subject and verb.

      B. Wordy. The construction *this has occurred as the result of* is wordy.

      D. Wordy. The phrase *as a resulting consequence of* is wordy and redundant.

      E. Faulty comparison. Because the adjective *favorite* is an absolute, it may not be used to make a comparison.

32. **C** A. Comma splice. Use a period or semicolon to separate two independent clauses.

      B. Faulty subordination. The conjunction *and* may not be used to show a contrast between ideas.

      D. Faulty subordination. The subordinating conjunction *whereas* fails to establish a logical relationship between clauses.

      E. Semicolon error. A semicolon may not be used to separate an independent clause from a dependent clause.

33. **D** A. Misplaced modifier. The clause *which he drank quickly* modifies *money* instead of *coffee.*

      B. Faulty pronoun reference. The pronoun *it* refers to *money*, not to *coffee.*

      C. Sentence fragment. The construction lacks a main verb. The *-ing* form of a verb (*using, buying*) may not be used as the main verb without a helping verb, as in *was using, is buying.*

      E. Verb tense. The sentence improperly shifts from the past tense to the present. Use *bought* instead of *buys.*

34. **C** A. The *-ing* form of a verb may not be used as the main verb in a sentence without a helping verb, as in *was coming* and *will be coming.*

      B. Mixed sentence structure. The clause beginning with *they came from* is grammatically unrelated to the previous part of the sentence.

      D. Mixed sentence structure. The clause beginning with *they have come from* is grammatically unrelated to the previous part of the sentence.

      E. Sentence fragment. The construction lacks a main verb.

35. **B** A. Dangling participle. The phrase that begins *After studying* has no noun or pronoun to modify.

      C. Dangling participle. The phrase that begins *After studying* has no noun or pronoun to modify.

      D. Dangling participle. The phrase that begins *After studying* modifies *F*, suggesting that *F*, not *Sally*, studied all night.

      E. Dangling participle. The phrase that begins *After studying* modifies *receiving* instead of *Sally.*

36. **A** B. Comma splice. Use a period or semicolon to separate two independent clauses.

   C. Semicolon error. Semicolons may not be used to separate an independent clause and a phrase.

   D. Faulty reference. *Lincoln* refers to *birthday* instead of to *president*, a word that is missing from the sentence.

   E. Misplaced modifier. The clause beginning with *who* modifies *birth* instead of *Lincoln*.

37. **D** A. Noun-verb agreement. *Freshman* is singular; *were* is plural.

   B. Pronoun choice. Prepositional phrases require objective case pronouns. Use *us* instead of *we*.

   C. Same as B.

   E. Subject-verb agreement. The subject *job* is singular; *were* is plural.

38. **A** B. Faulty parallelism. The phrase beginning with *also* is not grammatically parallel to *to care for the injured*.

   C. Comma splice. A period or semicolon, not a comma, is needed to separate independent clauses.

   D. Faulty parallelism. The phrase beginning *as well as* is not grammatically parallel to the phrase *to care for the injured*.

   E. Pronoun-antecedent agreement. *They* is a plural pronoun; *nurse* is singular.

39. **E** A. Faulty verb tense. The sentence is cast in the past tense but shifts to the present in the second clause.

   B. Faulty punctuation. A comma is needed between the clauses of a compound sentence.

   C. Comma splice. A period or semicolon is needed to separate two independent clauses.

   D. Faulty verb tense. The sentence is cast in the past tense but shifts to the present in the second clause

40. **B** A. Subject-verb agreement. *No one* is singular; *know* is plural.

   C. Pronoun choice. A pronoun from the nominative case (*she*) may not be paired with a pronoun in the objective case (*me*).

   D. Pronoun choice. An object of the preposition *but* (*but* is a preposition when it means "except") needs an objective case pronoun. The pronouns *she* and *I* are in the nominative case.

   E. Subject-verb agreement. *Nobody* is singular; *know* is plural.

41. **D** A. Subject-verb agreement. *Solution* is singular; *are* is plural.

   B. Dangling participle. *Thinking it over* modifies *our problems* instead of *I* (the speaker).

   C. Same as B.

   E. Noun-verb agreement. *Solution* is singular; *are* is plural.

42. **E**   A. Faulty comparison. In comparisons, the word *more* is used with adjectives in the positive degree (*easy*) instead of in the comparative degree (*easier*).
B. Wordiness. Repeating *from here* is redundant.
C. Faulty parallelism. The phrase *from here to Redding* is not grammatically parallel to *Red Bluff from here.*
D. Wordiness. Repeating *to get* is redundant.

43. **D**   A. Subject-verb agreement. The singular verb *is* fails to agree with the compound subject *shed and . . . pile.*
B. Subject-verb agreement. The compound subject *shed and . . . pile* requires a plural verb in the correct tense. Use *are* instead of *was.*
C. Subject-verb agreement. The singular verb *stands* fails to agree with the compound subject *shed and . . . pile.*
E. Faulty verb tense. A verb in the future perfect tense significantly alters the meaning of the original sentence.

SAT CHECKPOINT 2
ANSWER SHEET
(Total time: 25 minutes)

Improving Sentences

1. Ⓐ Ⓑ Ⓒ Ⓓ Ⓔ
2. Ⓐ Ⓑ Ⓒ Ⓓ Ⓔ
3. Ⓐ Ⓑ Ⓒ Ⓓ Ⓔ
4. Ⓐ Ⓑ Ⓒ Ⓓ Ⓔ

5. Ⓐ Ⓑ Ⓒ Ⓓ Ⓔ
6. Ⓐ Ⓑ Ⓒ Ⓓ Ⓔ
7. Ⓐ Ⓑ Ⓒ Ⓓ Ⓔ
8. Ⓐ Ⓑ Ⓒ Ⓓ Ⓔ

9. Ⓐ Ⓑ Ⓒ Ⓓ Ⓔ
10. Ⓐ Ⓑ Ⓒ Ⓓ Ⓔ
11. Ⓐ Ⓑ Ⓒ Ⓓ Ⓔ

Identifying Sentence Errors

12. Ⓐ Ⓑ Ⓒ Ⓓ Ⓔ
13. Ⓐ Ⓑ Ⓒ Ⓓ Ⓔ
14. Ⓐ Ⓑ Ⓒ Ⓓ Ⓔ
15. Ⓐ Ⓑ Ⓒ Ⓓ Ⓔ
16. Ⓐ Ⓑ Ⓒ Ⓓ Ⓔ
17. Ⓐ Ⓑ Ⓒ Ⓓ Ⓔ

18. Ⓐ Ⓑ Ⓒ Ⓓ Ⓔ
19. Ⓐ Ⓑ Ⓒ Ⓓ Ⓔ
20. Ⓐ Ⓑ Ⓒ Ⓓ Ⓔ
21. Ⓐ Ⓑ Ⓒ Ⓓ Ⓔ
22. Ⓐ Ⓑ Ⓒ Ⓓ Ⓔ
23. Ⓐ Ⓑ Ⓒ Ⓓ Ⓔ

24. Ⓐ Ⓑ Ⓒ Ⓓ Ⓔ
25. Ⓐ Ⓑ Ⓒ Ⓓ Ⓔ
26. Ⓐ Ⓑ Ⓒ Ⓓ Ⓔ
27. Ⓐ Ⓑ Ⓒ Ⓓ Ⓔ
28. Ⓐ Ⓑ Ⓒ Ⓓ Ⓔ
29. Ⓐ Ⓑ Ⓒ Ⓓ Ⓔ

Improving Sentences

30. Ⓐ Ⓑ Ⓒ Ⓓ Ⓔ
31. Ⓐ Ⓑ Ⓒ Ⓓ Ⓔ
32. Ⓐ Ⓑ Ⓒ Ⓓ Ⓔ
33. Ⓐ Ⓑ Ⓒ Ⓓ Ⓔ
34. Ⓐ Ⓑ Ⓒ Ⓓ Ⓔ

35. Ⓐ Ⓑ Ⓒ Ⓓ Ⓔ
36. Ⓐ Ⓑ Ⓒ Ⓓ Ⓔ
37. Ⓐ Ⓑ Ⓒ Ⓓ Ⓔ
38. Ⓐ Ⓑ Ⓒ Ⓓ Ⓔ
39. Ⓐ Ⓑ Ⓒ Ⓓ Ⓔ

40. Ⓐ Ⓑ Ⓒ Ⓓ Ⓔ
41. Ⓐ Ⓑ Ⓒ Ⓓ Ⓔ
42. Ⓐ Ⓑ Ⓒ Ⓓ Ⓔ
43. Ⓐ Ⓑ Ⓒ Ⓓ Ⓔ

Cut along dotted line.

Grammar Tests: SAT

CHECKPOINT 2
Time: 25 minutes

IMPROVING SENTENCES

INSTRUCTIONS: The underlined sentences and sentence parts below may contain errors in standard English, including awkward or ambiguous expression, poor word choice, incorrect sentence structure, or faulty grammar and usage. Read each sentence carefully and identify which of the five versions most effectively and correctly expresses the meaning of the underlined material. Indicate your choice by filling in the corresponding space on the answer sheet. Because Choice A always repeats the original, choose A if none of the other choices improves the original sentence.

1. St. Petersburg was renamed Leningrad after the <u>Russian Revolution, its original name was restored seventy years later</u>.
   (A) Russian Revolution, its original name was restored seventy years later
   (B) Russian Revolution and it got back its original name seventy years later
   (C) Russian Revolution; its original name was restored seventy years later
   (D) Russian Revolution, it was restored to its original name seventy years later
   (E) Russian Revolution; however, the restoration of its original name seventy years later

2. <u>The pilot guiding his plane to the aircraft carrier, he</u> had never encountered such dense fog in all his years of flying.
   (A) The pilot guiding his plane to the aircraft carrier, he
   (B) Guiding his plane to the aircraft carrier, the pilot he
   (C) Guiding his plane to the aircraft carrier, the pilot
   (D) To guide his plane to the aircraft carrier, the pilot
   (E) The pilot guided his plane to the aircraft carrier, and he

3. Can anything be more daring <u>than leaping from an airplane and to have your parachute open</u> just before you reach the ground?
   (A) than leaping from an airplane and to have your parachute open
   (B) than leaping from an airplane and having your parachute open
   (C) than leaping out an airplane and to have your parachute open
   (D) than to leap from an airplane and having your parachute opening
   (E) than after you leap from an airplane your parachute opened

4. The threat of thunderstorms and hail, in addition to the blistering heat, <u>makes it increasingly unlikely that the graduation will be held</u> outdoors.
   (A) makes it increasingly unlikely that the graduation will be held
   (B) make it increasingly unlikely that graduation will be held
   (C) are increasing the likelihood that graduation won't be held
   (D) increasingly making it unlikely that the graduation will be
   (E) makes the holding of the graduation increasingly unlikely

5. <u>Uncle Max was the kind of man which worked</u> long hours on behalf of the community.
   (A) Uncle Max was the kind of man which worked
   (B) Uncle Max, the kind of a man that worked
   (C) Uncle Max was the kind of man who works
   (D) Uncle Max was the sort of man whom worked
   (E) Uncle Max was the sort of a man that worked

6. <u>Melody is the most directly appealing element in pieces of music and are what we sing and hum and whistle.</u>
   (A) Melody is the most directly appealing element in pieces of music and are what we sing and hum and whistle.
   (B) Melody is the most directly appealing element in a piece of music, this explains why we sing and hum and whistle it.
   (C) Melody is the most directly appealing element in a piece of music, but it is what we sing and hum and whistle.
   (D) Melody, being both the part we sing and hum and whistle, and the most directly appealing element in a piece of music.
   (E) Melody, the part we sing and hum and whistle, is the most directly appealing element in a piece of music.

7. <u>Galileo, the first astronomer to accurately describe the solar system, doing so</u> against the teachings of the church.
   (A) Galileo, the first astronomer to accurately describe the solar system, doing so
   (B) Galileo was the first astronomer to accurately describe the solar system, doing so
   (C) Galileo was the first astronomer to have accurately described the solar system and does so
   (D) Galileo was the first astronomer to have accurately described the solar system, and who did so
   (E) Galileo, the first astronomer accurately describing the solar system

8. Hal Hedges and Troy Benson are candidates for the position of poet <u>laureate, their work in this having been excellent</u>.
   (A) laureate, their work in this having been excellent
   (B) laureate; they have excelled in this work
   (C) laureate, for they have worked excellent in writing poetry
   (D) laureate because of their excellence in poetry writing
   (E) laureate, their poetry writing being more excellent

9. A few students appeared to be on the verge of completing the test or <u>if they already have</u>.
   (A) if they already have
   (B) to have already completed it
   (C) as if they had already
   (D) as if already they had completed it
   (E) like they completed it already

10. <u>Although the actors never having rehearsed their lines</u>, they performed badly.
    (A) Although the actors never having rehearsed their lines
    (B) The actors never rehearsed their lines
    (C) Because the actors never rehearsed their lines
    (D) Never rehearsing their lines
    (E) The actors, however, never rehearsed their lines

11. <u>If they wait until spring to buy a new car</u>, they would have saved over a thousand dollars.
    (A) If they wait until spring to buy a new car
    (B) Had they waited until spring to buy a new car
    (C) If they would of waited until spring to buy a new car
    (D) If buying a new car was delayed until spring
    (E) They should have waited until spring to buy a new car

IDENTIFYING SENTENCE ERRORS

INSTRUCTIONS: The underlined and lettered parts of each sentence below may contain an error in grammar, usage, word choice (diction), or expression (idiom). Read each sentence carefully and identify which item, if any, contains an error. Indicate your choice by filling in the corresponding space on the answer sheet. No sentence contains more than one error. Some sentences may contain no error. In that case, the correct choice will always be E (<u>No error</u>).

12. The paper that Amy is <u>holding</u>, a letter written by
    　　　　　　　　　　　　(A)
    <u>she and her friends</u>, expresses thanks to the town for
    　　　(B)
    providing a recreation center for <u>teenagers'</u> use
    　　　　　　　　　　　　　　　　　　(C)
    after school and <u>on</u> weekends. <u>No error</u>.
    　　　　　　　　(D)　　　　　　(E)

13. The house, <u>constructed</u> <u>just</u> after World War II,
    　　　　　　(A)　　　　(B)
    stood in a working-class area of modest <u>one-family</u>
    　　　　　　　　　　　　　　　　　　　　(C)
    homes <u>along</u> a tree-lined street in southeast
    　　　　(D)
    Washington, D.C. <u>No error</u>.
    　　　　　　　　(E)

14. Weekend fishermen <u>are</u> called <u>to the water's edge</u> by
    　　　　　　　　　(A)　　　(B)
    either love of the outdoors <u>and</u> the companionship of
    　　　　　　　　　　　　　　(C)
    other anglers, <u>although</u> some hope to catch a fish
    　　　　　　　(D)
    for dinner. <u>No error</u>.
    　　　　　　(E)

15. Although the police are investigating break-ins at
    (A)   (B)
    the local high school, their efforts have been frustrating

    because it has produced no suspects. No error.
    (C)   (D)   (E)

16. What the twins have in common to each other are an
    (A)   (B)   (C)
    ability for swimming and high-diving and excellent
            (D)
    singing voices. No error.
                    (E)

17. Also condemned in the newspaper editorial was the
        (A)   (B)   (C)
    paving of Todd Road and the construction of a gazebo

    adjacent to the railroad station. No error.
    (D)   (E)

18. Because he is wearing earphones when the mail carrier
    (A)   (B)   (C)
    rang his doorbell, Mr. Ransome missed the delivery of

    the package he had been waiting for. No error.
                            (D)   (E)

19. Meteorologists agree that Katrina was

    not only the deadliest hurricane on record but also
                    (A)   (B)   (C)
    it destroyed the most property. No error.
    (D)   (E)

20. Two centuries after hanging the painting in the national art
    (A)   (B)
    museum, the hoax was revealed by the forger's
            (C)   (D)
    great-great-grandson. No error.
                          (E)

21. Some people believe that dowsing, a method
                        (A)
    of locating underground water with a Y-shaped
    (B)
    stick, is effective, and others considered the practice
                                    (C)
    a mere superstition. No error.
    (D)   (E)

22. <u>Persuaded by</u> our proposal to plant trees along 24th Street,
        (A)

    the <u>city's</u> parks commission awarded <u>Karl and I</u> several
        (B)   (C)

    thousand dollars to get the work <u>started</u>. <u>No error</u>.
        (D)   (E)

23. John Perlman, <u>whose</u> midwestern roots <u>have</u> affected
        (A)   (B)

    his thinking, <u>includes</u> many references <u>to his boyhood</u>
        (C)   (D)

    in Ohio in his poetry. <u>No error</u>.
        (E)

24. The quality of the athletic teams <u>is determined</u> by
        (A)

    <u>how much</u> money is budgeted for <u>it</u> and the morale
        (B)   (C)

    of the players <u>as well as</u> the coaches. <u>No error</u>.
        (D)   (E)

25. <u>In particular</u>, I remember the <u>constant</u> growing
        (A)   (B)

    tension <u>between</u> the widow of the deceased and
        (C)

    the creditors who <u>claimed</u> that her late husband
        (D)

    owed them money. <u>No error</u>.
        (E)

26. <u>That</u> Judge Rodman <u>would be</u> hard on the defendant
      (A)   (B)

    <u>was never made</u> <u>more clearer</u> than when she sentenced
       (C)   (D)

    the man to forty years in prison. <u>No error</u>.
        (E)

27. <u>Although</u> she <u>has always had</u> a happy-go-lucky
     (A)   (B)

    disposition, Ms. Parker performs her job <u>as principal</u>
        (C)

    <u>with</u> the utmost seriousness. <u>No error</u>.
    (D)   (E)

28. Because the mail <u>usually</u> consists of advertisements, glossy
                   (A)
    catalogs, and requests for money, Mrs. Pritchard <u>scarcely</u>
                                                         (B)
    bothers <u>to look</u> through <u>them</u> before throwing it away. <u>No error</u>.
            (C)   (D)   (E)

29. One difficulty that Maryann faces is <u>how applying</u> to college
                                          (A)
    <u>while keeping</u> up her schoolwork and <u>showing up</u> <u>at</u> her
     (B)   (C)   (D)
    part-time job every day. <u>No error</u>.
                             (E)

IMPROVING SENTENCES

30. Last February, <u>the amount of students absent from school with colds were</u> incredibly high.
    (A) the amount of students absent from school with colds were
    (B) the amounts of students absent from school with colds were
    (C) the number of students absent from school with colds was
    (D) the absenteeism of students from colds was
    (E) colds have kept the number of students absent from school

31. <u>As students, the school's administration aims to provide you with</u> the best education possible.
    (A) As students, the school's administration aims to provide you with
    (B) The aim of the school administration for students is about
    (C) You, as students, are the aim of the school administration to provide you with
    (D) The administrators of the school, who aim to provide you, as students
    (E) The administrators of the school aim to provide you, the students with

32. Gambling casinos will not be permitted to operate in this <u>state because it requires</u> changes in the law that the public is sure to reject.
    (A) state because it requires
    (B) state because it would require
    (C) state because they require
    (D) state, each requires
    (E) state since they are requiring

33. A new kind of cemetery, using microchips instead of tombstones to memorialize <u>the dead, and they are being developed in California</u>.
    (A) the dead, and they are being developed in California
    (B) the dead; and is being developed in California
    (C) the dead, is being developed in California
    (D) the dead being developed in California
    (E) the dead in California by developers of it

34. <u>At seven years of age, my mother took me on my first plane ride.</u>
    - (A) At seven years of age, my mother took me on my first plane ride.
    - (B) At seven years of age, my mother took me on my first plane ride for the very first time.
    - (C) My mother took me at seven years old on my first plane ride for the very first time.
    - (D) When I was seven, my mother took me on my first plane ride.
    - (E) At age seven, I was taken by my mother for my first plane ride, something I had never done before.

35. The composer grew up hearing the melodic guitar music of <u>Mexico, and these are what he included</u> in many of his songs.
    - (A) Mexico, and these are what he included
    - (B) Mexico, and the inclusion of these melodies were put
    - (C) Mexico, and these melodies having been included
    - (D) Mexico, and his inclusion of these melodies
    - (E) Mexico and included the melodies

36. <u>In Lane's review of the movie it compliments the director as being creative, inspired, and born in Austria in 1960.</u>
    - (A) In Lane's review of the movie it compliments the director as being creative, inspired, and born in Austria in 1960.
    - (B) The director, complimented in Lane's movie review as being creative, inspired, and born in Austria in 1960.
    - (C) Lane's review of the movie compliments the director as creative, inspired, and he was born in Austria in 1960.
    - (D) In Lane's review of the movie, the director, who was born in Austria in 1960, is complimented as creative and inspired.
    - (E) Lane's review of the movie, in which the director is complimented as being creative, inspired, and born in Austria in 1960.

37. English teachers do not return papers <u>as quickly as math teachers.</u>
    - (A) as quickly as math teachers
    - (B) as quick as do math teachers
    - (C) as quick as math teachers return papers
    - (D) as quickly as a math teacher
    - (E) as quickly as does math teachers

38. Last summer, more travelers passed through airports in Chicago than <u>New York</u>.
    - (A) New York
    - (B) New York airports
    - (C) compared with New York's
    - (D) New York ones
    - (E) in New York

39. Flowing through sand, rocks, and silt, <u>variations in the speed of underground water are many</u>.
    - (A) variations in the speed of underground water are many
    - (B) underground water travels at various speeds
    - (C) the speed of underground water varies
    - (D) underground speeds of water vary
    - (E) running underground water vary in speed

40. While strolling down Broadway, <u>that was when Marty and Keith decided to phone their former girlfriends</u>.
    - (A) that was when Marty and Keith decided to phone their former girlfriends
    - (B) it was decided to phone their former girlfriends by Marty and Keith
    - (C) Marty and Keith's phone was used to call their former girlfriends
    - (D) then the decision of Marty and Keith to phone their former girlfriends took place
    - (E) Marty and Keith decided to phone their former girlfriends

41. <u>Amelia and him should have been thanked for the gift, but appreciation was mistakenly given to Karly and I.</u>
    - (A) Amelia and him should have been thanked for the gift, but appreciation was mistakenly given to Karly and I.
    - (B) Amelia and he should have been thanked for the gift, but appreciation was mistakenly given to Karly and I.
    - (C) Amelia and him should have been thanked for the gift, but appreciation was mistakenly given to Karly and me.
    - (D) Amelia and he should have been thanked for the gift, but appreciation was mistakenly given to Karly and me.
    - (E) Appreciation for the gift should have gone to Amelia and him, but they were mistakenly given to Karly and me.

42. A responsibility of teachers is to set a good example for their students <u>and to instill in them</u> a love of learning.
    - (A) and to instill in them
    - (B) as well as instilling in them
    - (C) and, they should instill in them
    - (D) and as well, instill in them also
    - (E) at the same time simultaneously instilling in them

43. When the governor appointed his brother and sister to key positions in his administration, he was criticized for nepotism, <u>which became</u> a hot issue in the election.
    - (A) which became
    - (B) so, therefore, it became
    - (C) with the result being that it ultimately was
    - (D) therefore becoming
    - (E) it became

ANSWER KEY

1. C	11. B	21. C	31. E	41. D
2. C	12. B	22. C	32. C	42. A
3. B	13. E	23. E	33. C	43. A
4. A	14. C	24. C	34. D	
5. C	15. D	25. B	35. E	
6. E	16. B	26. D	36. D	
7. B	17. C	27. E	37. A	
8. D	18. B	28. D	38. E	
9. B	19. D	29. A	39. B	
10. C	20. C	30. C	40. E	

ANSWER EXPLANATIONS

Improving Sentences

Although some items have multiple errors, in most cases only one error is noted.

1. **C** A. Comma splice. A comma may not be used to separate two independent sentences.
    B. Faulty punctuation. A comma is needed between two clauses of a compound sentence.
    D. Comma splice. A comma may not be used to separate two independent sentences.
    E. Sentence fragment. The clause beginning with *however* lacks a verb.

2. **C** A. Mixed construction. The construction that begins with *The pilot* lacks a grammatical relationship with the main clause.
    B. Wordiness. The use of *he* and *pilot* is redundant. In addition, *the pilot he* is a nonstandard English construction.
    D. Mixed construction. The infinitive phrase *To guide . . .* is not logically related to the main clause of the sentence.
    E. Faulty coordination. The two clauses of this compound sentence are somewhat related but would be far more effective if stated in a complex sentence.

3. **B** A. Faulty parallelism. The phrases *leaping from* and *to have* lack the parallelism required of coordinate sentence elements.
    C. Faulty idiom. The phrase *leaping out an airplane* is not standard idiomatic English.
    D. Faulty parallelism. Coordinate elements in a sentence should be grammatically parallel. The phrases *to leap from* and *having your parachute open* are not parallel.
    E. Verb tense. The tense improperly shifts from present to past tense.

4. **A** B. Subject-verb agreement. The subject *threat* is singular; the verb *make* is plural.
    C. Subject-verb agreement. The subject *threat* is singular; the verb *are* is plural.
    D. Sentence fragment. The construction lacks a main verb.
    E. Awkwardness. The entire construction is awkward and unidiomatic.

5. **C**   A. Faulty pronoun choice. Use *who* or *that*, not *which*, to refer to people.

        B. Sentence fragment. The construction lacks an independent clause.

        D. Faulty pronoun choice. Use *who* when the pronoun stands for the subject and *whom* when the pronoun is the object.

        E. Idiom error. The standard phrase is *the sort of man*.

6. **E**   A. Subject-verb agreement. *Melody* is singular; *are* is plural.

        B. Comma splice. A comma may not be used to separate two independent clauses.

        C. Faulty coordination. The clause that begins the conjunction *but* lacks a logical relationship with the main clause.

        D. Sentence fragment. The construction lacks a main verb. As participle, *being* may not be used as the main verb.

7. **B**   A. Sentence fragment. The construction lacks a main clause.

        C. Faulty verb tense. The verb tense improperly shifts from past (*was*) to the present (*does*).

        D. Mixed construction. The clause beginning *and who did so* is grammatically unrelated to the first clause.

        E. Sentence fragment. The construction lacks a main verb.

8. **D**   A. Pronoun reference. The pronoun *this* fails to refer to a specific noun or other pronoun.

        B. Faulty reference. The phrase *this work* lacks a specific antecedent.

        C. Word choice. An adjective (*excellent*) may not be used to modify a verb (*worked*). Use the adverb *excellently* instead.

        E. Faulty comparison. The phrase *more excellent* makes an incomplete comparison. More excellent than what?

9. **B**   A. Verb tense. The sentence is cast in the past tense but improperly shifts to the present tense.

        C. Incomplete construction. The clause lacks a verb appropriate to the meaning of the sentence.

        D. Syntax error. The placement of *already* makes the phrase nonstandard and awkward

        E. Word choice. *Like* introduces a phrase; *as* introduces a clause. Use *as* in this construction.

10. **C**   A. Faulty subordination. The first clause lacks both a grammatical and a logical relationship with the second clause.

        B. Comma splice. A comma may not be used to separate two independent clauses. Use a period or semicolon instead.

        D. Tense shift. The verb *rehearsing* is in the present progressive tense, the remainder of the sentence in the past tense.

        E. Diction error. The word *however* makes little sense in the context.

11. **B** A. Shift in tense. Because the verb *wait* is in the present tense, it is inconsistent with the main verb of the sentence *would have saved*, which indicates action already completed.

C. Word choice. *Would of* is nonstandard; use *would have*.

D. Verb tense. The context calls for a verb in the past perfect tense (*had been delayed*) instead of the simple past (*was delayed*) to specify that the action has been completed. That is, they bought the car before the coming of spring.

E. Comma splice. A comma may not be used to separate two independent clauses. Use a period or semicolon instead.

IDENTIFYING SENTENCE ERRORS

12. **B** Faulty pronoun choice. When used as the object of a preposition, a pronoun should be in the objective case. Use *her* instead of *she*.

13. **E** No error.

14. **C** Faulty idiom. In parallel phrases *either* must be paired with *or*, not with *and*.

15. **D** Pronoun-antecedent agreement. The pronoun *it* is singular. Its antecedent *efforts* is plural. Use *they have*.

16. **B** Faulty idiom. In context the use of *to* is not standard English. Use *with*.

17. **C** Subject-verb agreement. The compound subject, *paving . . . and . . . construction*, requires a plural verb. Use *were* instead of *was*.

18. **B** Tense shift. The sentence is cast in the past tense. The verb *is wearing* is in the present tense. Use *was wearing*.

19. **D** Faulty parallelism. Coordinate elements in a sentence must be in the same grammatical form. The word *deadliest* is an adjective; *it destroyed property* is a clause. Use *most destructive*.

20. **C** Dangling modifier. The phrase *hanging the painting* should modify the hanger of the painting (unnamed in this sentence) instead of *hoax*.

21. **C** Verb tense. The sentence is cast in the present tense. The verb *considered* is in the past tense.

22. **C** Pronoun choice. Because the phrase *Karl and I* is the object of the verb *awarded*, the pronoun should be in the objective case. Use *me*.

23. **E** No error.

24. **C** Pronoun reference. The pronoun *it* fails to refer to a specific noun or other pronoun.

25. **B** Word choice. An adverb instead of an adjective is needed to modify the adjective *growing*. Use *constantly*.

26. **D** Faulty comparison. When using the word *more* to make a comparison, the accompanying adjective must be in the positive degree. Use *clear*.

27. **E** No error.

28. **D** Pronoun-antecedent agreement. The plural pronoun *them* fails to agree in number with the singular antecedent, *mail*.

29. **A.** Sentence fragment. The construction lacks a main verb. Use *how to apply* instead of *how applying*.

IMPROVING SENTENCES

30. **C** A. Subject-verb agreement. *Amount* is singular; *were* is plural.
   B. Word choice. Use *number* for quantities that can be counted.
   D. Faulty idiom. The phrase *from colds* is nonstandard. Use *with colds.*
   E. Faulty verb tense. The phrase *Last February* indicates that the event took place in the past. The verb *have kept* is in the present perfect tense.

31. **E** A. Misplaced modifier. *As students* should modify *you* instead of *administration.*
   B. Awkwardness. The construction is unidiomatic and clumsily expressed.
   C. Awkwardness. The construction is unidiomatic and clumsily expressed.
   D. Sentence fragment. The construction lacks a main verb.

32. **C** A. Pronoun-antecedent agreement. *Casinos* is plural; *it* is singular. Use *they.*
   B. Same as A.
   D. Comma splice. A comma may not be used to separate two independent clauses. Use a period or semicolon instead.
   E. Pronoun reference. The pronoun *they* lacks a specific antecedent.

33. **C** A. Pronoun-antecedent agreement. The plural pronoun *they* fails to agree with its singular antecedent, *kind.*
   B. Semicolon error. Semicolons are used to separate independent clauses, not sentence fragments.
   D. Sentence fragment. The construction lacks a main verb.
   E. Same as D.

34. **D** A. Misplaced modifier. *At seven years of age* should modify *I* (the speaker), not *my mother.*
   B. Same as A.
   C. Wordiness. The phrases *my first plane ride* and *for the very first time* are redundant.
   E. Passive construction. The sentence would be more effectively expressed if it were less wordy and written in the active voice.

35. **E** A. Faulty pronoun reference. The pronoun *these* fails to refer to a specific noun or other pronoun.
   B. Subject-verb agreement. The subject *inclusion* is singular. The verb *were put* is plural.
   C. Sentence fragment. The second clause lacks a main verb.
   D. Same as C.

36. **D** A. Faulty pronoun reference. The pronoun *it* fails to refer to a specific noun or other pronoun.
        B. Sentence fragment. The construction lacks a main verb.
        C. Faulty parallelism. The clause *he was born ...* is not parallel in structure to the adjectives *creative* and *inspired.*
        E. Sentence fragment. The subject, *review,* lacks a verb.

37. **A** B. Word choice. To modify the verb *return,* use an adverb (*quickly*) instead of an adjective (*quick*).
        C. Same as B.
        D. Faulty comparison. The sentence improperly tries to compare unequivalent entities: *English teachers* (plural) and *a math teacher* (singular).
        E. Noun-verb agreement. The noun *teachers* is plural; the verb *does* is singular.

38. **E** A. Faulty comparison. The sentence improperly compares Chicago's airports with the city of New York, an illogical comparison.
        B. Faulty parallelism. The phrase *airports in Chicago* is not structurally parallel to *New York airports.*
        C. Faulty parallelism. The phrase *to New York's* is not parallel in structure to the phrase *in Chicago.*
        D. Awkwardness. The phrase *New York ones* is awkwardly expressed.

39. **B** A. Dangling participle. The phrase that begins *Flowing through* should modify *water* instead of *variations.*
        C. Dangling participle. The phrase that begins *Flowing through* should modify *water* instead of *speed.*
        D. Dangling participle. The phrase that begins *Flowing through* should modify *water* instead of *speeds.*
        E. Subject-verb agreement. The subject *water* is singular; the verb *vary* is plural.

40. **E** A. Wordiness. The use of both *While* and *that was when* is redundant.
        B. Passive construction. Using *it* as the grammatical subject leads to a passive, awkwardly worded sentence.
        C. Dangling participle. The phrase that begins *While strolling* should modify *Marty and Keith,* not *phone.*
        D. Unrelated sentence parts. The clause that begins with *then* is grammatically unrelated to the earlier part of the sentence.

41. **D** A. Pronoun choice. Use *he* instead of *him* in the subject of a sentence; use *me* instead of *I* as the object of a preposition.
        B. Pronoun choice. Use *me* instead of *I* in a prepositional phrase.
        C. Pronoun choice. Use *he* instead of *him* in the subject of a sentence.
        E. Pronoun-antecedent agreement. *Appreciation* is singular; *they* is plural.

42. **A**   B. Faulty parallelism. Coordinate elements in a sentence must be in parallel form. *To set a good example* and *as well as instilling in them* are not in parallel form.

C. Faulty parallelism. *To set a good example* is a phrase that is not parallel to the clause *they should instill in them.*

D. Wordiness. *As well* and *also* are redundant.

E. Wordiness. *At the same time* and *simultaneously* are redundant.

43. **A**   B. Comma splice. A comma may not be used to separate independent clauses. Use a period or semicolon between *nepotism* and *so.*

C. Wordiness. The phrase *with the result being that* is unnecessarily wordy. Use *resulting in* or some other more concise phrase.

D. Mixed sentence construction. The phrase *therefore becoming* is grammatically unrelated to the previous part of the sentence.

E. Same as B. Use a period or semicolon between *nepotism* and *it.*

Chapter 5

ACT Grammar Questions

The ACT Assessment is made up of four separate tests: English, Math, Reading, and Science. Students applying to some colleges also take an optional ACT Writing Test.

Grammar questions appear only on the ACT English Test, which consists of 75 multiple-choice questions to be answered in 45 minutes. All the questions are presented in the context of five different essays, or passages, each about 300 words long. Portions of each passage are underlined, and your job is to decide whether the underlined segment is correct as it is or whether it needs to be changed.

Each multiple-choice question gives you four choices. The first choice is always NO CHANGE. The choices for odd-numbered questions are labeled A, B, C, and D, and those for even-numbered questions F, G, H, and J.

Topics Covered on the ACT English Test

Each passage includes items in two main categories:

- English grammar and usage, including punctuation and sentence structure (40 questions)

and

- Rhetoric, including organization, style, and writing strategy (35 questions)

Some passages will contain more questions on grammar than on rhetoric. Others emphasize rhetoric more than grammar. All the questions pertain to matters of everyday grammar, usage, and rhetoric. They won't ask you about obscure rules of grammar, parts of speech, or vocabulary. Nor will you be asked to interpret the meaning of the essay.

The following chart shows the topics covered on the test. Note that the test offers more questions on sentence structure than on any other topic, and that the fewest questions pertain to punctuation. Use this information as you develop a study plan in preparation for the ACT.

Content		Number of Questions
Grammar		12
Sentence structure		18
Punctuation		<u>10</u>
Grammar, usage, and mechanics questions	Total	40
Organization		11
Style		12
Strategy		<u>12</u>
Questions on rhetoric	Total	35

Sample ACT Questions

Grammar questions

Questions on grammar ask about such matters as:

- Agreement between subject and verb
- Pronoun references
- Modification
- Pronoun-antecedent agreement
- Verb forms and tenses
- Pronoun choice
- Making comparisons
- English idiom
- Word choice

What follows is a random sample of ACT questions based on sentences taken from a 200-word passage (not reprinted here). The questions are numbered 3, 10, and 15.

EXAMPLE #1

Saudi Arabia, along with other oil-exporting countries,
<u>are continuing</u> to raise the price of crude oil.
     3

3. **A.** NO CHANGE
   B. continue
   C. continuing
   D. is continuing

Explanation: *Saudi Arabia* is the subject of the sentence. It is singular. Because the verb *are continuing* is plural, the subject fails to agree with the verb. The phrase *along with other . . .* that comes between the subject and verb may suggest a plural subject. But this and similar phrases, including *in addition to, as well as,* and *together with,* are not conjunctions and, therefore, do not change singular subjects to plural. In other words, the noun *countries* is not part of the subject.

Choice B is not a good alternative because *continue,* like *are continuing,* is a plural verb. Choice C turns the entire construction into a sentence fragment because it lacks a verb. Although *continuing* sounds like a verb, the *-ing* form of any verb may not serve as the main verb of a sentence without an additional helping verb, as in *was continuing* or *will be continuing.*

That leaves D as the best answer. Indeed, the singular verb *is* agrees with the singular subject of the sentence, *Saudi Arabia.*

(*For details on subject-verb agreement, turn to page 30.*)

EXAMPLE # 2

At the White House, the President and the Saudi ambassador met to discuss the issue. "Do you remember," <u>he asked</u>, "that we met once

                                        10

before—in 1996 at a conference in Singapore?"

10. F. NO CHANGE
    G. he was asked
    H. the President asked
    J. the ambassador was asked by the President

Explanation: The underlined phrase is problematical because pronouns must refer specifically to a noun or another pronoun. In the given sentence, it's anybody's guess who asked the question. Was it the guest or the host? Because neither Choice F nor Choice G identifies the speaker, disregard those answers. Choice J specifies who was speaking, but the construction is written in the passive voice and is wordy. That leaves Choice H as the best answer because it concisely identifies the speaker.

(*For details on pronoun references, turn to page 12.*)

EXAMPLE # 3

Meanwhile, the chairperson of the committee appointed Ms. Dickinson to investigate possible corruption in the oil industry, <u>where she has long worked</u>.

                                        15

15. A. NO CHANGE
    B. in which she has long been involved
    C. a business to which she has long been working
    D. in which a long career has been spent

Explanation: The underlined segment raises an issue of modification. That is, each of the choices is meant to modify the noun *industry*. Your job is to decide which one does it most accurately and clearly. Choice B suggests that the chairperson's appointee has been involved in corruption—surely not the intent of the writer. Choice C contains *to which*, a phrase containing an error in English idiom (use *in* instead of *to*). And D, in the passive voice, fails to say whose career has been spent in the industry. Choice A, therefore, is the best, and, incidentally, the most concise answer.

(*For details on modification, turn to page 34.*)

Other grammatical problems found in the ACT are illustrated below by the sentences that follow:

- Pronoun-antecedent agreement (*Page 10*)

    A high school student needs to be well organized if *they* want to succeed.
    REVISED: *High school students need* to be well organized if *they* want to succeed.

- Verb forms and tenses (*Page 21*)

  After the bell had *rang*, the boys rushed to the cafeteria.
  REVISED: After the bell had *rung*, the boys rushed to the cafeteria.

  Tomorrow, when the president *walked* into the hall, everyone should stand.
  REVISED: Tomorrow, when the president *walks* into the hall, everyone should stand.

- Pronoun choice (*Page 6*)

  This is just between you and *I*, but I can't stand Boris.
  REVISED: This is just between you and *me*, but I can't stand Boris.

  Everyone should wear a hat unless you want to freeze.
  REVISED: *You* should wear a hat unless you want to freeze.

- Making comparisons (*Page 35*)

  That star is *more brighter* than the other one.
  REVISED: That star is *brighter* than the other one.

  Mars is closer to the Earth than *any planet*.
  REVISED: Mars is closer to the Earth than *any other planet*.

- English idiom (*Page 75*)

  Martha intends *on going* to the beach on Saturday.
  REVISED: Martha intends *to go* to the beach on Saturday.

- Word choice (*Page 70*)

  The ghost was seen walking *slow* around the reservoir.
  REVISED: The ghost was seen walking *slowly* around the reservoir.

Sentence structure questions

Questions on the structure of sentences may ask you to recognize and correct:

- Incomplete sentences
- Run-on sentences and comma splices
- Faulty parallelism
- Shifts between the active and passive voice
- Shifts in pronoun person or number
- Shifts in verb tenses
- Faulty coordination and subordination

EXAMPLE # 1

Shopping malls across the country <u>reporting</u> the usual
4

increase during the holiday season and the annual
decline in midsummer.

4. F. NO CHANGE
   G. issuing a report of
   H. have reported,
   J. report

Explanation: Here you are being asked to recognize a sentence fragment. The construction has a subject, *malls*, and also what looks like a verb, *reporting*. But the *-ing* form of a verb cannot serve as the main verb of a sentence without an accompanying helping verb, as in *is reporting* or *will be reporting*. Choice G has the same problem—an unusable *-ing* verb. Choice H contains a correct verb, but the addition of a comma between the verb and its object turns a reasonable answer into a wrong one. Only Choice J offers a verb that properly fits the subject and makes the sentence whole.

(*For details on complete sentences, turn to page 57.*)

EXAMPLE # 2

Consumers have grown accustomed to receiving holiday
catalogs <u>by mail they arrive</u> as early as Labor Day each year.
7

7. A. NO CHANGE
   B. that arrive by mail
   C. by mail, which arrives
   D. in the mail, many of them arrive

Explanation: The underlined words appear at a turning point in the sentence, the end of the first clause and the start of the second, where a change in the subject and verb occurs. The phrase *Consumers have grown* contains the subject and verb of the first clause. The second clause uses *they* as its subject, and *arrive* as its verb. Because the two clauses have separate subjects and verbs, and because no conjunction or mark of punctuation comes between them, the sentence consists of two independent clauses that have improperly been run together. Therefore, eliminate Choice A as a possible answer. Choice C contains *which*, a relative pronoun meant to refer to *catalogs,* but instead it appears to refer to *mail* because the verb *arrives*, like the noun *mail*, is singular. This ambiguity disqualifies C as a good choice. Choice D is similar to A except that the two sentences are erroneously joined by a comma. That leaves Choice B as the correct answer because it turns the second clause into a dependent clause beginning with *that*.

(*For details on run-on sentences and comma splices, turn to page 64.*)

EXAMPLE # 3

The holiday season causes anxiety and depression
in many people who can't cope with crowded stores,
endless advertisements, <u>and less than cheerful feelings</u>.
8

8. F. NO CHANGE
   G. and they don't feel cheerful
   H. and less feeling of cheerfulness
   J. and their feelings of cheer are less

Explanation: This question tests your understanding of parallel structure. The sentence lists three problems that many people face during the holiday season. Each problem is stated in the same grammatical form—as the object of the preposition *with*. Each object—*stores, advertisements* and *feelings*—is preceded and modified by an adjective. Because Choices G, H, and J fail to maintain this pattern, they are incorrect. Choice F is the best answer.

(*For details on parallel structure, turn to page 65.*)

Additional issues of sentence structure are illustrated by the following pairs of sentences:

- Shifts between the active and passive voice (*Page 69*)

   In the early spring colleges tell applicants whether they have been admitted, and decisions about which college to attend are made by students.
   REVISED: In the early spring colleges tell applicants whether they have been admitted, and students decide which college to attend.

- Shifts in pronoun person or number (*Page 6*)

   In our cooking class, you were graded on how well you seasoned the pea soup.
   REVISED: In our cooking class, we were graded on how well we seasoned the pea soup.

   An owl hoots at night, but they are silent during the day.
   REVISED: An owl hoots at night, but it is silent during the day.

- Faulty coordination and subordination (*Pages 46 and 47*)

   The canoe turned over in the rapids and a rock hit it.
   REVISED: The canoe hit a rock and turned over in the rapids.

   Ellie lost her sneakers because she found them again.
   REVISED: Ellie lost her sneakers, but she found them again.

Punctuation questions

Questions ask you to apply rules governing the use of:

- Commas (*page 82*)
- Semicolons, colons, and dashes (*page 83*)
- Question marks and exclamation points (*page 85*)

EXAMPLE

For untold ages the game of life played according to
certain <u>rules</u>; meant that some of us won and others lost.
        7

7. A. NO CHANGE
   B. rules
   C. rules:
   D. rules,

Explanation: This is a punctuation question, pure and simple, because the choices differ from each other only in the mark of punctuation that follows *rules*. Read the whole sentence from start to finish before analyzing its parts. If you read only the first few words it may seem that the subject of the sentence is *game* and that its verb is *played*. A complete reading, however, reveals that *played* is really part of a clause, *played according to certain rules*, which modifies *game*.

Choice A is not a good choice because the material before the semicolon is a sentence fragment, and since semicolons may not be used to separate incomplete sentences, the punctuation is faulty. Choice C is equally poor because colons are used to introduce independent clauses that explain or illustrate previously stated ideas, or to introduce lists of items.

If you are drawn to Choice D, you may be thinking that commas sometimes come before and after a subordinate clause to set it apart from the rest of the sentence. That's true, but here, because no comma precedes the clause, no comma is needed to follow it. Moreover, commas don't normally separate subjects and predicates. In other words, D is incorrect because no comma is needed. Choice B, then, is the best answer.

During the timed ACT, a lengthy, time-consuming analysis such as this isn't necessary, or even possible. Most students would probably land on the right answer after a few seconds of checking which punctuation mark best fits the context.

The ACT almost never asks punctuation questions *per se*. That is, no question is devoted exclusively to the use of semicolons, commas, dashes, and so on. Rather, you'll encounter punctuation problems in the context of compound and complex sentences, appositives, sentence fragments, run-on sentences, comma splices, conjunction usage—all matters discussed earlier in this book.

Questions on Rhetoric

Questions relate to:

- Organization, including sequence of ideas, coherence, paragraphing, introductions, and conclusions
- Style, including word choice, wordiness, tone, use of language
- Strategy, including overall purpose, use of appropriate details, relevance to audience

To answer questions on rhetoric, it helps to be aware of the point and purpose of a given passage and each of its paragraphs. Understanding the passage and the role of each paragraph will help you decide whether the author has used an appropriate style, organized the material sensibly, and fully developed ideas in a clear, coherent manner.

EXAMPLE # 1

Divorce is a concept that many American children have come to
understand by bitter experience. <u>Indeed, it has obligated</u> suffering
                                                      5
on countless young people.

5. A. NO CHANGE
   B. Though, it has caused
   C. In fact, it has imposed
   D. However, it has compelled

Before answering, examine the relationship between the two sentences by asking questions like these:

Does one sentence follow logically from the other? Are the tone and style of the two sentences consistent both with each other and with the whole passage?

What is the function of the second sentence? To develop an idea stated in the first? To offer an alternative point of view? To contradict the validity of the first sentence? In other words, it is important to read the sentences as a pair, and to consider their role in the given passage.

Choice A uses the conjunctive adverb *indeed* to link the two sentences. The word indicates that the second sentence is intended to develop the idea stated in the first. So far, so good, but a problem exists with the word *obligated.* In this context, a word that means *required* or *demanded* makes little sense.

The conjunctive adverb *Though,* used in Choice B, ordinarily introduces a contrasting thought. But the second sentence seems to support rather than depart from the idea of the preceding sentence. Therefore, eliminate B as a possible answer. Keep in mind, however, that the phrase *it has caused* suits the context well.

Choice D is similar to Choice B because the word *However* also implies the introduction of a contrasting idea. Because no contrast is stated in the sentence that follows, however, D is not a good answer. What's more, the use of *compelled* is inappropriate in the context.

Choice C is the best answer because the phrase *In fact* serves as a clear and logical link between the two sentences. In addition, the verb *imposed* accurately expresses the writer's intended meaning.

EXAMPLE # 2

The attorney's official report concluded that the root of the district's
problem is that the school administration customarily hires teachers who
<u>are incompetent toward</u> the subject they teach.

10. F. NO CHANGE
   G. are inadequately trained in
   H. haven't a clue about
   J. are complete ditzes in

This sentence seems to come from a document that describes a serious problem in a particular school district. Your task is to determine which of the choices is most likely to be used in such a passage.

Choice F certainly reveals a reason that the district is in trouble, but the phrase *incompetent toward* is not idiomatic. Rather, *incompetent in* is standard English usage.

Choices H and J are strong, colorfully worded phrases, but they are inconsistent with the formal tone of the passage. Colloquial language has its place, of course, but the discussion of an attorney's official report on a school district's educational problem is not one of them.

That leaves Choice G, a grammatical and appropriately worded description of the problem. G is the best answer.

ACT CHECKPOINT 1
ANSWER SHEET

Passage 1 The Good Old Days

1. Ⓐ Ⓑ Ⓒ Ⓓ
2. Ⓕ Ⓖ Ⓗ Ⓙ
3. Ⓐ Ⓑ Ⓒ Ⓓ
4. Ⓕ Ⓖ Ⓗ Ⓙ
5. Ⓐ Ⓑ Ⓒ Ⓓ

6. Ⓕ Ⓖ Ⓗ Ⓙ
7. Ⓐ Ⓑ Ⓒ Ⓓ
8. Ⓕ Ⓖ Ⓗ Ⓙ
9. Ⓐ Ⓑ Ⓒ Ⓓ
10. Ⓕ Ⓖ Ⓗ Ⓙ

11. Ⓐ Ⓑ Ⓒ Ⓓ
12. Ⓕ Ⓖ Ⓗ Ⓙ
13. Ⓐ Ⓑ Ⓒ Ⓓ
14. Ⓕ Ⓖ Ⓗ Ⓙ
15. Ⓐ Ⓑ Ⓒ Ⓓ

Passage 2 Policeman on Patrol

16. Ⓕ Ⓖ Ⓗ Ⓙ
17. Ⓐ Ⓑ Ⓒ Ⓓ
18. Ⓕ Ⓖ Ⓗ Ⓙ
19. Ⓐ Ⓑ Ⓒ Ⓓ
20. Ⓕ Ⓖ Ⓗ Ⓙ

21. Ⓐ Ⓑ Ⓒ Ⓓ
22. Ⓕ Ⓖ Ⓗ Ⓙ
23. Ⓐ Ⓑ Ⓒ Ⓓ
24. Ⓕ Ⓖ Ⓗ Ⓙ
25. Ⓐ Ⓑ Ⓒ Ⓓ

26. Ⓕ Ⓖ Ⓗ Ⓙ
27. Ⓐ Ⓑ Ⓒ Ⓓ
28. Ⓕ Ⓖ Ⓗ Ⓙ
29. Ⓐ Ⓑ Ⓒ Ⓓ
30. Ⓕ Ⓖ Ⓗ Ⓙ

Passage 3 Romping in the Pumpkin Patch

31. Ⓐ Ⓑ Ⓒ Ⓓ
32. Ⓕ Ⓖ Ⓗ Ⓙ
33. Ⓐ Ⓑ Ⓒ Ⓓ
34. Ⓕ Ⓖ Ⓗ Ⓙ
35. Ⓐ Ⓑ Ⓒ Ⓓ

36. Ⓕ Ⓖ Ⓗ Ⓙ
37. Ⓐ Ⓑ Ⓒ Ⓓ
38. Ⓕ Ⓖ Ⓗ Ⓙ
39. Ⓐ Ⓑ Ⓒ Ⓓ
40. Ⓕ Ⓖ Ⓗ Ⓙ

41. Ⓐ Ⓑ Ⓒ Ⓓ
42. Ⓕ Ⓖ Ⓗ Ⓙ
43. Ⓐ Ⓑ Ⓒ Ⓓ
44. Ⓕ Ⓖ Ⓗ Ⓙ
45. Ⓐ Ⓑ Ⓒ Ⓓ

Grammar Tests: ACT

Cut along dotted line.

Passage 4 Preparing for Success

46. Ⓕ Ⓖ Ⓗ Ⓙ   51. Ⓐ Ⓑ Ⓒ Ⓓ   56. Ⓕ Ⓖ Ⓗ Ⓙ

47. Ⓐ Ⓑ Ⓒ Ⓓ   52. Ⓕ Ⓖ Ⓗ Ⓙ   57. Ⓐ Ⓑ Ⓒ Ⓓ

48. Ⓕ Ⓖ Ⓗ Ⓙ   53. Ⓐ Ⓑ Ⓒ Ⓓ   58. Ⓕ Ⓖ Ⓗ Ⓙ

49. Ⓐ Ⓑ Ⓒ Ⓓ   54. Ⓕ Ⓖ Ⓗ Ⓙ   59. Ⓐ Ⓑ Ⓒ Ⓓ

50. Ⓕ Ⓖ Ⓗ Ⓙ   55. Ⓐ Ⓑ Ⓒ Ⓓ

Passage 5 Getting Along with the Amish

60. Ⓕ Ⓖ Ⓗ Ⓙ   66. Ⓕ Ⓖ Ⓗ Ⓙ   72. Ⓕ Ⓖ Ⓗ Ⓙ

61. Ⓐ Ⓑ Ⓒ Ⓓ   67. Ⓐ Ⓑ Ⓒ Ⓓ   73. Ⓐ Ⓑ Ⓒ Ⓓ

62. Ⓕ Ⓖ Ⓗ Ⓙ   68. Ⓕ Ⓖ Ⓗ Ⓙ   74. Ⓕ Ⓖ Ⓗ Ⓙ

63. Ⓐ Ⓑ Ⓒ Ⓓ   69. Ⓐ Ⓑ Ⓒ Ⓓ   75. Ⓐ Ⓑ Ⓒ Ⓓ

64. Ⓕ Ⓖ Ⓗ Ⓙ   70. Ⓕ Ⓖ Ⓗ Ⓙ

65. Ⓐ Ⓑ Ⓒ Ⓓ   71. Ⓐ Ⓑ Ⓒ Ⓓ

INSTRUCTIONS: In each of the five passages printed on the left you will find sentences with segments underlined and numbered. A multiple-choice question about each underlined segment appears on the right. To answer the question, choose the alternative that best expresses the underlined word or phrase in standard written English or is most consistent with the style or tone of the passage. If you decide that the original is best, choose either A or F, indicating that NO CHANGE is needed.

Some questions will direct your attention to specific words or phrases, others to a broader section of the passage or to the passage as a whole. These questions are indicated with a number inside brackets or inside a box.

Once you have decided on an answer, fill in the blank space on the answer sheet. You are advised to read each passage completely before answering the questions. Also be mindful that to answer some questions you may need to read one or more sentences that precede or follow the sentence containing a question.

Passage 1

The Good Old Days

America's consumers spend thirty to fifty dollars to
fill up their gasoline tanks with fuel costing
between two and three dollars a gallon, many yearn
for the good old days. Older drivers recall the
decades when gasoline cost thirty cents a gallon
and price wars among competing service stations
sometimes have sent the cost of a gallon
plummeting into the teens. Imagine; Only nineteen
cents a gallon! The bottled water so popular today
costs more than that.

1. **A.** NO CHANGE
   B. American consumers
   C. Because Americans
   D. Americas' consumers

2. **F.** NO CHANGE
   G. decades of time when gasoline
   H. decades, in which gasoline
   J. decades, when gasoline

3. **A.** NO CHANGE
   B. sended
   C. sent
   D. sending

4. **F.** NO CHANGE
   G. Imagine! only nineteen cents a gallon.
   H. Imagine nineteen cents a gallon.
   J. Imagine—only nineteen cents a gallon!

5. **A.** NO CHANGE
   B. A fill-up would cost less than two dollars.
   C. Automobiles had smaller gas tanks in those days, however.
   D. For five dollars you could buy a fill-up and then take your sweetheart out to dinner.

Yes, it's tempting sometimes to think back to old times and wish that life today were as easy, not to mention as cheap, <u>as the past</u>. If you go back <u>half a</u> **6** **7** <u>century, fifty years ago,</u> it seems that people lived **7** in a consumer's paradise. <u>Because credit cards</u> **8** <u>hadn't yet been invented, prices were low and</u> **8** <u>people paid for goods in cash.</u> **8**

In the 1950's, food staples for a family of five might cost $40 a week. Milk was almost as cheap as gasoline, and a loaf of bread cost a quarter. Eggs sold for a nickel apiece. Butter, sugar, cheese, potatoes, beef—all were available at a fraction of today's cost. <u>Returning</u> to the mid-19th century, **9** the cost of living would be <u>lesser than</u> one- **10** twentieth of what it is today. The price for a quart of milk in 1849, for example, was 10 cents <u>a quart</u>. **11** To buy a hundred pounds of flour would set you back $2. A pound of potatoes cost a penny and a half. In some places, especially rural areas, the market value of both food and nonfood items <u>was</u> **12** immaterial. For a bushel of rice, a pair of shoes, or an iron kettle, a housewife had <u>to barter, she</u> **13** <u>paying,</u> not in dollars but in sacks of homegrown **13**

6. **F.** NO CHANGE
   G. as it was in the past
   H. as the past was
   J. like in the past

7. **A.** NO CHANGE
   B. half a century
   C. half a century,
   D. fifty years ago,

8. **F.** NO CHANGE
   G. Prices were low, and people could not spend their money recklessly.
   H. Although people paid for low-priced goods in cash.
   J. Prices were low and people paid for goods in cash.

9. **A.** NO CHANGE
   B. By going back
   C. If you went back
   D. To return

10. **F.** NO CHANGE
    G. less than
    H. still lesser than
    J. fewer than

11. **A.** NO CHANGE
    B. for a quart
    C. per quart
    D. OMIT the underlined words

12. **F.** NO CHANGE
    G. were
    H. had been
    J. had to have been

13. **A.** NO CHANGE
    B. bartered, her paying
    C. to barter. She paid
    D. bartered, and paid,

potatoes, a blanket, or outgrown children's clothing.

Considering today's prices, you might think that our ancestors had it easy. But look at the facts and figures: Wages and the cost of living <u>having grown</u>
14
in virtually equal proportions through the generations. A minimum-wage worker in 1850, spending forty hours on the job each week, brought home about $15. For an equivalent work week today, the wages would be $250. [15]

14. **F.** NO CHANGE
   G. have grown
   H. growing
   J. grows

15. Which of the following factual statements, if inserted at the end of the passage, would serve as the conclusion most consistent with the purpose and tone of the passage?
   A. The numbers differ significantly, of course, but in real dollars, or more important, in buying power, the amount is virtually the same.
   B. In "the good old days," people suffered from poorer health, lower life expectancy, greater lawlessness, and fewer recreational opportunities.
   C. The U.S. GNP (Gross National Product) in the 21st century exceeds the country's mid-19th century GNP by over 5,000 percent.
   D. Today we still spend roughly 40 percent of our income on food, clothing, and other essentials.

Passage 2

Policeman on Patrol

[1] Dan Lewis is an <u>officer, in his seventh year,</u>
16
with the Washington, D.C., police force. [2] Dan's beat <u>was</u> the northeast quadrant of the <u>city; one</u> of
17   **18**
the more dangerous sections of town. [3] On patrol, he wears a bulletproof vest and carries a nightstick, a gun, extra ammunition, two pairs of

16. **F.** NO CHANGE
   G. officer, in his seventh year
   H. officer in his seventh, year
   J. officer in his seventh year

17. **A.** NO CHANGE
   B. is
   C. was located
   D. being

18. **F.** NO CHANGE
   G. city one
   H. city, one
   J. city one,

handcuffs, pepper spray, <u>and his two-way radio</u> is
                                    19
portable. [4] Whatever comes up he investigates.

[5] For most of his years on the force he's been

doing "midnights," the only shift that starts on one

date and ends on the next. [6] Between 11 PM and

7 AM Dan listens to his police radio and responds

to the situations that crackle over the airwaves—a

collision at New York Avenue near P Street, reports

of broken glass or a stolen car, a bunch of guys

shouting obscenities in the street. 20

Sometimes Dan's nights are manic—moments of

intense activity followed by endless lulls. On a quiet

night, Dan might pick up a couple of domestic

disputes or <u>assist</u> in an emergency medical
                        21
evacuation. 22

One wintry night last December, responding to a

"man-with-a-gun" call, Dan shot someone to

death, a man gone berserk on PCP. <u>Recalling the</u>
                                            23
<u>incident,</u> the man <u>had barged into the backseat</u>
23   **24**
of a passing car stopped at a red light. As Dan ran

toward the car, a late-model BMW with vanity

plates, he yelled to the motorist that the man had a

19. **A.** NO CHANGE
  B. and a two-way radio that is portable
  C. and a two-way radio
  D. and a portable, two-way radio

20. The logic and coherence of the passage are
  best served by placing sentence 4:
  F. where it is now
  G. before sentence 2
  H. after sentence 2
  J. after sentence 6

21. **A.** NO CHANGE
  B. he is assisting
  C. would assist
  D. had assisted

22. The writer of the passage now wants to develop
  the idea of "intense activity" introduced earlier
  in the paragraph. Which of the following sen-
  tences would best accomplish this?
  F. A policeman must be prepared to handle an
    emergency at any time.
  G. On most nights Dan takes a coffee break,
    but sometimes he can't.
  H. Then there are nights when the city
    explodes, and Dan repeatedly puts his
    health and safety—even his life—on the
    line.
  J. His shift lasts eight hours, and during every
    one he is busy as a little beaver.

23. **A.** NO CHANGE
  B. Dan explained what happened
  C. Reviewing what happened,
  D. As Dan recalls the incident,

24. **F.** NO CHANGE
  G. had barged in the backseat
  H. barged in the rear seat
  J. into the rear seat had barged

gun. 25 Immediately, the driver and front seat passenger leaped out. Approaching the car, Dan ordered the man to raise both of his hands to the roof. The man looked at Dan <u>through vacantly eyes</u>
26
and said, "Shoot me." Then his body turned toward Dan, who sensed that the man was about to bring the muzzle of his pistol around to fire at him through the window. But Dan fired first. Yet the man kept turning toward Dan. It took three more rounds before the man was still.

Immediately Dan was put on administrative leave, a standard procedure following a shooting. An investigation <u>took place and five months later</u>
27
Dan was exonerated and returned to active duty. During his first night back, another <u>incident that</u>
28
<u>has changed the course</u> of Dan's life: Responding to
28
another "man-with-a-gun" call, Dan went to the address <u>he'd been given, it turned</u> out to be a bad
29
call. That is, <u>neither a gun nor a suspect was</u> found.
30
Ever since, Dan has been worrying whether he has it in him to shoot again. He's grown tense on the job. He is short-tempered and brusque with his fellow officers. Anxious about doing the right thing, he's tempted to find a less dangerous way to earn a living.

25. The writer of the passage is thinking about deleting the phrase *a late-model BMW with vanity plates* from the previous sentence. By doing so, the main effect on the passage would be:
A. NO CHANGE
B. the removal of irrelevant material
C. a loss of suspense in the account of the shooting incident
D. a heightening of reality

26. F. NO CHANGE
G. through eyes which are vacant
H. with vacant eyes
J. with vacancy

27. A. NO CHANGE
B. took place, and five months later
C. took place and in five months later
D. took place, and, five months later

28. F. NO CHANGE
G. incident, changing the course
H. incident, that has changed the course
J. incident occurred that has changed the course

29. A. NO CHANGE
B. address he received, but it turned
C. address that he'd been given, it turned
D. address, it turned

30. F. NO CHANGE
G. neither a gun or a suspect was
H. neither a gun nor a suspect were
J. a gun and a suspect was not

Passage 3

Romping in the Pumpkin Patch

Labor Day <u>commences</u> the start of pumpkin
                    31
season. Piled on supermarket shelves, stacked on

roadside veggie stands, and displayed on countless

<u>front porches from</u> Maine to California, <u>an</u>
          32   33
<u>epidemic of pumpkins sweeps</u> across the land
          33
<u>between September to Halloween</u>. America buys
          34
most of <u>their</u> pumpkins in grocery stores, but
          35
<u>increasing amounts of consumers</u> make their way
          36
to the <u>countryside, in an effort</u> to be closer to
          37

31. **A.** NO CHANGE
    B. marks
    C. will symbolize
    D. has commenced

32. **F.** NO CHANGE
    G. front, porches from
    H. front porches; from
    J. front, porches, from

33. **A.** NO CHANGE
    B. an epidemic of pumpkins sweep
    C. millions of pumpkins sweep
    D. pumpkins in the million sweeps

34. **F.** NO CHANGE
    G. in between September to Halloween
    H. from September to Halloween
    J. from September and Halloween

35. **A.** NO CHANGE
    B. they're
    C. its
    D. it's

36. **F.** NO CHANGE
    G. consumers in larger amounts
    H. increasing numbers of consumers
    J. numbers of consumers in increasing
       amounts

37. **A.** NO CHANGE
    B. countryside in an effort
    C. countryside, trying
    D. countryside. In an effort

nature they pick pumpkins right off the ground. ⬚38

Alas, harvesting a fresh pumpkin may not thrill every member of the family. ⬚39 For an additional fee they'll drive you around on a hay wagon, serve you cider and pie, <u>let one feed the goats</u>, and
<u>40</u>
promise you a hair-raising trip <u>through man-made</u>
<u>41</u>
<u>artificial caves, where</u> witches will shriek at you,
<u>41</u>
wolves will howl, and spooks will try to scare you out of your wits. Such attractions have taken on a

Grammar Tests: ACT

38. The writer wants to add a concluding sentence to the first paragraph. Which of the following would provide the most effective ending?
- **F.** Around every bend in the road, they look for signs bearing such come-ons as "Find perfect pumpkins at Pete's U-Pik-It Pumpkin Patch" or "Polly's Pumpkin Farm. Free Doughnuts. Since 1975."
- **G.** According to the U.S. Department of Agriculture, pumpkin farming has grown over 60 percent during the last decade.
- **H.** Pumpkin meat has found its way into such food specialties as pumpkin pie, pumpkin jam, pumpkin fritters, pumpkin bread, and the ever-popular french fried pumpkin.
- **J.** The increased commercialization of Halloween has helped pumpkin farmers make huge profits.

39. The writer is thinking of revising this paragraph by inserting a sentence between the first and second sentences. Which of the following would be LEAST appropriate?
- **A.** To leave the passage as it is.
- **B.** To add this sentence: "To keep their customers happy, growers have turned their farms into mini-amusement parks."
- **C.** To add this sentence: "So, enterprising pumpkin growers have added glitzy diversions to the picking ritual."
- **D.** To add this sentence: "Knowing this, growers have tried to broaden the appeal of the pumpkin-picking experience."

40. **F.** NO CHANGE
- **G.** feed the goats
- **H.** let you feed the goats
- **J.** have the goats be fed

41. **A.** NO CHANGE
- **B.** through man-made, artificial caves in which
- **C.** through artificial caves throughout which
- **D.** through man-made caves, where

name: agri-tainment. What <u>it has</u> to do with

⁴²

picking pumpkins is anyone's guess, <u>but</u> amuse-

⁴³

ment park distractions have become as fundamen-

tal to pumpkin-picking as jack-o'-lanterns are to

Halloween.

 Few pickers realize that the annual rite is largely

a ruse foisted on unwary consumers. It's true that

some pumpkins are picked right where they grew

from seeds, but the major portion of pumpkins

dragged home from the patch have been grown

somewhere else and placed strategically in an open

field. In effect, the pumpkins have become stage

props <u>prettily arranged</u> to entice unwitting

⁴⁴

shoppers. Farmers claim that cutting pumpkins off

the vine ahead of time makes the picking process

<u>cleaner, easier, and more safer</u>: no knives, no

⁴⁵

pruning shears, no dirt to wash off.

42. **F.** NO CHANGE
 G. it is having
 H. they have
  J. these have had

43. **A.** NO CHANGE
 B. nevertheless
 C. but nevertheless
 D. but, nevertheless

44. **F.** NO CHANGE
 G. whose pretty arrangement are for
 H. arranged careful and pretty
  J. carefully, and prettily, arranged

45. **A.** NO CHANGE
 B. cleaner, easier, and safer
 C. more cleaner, more easier, and safer
 D. more clean, easier, and more safer

Passage 4

Preparing for Success

Success means different things to different people, but everyone wants it. <u>To have wealth is also something that people want.</u> A desire to be
₄₆
successful <u>which seems to be </u>built into the human
₄₇
nervous system. It's an instinct, like self-preservation, and <u>as natural to do as breathing</u>.
₄₈
<u>Unlike breathing however success</u> doesn't come
₄₉
naturally for most people. It must be worked for.

Most ordinary success stories <u>begin in
₅₀
childhood</u>, frequently with parents or other adults
₅₀
taking a special interest in <u>his or her</u> development
₅₁
and helping the youngster to acquire habits that typically lead to success. Some children are taught a work ethic early on and respond favorably to discipline and high expectations. Others thrive under <u>the freedom that is guaranteed by the Constitution,</u>
₅₂
youthful self-expression, and an abundance of positive reinforcement. Some child-development experts comment, <u>though,</u> that overabundant
₅₃
praise can be damaging. Children accustomed to effusive praise for everything they do may develop a good self-image, but when reality sets in, they often discover that the real world is relatively indif-

46. **F.** NO CHANGE
   G. Everyone also wants wealth.
   H. (Only wealth is something that people want more.)
   J. OMIT the underlined section.

47. **A.** NO CHANGE
   B. which seems to have been
   C. seems to have been
   D. would seem to be

48. **F.** NO CHANGE
   G. as natural as breathing
   H. as natural as doing breathing
   J. as natural like breathing

49. **A.** NO CHANGE
   B. Unlike breathing, however,
   C. Different than breathing, however,
   D. Different from, breathing however

50. **F.** NO CHANGE
   G. begin with childhood
   H. are introduced at the time of childhood
   J. start by the time of the elementary grades

51. **A.** NO CHANGE
   B. their
   C. children's
   D. a child's

52. **F.** NO CHANGE
   G. freedom,
   H. freedom, which is a guarantee of the Constitution
   J. freedom, which, under the Constitution, is our right

53. Which of the following alternatives to the underlined word would be the LEAST desirable?
   A. therefore
   B. however
   C. nevertheless
   D. while

ferent to the behaviors that, once won generous
        54

approval.

Growing up in a highly regimented and tightly
        55

disciplined atmosphere, on the other hand, can
        55

teach children to value high achievement through
        55

hard work. Many successful people attribute
     55

their becoming successful people not only to the
        56

discipline that had been imposed on them, but on
                                           57

the example set by their parents who dedicated

themselves for hours every day, sometimes
                                    58

patiently sometimes in frustration teaching them to
        58

use their time and talent constructively. They may

not have appreciated their parents' attentiveness at

the time, but in the end they think it paid off.

Observers note that some children raised in

unceasing strict and demanding circumstances
   59

grow up inhibited and feeling shortchanged about

having missed a real childhood. A sheltered

upbringing has kept these children from seeing the

world as it really is. Later in life they may rebel,

especially when they are let go, say, during their

54. **F.** NO CHANGE
    G. that once
    H. that, once,
    J. that once,

55. Which choice would be the most effective sentence for leading the reader from the previous paragraph to this one?
    A. NO CHANGE
    B. Theories about how children should be raised have changed over the years and often go through cycles.
    C. Standards of good behavior are difficult to enforce, as any parent will tell you.
    D. Teachers, for example, must often decide whether to reward students for trying hard even when the work is mediocre.

56. **F.** NO CHANGE
    G. fame
    H. success
    J. OMIT the underlined words

57. **A.** NO CHANGE
    B. but also on
    C. but to
    D. but also to

58. **F.** NO CHANGE
    G. sometimes patiently, sometimes in frustration,
    H. sometimes patiently; sometimes not
    J. sometimes with patience, and, sometimes not

59. **A.** NO CHANGE
    B. unceasingly
    C. unending
    D. nonstop

freshman year in college. Feeling insecure, they may withdraw socially, and in the worst cases, become self-destructive. 60

60. This question deals with the entire passage. If the writer had intended to write an essay showing that success is more regularly achieved by people who had been brought up in strict, demanding circumstances, would this essay fulfill the writer's intention?
   F. Yes, because the essay contains more evidence to support the position that strict discipline is a prerequisite for success.
   G. Yes, because the writer implies that adults who lacked freedom as children learn to make choices regardless of their upbringing.
   H. No, because the writer doesn't say that one type of upbringing is better than another.
   J. No, because the writer suggests that child development experts cannot make up their minds about which kind of upbringing works best.

Passage 5

Getting Along with the Amish

[1]

The Amish are a Christian group with roots going back to sixteenth-century Europe. It has distinguished themselves in America by their plain clothing, simple living, and rejection of everyday conveniences as electricity, telephones, and cars. In short, they favor traditional customs that, go back hundreds of years.

61. A. NO CHANGE
   B. It's distinguished
   C. Distinguishing themselves
   D. They have distinguished themselves

62. F. NO CHANGE
   G. customs that go back
   H. customs, that, go back
   J. customs, going back,

[2]

Most Amish in the United States live in: rural Pennsylvania, Ohio, and Indiana. More than 10,000 also live in Wisconsin, some of them near the little

63. A. NO CHANGE
   B. in: rural Pennsylvania, Ohio, and Indiana
   C. in rural Pennsylvania, Ohio, and Indiana
   D. in rural Pennsylvania; Ohio; and Indiana

town of Loyal. Although the Amish <u>live independ-</u>
₆₄
<u>ently separate lives</u> from "the English," as they call
₆₄
non-Amish people, they have a history of <u>getting</u>
₆₅
<u>along peaceful with</u> the citizens of Loyal.
₆₅
<u>Nevertheless</u>, a rift has grown <u>between</u> them in
₆₆ ₆₇
recent years. At the root of the problem is the

Amish use of horses and buggies. Whenever Amish

farmers or family <u>drives to</u> town for shopping or
₆₈
banking, they go by horse and buggy.

[3]

69 The citizens of Loyal have wearied of the

stench left by Amish horses and have grown tired

of stepping with care whenever they walk around

64. **F.** NO CHANGE
   G. live apart from
   H. live separately and independent lives
   J. live lives that are separate and independent

65. **A.** NO CHANGE
   B. peacefulness to
   C. peaceful getting along with
   D. getting along peacefully with

66. Which of the following would be the LEAST effective transition between this and the previous sentence?
   F. NO CHANGE
   G. However,
   H. By all means,
   J. Yet,

67. **A.** NO CHANGE
   B. among
   C. amongst
   D. up in between

68. **F.** NO CHANGE
   G. drives into town
   H. drive to
   J. were to drive into

69. The writer is thinking of adding a new sentence to introduce paragraph 3. Which of the following would be the most effective addition?
   A. Conversation at the town's post office and in coffee shops is usually about keeping the streets clean.
   B. The Amish tend to their horses and buggies as avidly as teenagers care for their first cars.
   C. Buggies present no problem, but horses, being horses, have a habit of dropping manure wherever they go.
   D. "The issue is that those people are different from us, and that's unfortunate," says Martha Peterson, a lifelong resident of Loyal.

town. <u>Besides</u>, they resent paying for crews to clean
     70
their streets almost every day.

[4]

<u>Three years ago the Amish and the townspeople</u>
                    71
<u>tried to negotiate an agreement:</u> The Amish would
                    71
drive their horses only on certain streets and would

pay a fine if they neglected to clean up the areas

where they hitched their horses. In return, the town

would drop its insistence that the Amish put a

manure-catching device—a kind of diaper—on

their horses. But negotiations got nasty, causing the

Amish to withdraw their money from the local

banks and to boycott Loyal's stores and other busi-

nesses for a year. Since then, the town council has

discussed the matter repeatedly, but a solution has

yet to be found.

[5]

In the meantime, some members of the non-

Amish community harbor ill feelings about the

strangers who live so close by <u>but remain aloof.</u>
                                        72
<u>Others welcome</u> the Amish, not for their sociability
     72
but for their trade. For example, the owner of the

70. What is the best location for the underlined word?
- **F.** Where it is now
- **G.** After the word *resent*
- **H.** After the word *paying*
- **J.** After the word *day*

71. **A.** NO CHANGE
- **B.** An agreement was attempted to be negotiated three years ago by the Amish and the townspeople.
- **C.** At attempt at negotiations for an agreement three years ago by the Amish and the townspeople.
- **D.** OMIT the underlined sentence.

72. **F.** NO CHANGE
- **G.** and remain aloof, others welcome
- **H.** remaining aloof. Others welcome
- **J.** and are aloof and others welcome

Grammar Tests: ACT

town's hardware store, Tom Zettler, <u>asserts,</u> he
                                         73
makes 25 percent of his sales to the Amish.

73. **A.** NO CHANGE
    B. asserts
    C. asserts, that
    D. asserts, that,

74. Having reread the passage, the writer decides to add a sentence containing information that had been left out. The sentence is:

    The head of the Amish community claimed that it was unsafe for buggies to be stopped in the middle of the street every time a horse relieved itself.

    The most logical and effective place to insert this sentence is paragraph
    F. 2
    G. 3
    H. 4
    J. 5

75. Suppose the writer had planned to compose an essay comparing and contrasting the Amish way of life with that of other Loyal residents. Would this essay successfully achieve the writer's purpose?
    A. No, because the essay has a limited purpose—to describe one source of disagreement between the Amish and the townspeople.
    B. No, because the essay focuses on secret deals made between the Amish and the town administration.
    C. Yes, because the essay shows that diverse religious beliefs have led to longstanding hostility between the Amish and the townspeople.
    D. Yes, because the essay points out that the Amish use horses and buggies, whereas the residents of Loyal prefer cars.

ANSWER KEY

1. C	11. D	21. A	31. B	41. D	51. D	61. D	71. A
2. F	12. F	22. H	32. F	42. H	52. G	62. G	72. F
3. C	13. C	23. D	33. C	43. A	53. D	63. C	73. B
4. J	14. G	24. F	34. H	44. F	54. G	64. G	74. H
5. B	15. A	25. B	35. C	45. B	55. A	65. D	75. A
6. G	16. J	26. H	36. H	46. J	56. H	66. H	
7. C	17. B	27. B	37. D	47. C	57. D	67. A	
8. J	18. H	28. J	38. F	48. G	58. G	68. H	
9. C	19. C	29. B	39. A	49. B	59. B	69. C	
10. G	20. J	30. F	40. H	50. F	60. H	70. F	

ANSWER EXPLANATIONS

Passage 1

1. **C** Leaving the original version intact makes *consumers* the subject of the sentence and leads to a comma splice after the word *gallon*. Choice B has the same problem as Choice A. By maintaining *consumers* as the subject, you are left with a comma splice following the word *gallon*. Choice D is similar to A and B, with the additional problem of an apostrophe after the *-s* in *Americas*, suggesting that America is plural. The use of *because* in Choice C turns the construction into a dependent clause, thereby eliminating the comma splice.

2. **F** Choice G contains a redundancy: *decades* and *time*. Use one or the other but not both words. Choices H and J both include a misplaced and unnecessary comma.

3. **C** Choice A contains faulty verb tense. Because the sentence is cast in the past tense, *have sent*, a verb in the present perfect tense, is not appropriate. Choice B is wrong because *sended* is not standard English. Choice C is correct because the past tense of the verb *to send* is *sent*. Choice D attempts to use *sending* as the

main verb of the clause beginning with *price wars*. The problem is that the *-ing* form of a verb may not serve as the main verb without a helping verb, as in *is sending* or *were sending*.

4. **J** Choice F misuses a semicolon to separate a word from a phrase. Choice G places the exclamation point in the wrong place—after the interjection *Imagine* instead of after the exclamation itself. The meaning expressed by Choice H is unrelated to the point of the passage. The use of the dash in Choice J creates an effective pause between *Imagine* and the rest of the sentence.

5. **B** Although interesting, the information given by the underlined statement wanders from the point of the paragraph. Choice B succinctly highlights the difference in gasoline prices between then and now. It is the best answer. Choices C and D include irrelevancies that weaken the coherence of the passage.

6. **G** The original version tries to compare *life* and *the past*, two things that cannot logically be compared. Choice H is the same as G. Choice J uses nonstandard English idiom. A properly worded comparison

may use an *as . . . as* construction: "*as* wild *as* a tiger," but never an *as . . . like* construction.

7. **C** The underlined portion of the sentence should be changed because the phrases *half a century* and *fifty years ago* are redundant. Choice B leaves out a necessary comma after the "*If*" clause. Choice D contains an error in standard English expression because one does not go back *fifty years ago* but one goes back *fifty years.* Delete *ago.*

8. **J** The transitional sentence needed here should provide a link between a paragraph discussing an idealized image of a long-ago consumer's paradise and the actual prices of everyday products. The original sentence (Choice A) attempts to attribute low prices to the absence of credit cards, an inappropriate and essentially wrong-headed idea. Choice G introduces an idea about reckless spending that is not relevant to the passage. Choice H relates to the content of the passage but is a sentence fragment. Choice J is the best answer because it reiterates the idea that prices were low and introduces a discussion of a family's expenditures.

9. **C** Choice A contains a dangling participle. *Returning* modifies *cost* instead of a performer of the action such as *you* or some other pronoun or a noun. Choice B is similar to A. It fails to say who is "going back." D suggests that the writer is about to discuss the 19th century again, but the passage previously made no mention of the 19th century. C is the best answer: It uses an "if" clause followed by the conditional verb, *would be.*

10. **G** Choice F is incorrect because the comparative form of *less* is not *lesser* but *less.*

Choice H is the same as F. Choice J uses *fewer*, a word reserved for comparing things that are countable, such as marbles and cars. G is the best answer.

11. **D** Choices A, B, and C are all grammatically correct, but are also redundant because *quart* was used earlier in the sentence.

12. **F** Choice G contains disagreement between the singular subject (*value*) and the plural verb (*were*). Choices H and J improperly shift the verb away from the simple past tense.

13. **C** The underlined segment contains a pronoun, *she*, that serves as the subject of the second clause. The verb *paying*, however, is incorrect because an *-ing* verb requires a helping verb, as in *was paying* and *has been paying* to serve as the main verb in a clause or sentence. Choice B is the same as A, but is an even poorer choice because *her* is an objective pronoun ineligible to be used as a subject. Choice D includes two superfluous commas.

14. **G** The underlined verb causes the construction to be a sentence fragment because a verb in the past progressive form may not act as the main verb of a sentence. H is a sentence fragment because the construction lacks a verb. The *-ing* form of a verb may not be the main verb without a helping verb as in *is growing* or *had been growing.* J is a singular verb that disagrees with its plural subject—*wages* and *cost.*

15. **A** The passage, which compares the cost of living then and now, makes the point that, although prices seemed lower in the past, in terms of purchasing power and wages they were not much different. Choices B, C, and D state ideas that are only marginally related to the point of the passage.

Passage 2

16. **J** The underlined words require no punctuation.

17. **B** Because the passage is in the present tense, the use of *was*, a verb in the past tense, is incorrect. Choice C also uses a verb in the past tense. Choice D improperly uses an *-ing* verb as the main verb of the sentence, causing the construction to be a sentence fragment.

18. **H** Choice F is incorrect because semicolons may not be used to separate a clause and a phrase. Choice G fails to include a comma to indicate that the phrase beginning with the word *one* is an appositive that defines the *northeast quadrant of the city*. Choice J includes a misplaced and unnecessary comma.

19. **C** The underlined phrase is not grammatically parallel to the other items on Dan's equipment list. Choice B is parallel to the other items but contains the word *portable*, a redundancy, because anything that is carried is portable by definition. Choice D includes an unnecessary comma and has the same redundancy as B.

20. **J** The sentence fits best where the passage deals with the types of problems that Dan encounters on patrol.

21. **A** The verb *assist* is structurally parallel to the verb *pick up*. Choices B, C, and D lack the necessary parallelism.

22. **H** Choice F is unrelated to the idea of intense activity. Choice G does no more than weakly suggest nights of intense activity. Choice J supports the idea of intense activity, but the tone of "busy as a little beaver" is inconsistent with the rest of the passage. Only Choice H fulfills the writer's purpose.

23. **D** Choice A is a dangling modifier because he phrase *Recalling the incident* modifies *man* instead of *Dan*. Choice B is an independent clause that lacks punctuation, thereby forming a run-on sentence. Choice C has a modification problem similar to that of Choice A.

24. **F** Choice G contains a faulty word choice. The word *in* means "within," not "into," which refers to the motion of going from outside to inside. Choice H is the same as G with the addition of the incorrect use of the past tense of the verb. The past perfect *had barged* is called for because the action described took place before another past action, namely Dan's shooting of the man. Choice J uses inverted word order in an inappropriate context.

25. **B** Because the description of the car is unimportant, especially at a moment of tension in Dan's story, the passage is improved by the deletion.

26. **H** The underlined words include an adverb where an adjective is needed to modify the noun *eyes*. Choice G is wordy and shifts the verb tense from past to present. Choice J is awkwardly expressed.

27. **B** Choice A lacks a comma that is needed to separate the clauses of a compound sentence. In Choice C the phrase *in five months later* is a nonstandard English idiom. Choice D includes an unnecessary comma after *and*.

28. **J** Choices F, G, and H are sentence fragments. Each clause has a subject but lacks a viable verb.

29. **B** Choices A, C, and D contain a comma splice. Only Choice B recognizes the construction as a compound sentence requiring the use of a comma and a conjunction (*but*) between clauses.

30. **F** Choice G incorrectly pairs *or* and *neither*. Choice H uses a plural verb (*were*) with a singular subject. Choice J uses a singular verb (*was*) with the plural subject *gun and suspect*.

Passage 3

31. **B** Choice A, which contains *commences* and *start*, is redundant. Choice C uses the future tense instead of the present tense of the verb. Choice D contains a redundancy similar to that in A.

32. **F** Choice G includes a misplaced comma between the adjective *front* and *porches*, the noun it modifies. The semicolon in Choice H is an error because semicolons should function like periods, separating independent clauses. Choice J contains two superfluous commas.

33. **C** Both Choices A and B suffer from a problem in modification. The phrases beginning with *piled*, *stacked*, and *displayed* should modify *pumpkins*, not *epidemic*. Choice D contains a lack of agreement between the plural subject *pumpkins* and the singular verb *sweeps*.

34. **H** Choices F, G, and J contain nonstandard English idiom.

35. **C** The plural pronoun *their* lacks agreement with *America*, its singular antecedent. Choice B uses a contraction meaning *they are*. Choice D is a contraction meaning *it is*.

36. **H** The word *amounts* refers to uncountable quantities. *Numbers* refers to things that can be counted. Because consumers can be counted, *numbers* is the word to use in this context.

37. **D** Choices A and C are incorrect because each consists of two sentences separated by a comma instead of an end mark of punctuation. Choice B is a run-on sentence.

38. **F** Only Choice F continues to add details about the phenomenon of picking your own pumpkin. The other choices pertain to other aspects of the pumpkin industry.

39. **A** Choices B, C, and D contain sentences that improve the coherence of the paragraph by providing a link between the first and second sentences. Choice A leaves a gap.

40. **H** In Choice F the pronoun person shifts from second to third person. Choices G and J are not grammatically parallel to the other phrases in the list of activities at the pumpkin patch.

41. **D** Choices A and B contain redundancies because *man-made* and *artificial* mean essentially the same thing. Choice C is wordy and awkwardly expressed.

42. **H** Choices F and G contains the singular pronoun *it*, which lacks agreement in number with its plural antecedent *attractions*. Choice J shifts the sentence from the present to the past perfect tense.

43. **A** The use of *nevertheless* in Choice B creates a comma splice between two independent clauses. Both Choices C and D contain redundancies. Use *but* or *nevertheless*, not both.

44. **F** Choice G is wordy and awkward. It also lacks noun-verb agreement. Choice H uses adjectives instead of adverbs to modify the verb *arranged*. Choice J includes superfluous, inappropriate punctuation.

45. **B** Choices A, C, and D are incorrect because comparisons using *more* may not be made with adjectives in the comparative degree.

Passage 4

46. **J** The sentences in Choices F, G, and H digress from the main idea of the paragraph and detract from the paragraph's unity.

47. **C** Choices A and B are sentence fragments because each lacks a main verb. Choice D uses *would seem,* a weak conditional phrase.

48. **G** Choice A contains the awkward, nonstandard construction *to do breathing.* Similarly, Choice H uses *doing breathing.* In Choice J, *like* may not be used in place of *as.*

49. **B** Because *however* functions like a conjunction in Choice A, it must be set off by commas. Choice C contains *different than,* a nonstandard phrase. Choice D uses the standard phrase *different from,* but includes an unnecessary comma after *from* and fails to provide commas before and after *however.*

50. **F** In Choice G, the use of *with* instead of *in* is nonstandard English idiom. Choice H, a construction in the passive voice, suggests that most success stories are told to children—surely not the intent of the writer. Choice J makes little sense in the context of the passage.

51. **D** The pronouns in Choices A and B fail to refer to a specific noun or other pronoun. Choice C uses the plural *children* when the discussion is about a single *youngster.*

52. **G** References to the Constitution are irrelevant. The passage discusses freedom in a more personal sense—that is, parents giving children opportunities to make choices for themselves.

53. **D** Choices A, B, and C provide an appropriate link between contrasting ideas in the passage.

54. **G** In this context, no commas are needed.

55. **A** The underscored sentence introduces a paragraph on the effects of strict discipline. The other choices wander from this purpose.

56. **H** Choice F is wordy and needlessly repetitive. Choice G improperly narrows the focus of the passage, which discusses success in general, not *fame.* Choice J leaves the sentence without a coherent meaning.

57. **D** Choices A and B lack grammatical parallelism to the phrase *to the discipline.* Choice C lacks the word *also,* needed to complete the paired expression *not only . . . but also.*

58. **G** Choice F needs commas to separate the phrases inserted almost parenthetically into the structure of the sentence. Choice H misuses a semicolon, which should function like a period, separating two independent clauses. Choice J contains two superfluous commas.

59. **B** Choices A, C, and D are adjectives, but an adverb is needed to modify the adjectives *strict* and *demanding.*

60. **H** Choice H accurately describes the essay, which presents the pros and cons of each point of view.

Passage 5

61. **D** Choice A uses the singular pronoun *It* to refer to *The Amish*, a plural noun. In Choice B, the use of the contraction meaning *it is* turns the rest of the sentence into nonstandard English. Choice C is a sentence fragment because it lacks a main verb.

62. **G** Choices F, H, and J include improperly placed and unnecessary commas.

63. **C** Choices A and B are incorrect because colons should not be used to introduce a list or series when the list or series grammatically completes the introductory statement. Choice D is incorrect because semicolons should be used in lists only when items in the list contain commas, as in *Boston, Massachusetts; Bangor, Maine*, etc.

64. **G** Eliminate Choice F because *independently* and *separate* express essentially the same meaning, and *live . . . lives* is repetitive. Choices H and J are similar to Choice F.

65. **D** Choice A is incorrect because it uses the adjective *peaceful* instead of an adverb to modify the verb *getting along*. The use of *to* instead of *with* in Choice B is nonstandard English idiom. Choice C is the same as A.

66. **H** Choices F, G, and J are words that are used to introduce ideas that contrast with those stated previously. Choice H fails to do that.

67. **A** Choice B is incorrect because *among* refers to division of more than two. Choice C is a word that means *surrounded by*. Choice D uses the prepositions *up* and *in*, both unnecessary.

68. **H** In Choice F the singular verb *drives* fails to agree with the plural subject *farmers*. Choice G is the same as F. Choice J improperly shifts the verb to the subjunctive.

69. **C** Choice C, which alludes to the problem mentioned in the previous paragraph, deals with the substance of paragraph 3 and provides a bridge between the paragraphs. None of the other choices work as effectively.

70. **F** To move the underlined word to the places specified by Choices G, H, and J would do nothing but make the language awkward and unidiomatic.

71. **A** Choice B uses awkward passive construction. Choice C is a sentence fragment because it lacks a verb. Choice D would deprive the paragraph of a topic sentence.

72. **F** Choice G contains faulty punctuation because a period or semicolon (instead of a comma) must be used to separate sentences. Choice H contains faulty parallelism. The phrase *remaining aloof* is not grammatically parallel to *live so close by*. Choice J suffers from a stylistic flaw: Because it is a compound sentence meant to contrast opposing attitudes toward the Amish, the conjunction *and* is a weak choice of words. *But* would be better. In addition, the clauses of a compound sentence should be separated by a comma.

73. **B** Choices A and C include an unnecessary comma between the verb and the indirect quotation. Choice D contains two superfluous commas, the first between the verb and the indirect quotation, the other between *that* and the clause it introduces.

74. **H** Paragraph 4 discusses the details of the agreement between the town and the Amish. The sentence in question adds a new dimension to the discussion.

75. **A** Choice A accurately describes the purpose of the passage.

ACT CHECKPOINT 2
ANSWER SHEET

Passage 1 Runners Beware!

1. Ⓐ Ⓑ Ⓒ Ⓓ
2. Ⓕ Ⓖ Ⓗ Ⓙ
3. Ⓐ Ⓑ Ⓒ Ⓓ
4. Ⓕ Ⓖ Ⓗ Ⓙ
5. Ⓐ Ⓑ Ⓒ Ⓓ

6. Ⓕ Ⓖ Ⓗ Ⓙ
7. Ⓐ Ⓑ Ⓒ Ⓓ
8. Ⓕ Ⓖ Ⓗ Ⓙ
9. Ⓐ Ⓑ Ⓒ Ⓓ
10. Ⓕ Ⓖ Ⓗ Ⓙ

11. Ⓐ Ⓑ Ⓒ Ⓓ
12. Ⓕ Ⓖ Ⓗ Ⓙ
13. Ⓐ Ⓑ Ⓒ Ⓓ
14. Ⓕ Ⓖ Ⓗ Ⓙ
15. Ⓐ Ⓑ Ⓒ Ⓓ

Passage 2 The World's Worst Nuclear Accident

16. Ⓕ Ⓖ Ⓗ Ⓙ
17. Ⓐ Ⓑ Ⓒ Ⓓ
18. Ⓕ Ⓖ Ⓗ Ⓙ
19. Ⓐ Ⓑ Ⓒ Ⓓ
20. Ⓕ Ⓖ Ⓗ Ⓙ

21. Ⓐ Ⓑ Ⓒ Ⓓ
22. Ⓕ Ⓖ Ⓗ Ⓙ
23. Ⓐ Ⓑ Ⓒ Ⓓ
24. Ⓕ Ⓖ Ⓗ Ⓙ
25. Ⓐ Ⓑ Ⓒ Ⓓ

26. Ⓕ Ⓖ Ⓗ Ⓙ
27. Ⓐ Ⓑ Ⓒ Ⓓ
28. Ⓕ Ⓖ Ⓗ Ⓙ
29. Ⓐ Ⓑ Ⓒ Ⓓ
30. Ⓕ Ⓖ Ⓗ Ⓙ

Passage 3 Ghosts in the House

31. Ⓐ Ⓑ Ⓒ Ⓓ
32. Ⓕ Ⓖ Ⓗ Ⓙ
33. Ⓐ Ⓑ Ⓒ Ⓓ
34. Ⓕ Ⓖ Ⓗ Ⓙ
35. Ⓐ Ⓑ Ⓒ Ⓓ

36. Ⓕ Ⓖ Ⓗ Ⓙ
37. Ⓐ Ⓑ Ⓒ Ⓓ
38. Ⓕ Ⓖ Ⓗ Ⓙ
39. Ⓐ Ⓑ Ⓒ Ⓓ
40. Ⓕ Ⓖ Ⓗ Ⓙ

41. Ⓐ Ⓑ Ⓒ Ⓓ
42. Ⓕ Ⓖ Ⓗ Ⓙ
43. Ⓐ Ⓑ Ⓒ Ⓓ
44. Ⓕ Ⓖ Ⓗ Ⓙ
45. Ⓐ Ⓑ Ⓒ Ⓓ

Cut along dotted line.

Grammar Tests: ACT

Passage 4 Pros and Cons of Child Care

46. Ⓕ Ⓖ Ⓗ Ⓙ   51. Ⓐ Ⓑ Ⓒ Ⓓ   56. Ⓕ Ⓖ Ⓗ Ⓙ
47. Ⓐ Ⓑ Ⓒ Ⓓ   52. Ⓕ Ⓖ Ⓗ Ⓙ   57. Ⓐ Ⓑ Ⓒ Ⓓ
48. Ⓕ Ⓖ Ⓗ Ⓙ   53. Ⓐ Ⓑ Ⓒ Ⓓ   58. Ⓕ Ⓖ Ⓗ Ⓙ
49. Ⓐ Ⓑ Ⓒ Ⓓ   54. Ⓕ Ⓖ Ⓗ Ⓙ   59. Ⓐ Ⓑ Ⓒ Ⓓ
50. Ⓕ Ⓖ Ⓗ Ⓙ   55. Ⓐ Ⓑ Ⓒ Ⓓ   60. Ⓕ Ⓖ Ⓗ Ⓙ

Passage 5 Cinderella: A Rags to Riches Story

61. Ⓐ Ⓑ Ⓒ Ⓓ   66. Ⓕ Ⓖ Ⓗ Ⓙ   71. Ⓐ Ⓑ Ⓒ Ⓓ
62. Ⓕ Ⓖ Ⓗ Ⓙ   67. Ⓐ Ⓑ Ⓒ Ⓓ   72. Ⓕ Ⓖ Ⓗ Ⓙ
63. Ⓐ Ⓑ Ⓒ Ⓓ   68. Ⓕ Ⓖ Ⓗ Ⓙ   73. Ⓐ Ⓑ Ⓒ Ⓓ
64. Ⓕ Ⓖ Ⓗ Ⓙ   69. Ⓐ Ⓑ Ⓒ Ⓓ   74. Ⓕ Ⓖ Ⓗ Ⓙ
65. Ⓐ Ⓑ Ⓒ Ⓓ   70. Ⓕ Ⓖ Ⓗ Ⓙ   75. Ⓐ Ⓑ Ⓒ Ⓓ

INSTRUCTIONS: In each of the five passages printed on the left you will find sentence segments that are underlined and numbered. A multiple-choice question about each underlined segment appears on the right. To answer the question, choose the alternative that best expresses the underlined word or phrase in standard written English, or the one that is most consistent with the style or tone of the passage. If you decide that the original is best, choose either A or F, indicating that NO CHANGE is needed.

Some questions will direct your attention to specific words or phrases, others to a broader section of the passage or to the passage as a whole. These questions are indicated with a number inside brackets or inside a box.

Once you have decided on an answer, fill in the blank space on the answer sheet. You are advised to read each passage completely before answering the questions. Also be mindful that to answer some questions you may need to read one or more sentences that preccde or follow the sentence containing a question.

Passage 1

Runners Beware!

Whether or not knowing it, marathoners and

1
other long-distance runners face a host of common

perils. A little-known one that surprise most

2
runners however, is one of the most dangerous. Its

3   4
the threat that comes from drinking too much

4
water.

To stave off dehydration, runners, as well as

5
athletes, in virtually every sport, tend to drink

5

1. **A.** NO CHANGE
   B. They have the knowledge or not
   C. Wanting to be informed,
   D. OMIT the underlined portion

2. **F.** NO CHANGE
   G. that surprises
   H. had been surpising
   J. surprised

3. **A.** NO CHANGE
   B. runners, however
   C. runners, however,
   D. runners however

4. **F.** NO CHANGE
   G. dangerous, it is the threat
   H. dangerous—the threat
   J. dangerous threats

5. **A.** NO CHANGE
   B. runners, as well as athletes in virtually every sport,
   C. including runners and athletes, in virtually every sport
   D. runners as well as athletes,

plenty of water, especially in hot weather. <u>Before a</u>
<u>race, runners cast off extra clothing they may</u>
<u>have brought to the starting gate.</u> Because a
marathon takes hours to complete, most partici-
pants drink still more during the race itself in order
to replenish the liquids they've lost through perspi-
ration. Unaware of the dangers of drinking too
much, their health and well-being are <u>put to risk</u>.
An excessive amount of water <u>dilutes your</u>
blood. Water seeps into cells throughout they're
body, including the brain. Swollen brain cells then
press against the inside of the skull, resulting in
hyponatremia—a condition that <u>completes the</u>
<u>score.</u>
 <u>Marathon authorities have lately spread the word</u>
that runners should <u>limit and restrict their water</u>
<u>intake</u> to no more than eight ounces of water every
20 minutes. They want to avoid situations such as
<u>that having occurred</u> during the New York City

6. Given that all the choices are true, which one develops the paragraph most logically and effectively?
   F. NO CHANGE
   G. Sponsors provide bottled water and Gatorade free of charge.
   H. Before the race they often guzzle water or popular sports drinks such as Gatorade.
   J. Some runners carry plastic bottles filled with water or a sports drink.

7. A. NO CHANGE
   B. in risk
   C. risky
   D. put at risk

8. F. NO CHANGE
   G. dilutes the
   H. diluted
   J. has diluted your

9. A. NO CHANGE
   B. has its limits
   C. can be fatal
   D. is without exception

10. F. NO CHANGE
    G. The word spread by marathon authorities have lately been
    H. Spreading the word, which marathon authorities say lately
    J. To spread the word, marathon authorities, say

11. A. NO CHANGE
    B. restrict the amount of water they drink
    C. limit the amount and restrict the quantity of their water intake
    D. limit their water drinking by restricting the amount

12. F. NO CHANGE
    G. those occurring
    H. them which had occurred
    J. those which occurred

Marathon <u>in 2004, when more than</u> 350 runners
                    13
were hospitalized with hyponatremia. Because the

symptoms of hyponatremia—leg cramps, dizzi-

ness, nausea—<u>are similar with those of</u> dehy-
                        14
dration, or too little water, doctors treated some

patients by giving them intravenous fluids, <u>making</u>
                                             15
<u>medical malpractice lawsuits more widespread.</u>
                    15

13. **A.** NO CHANGE
    B. in 2004, when more then
    C. in 2004 as over
    D. in 2004; when, over

14. **F.** NO CHANGE
    G. are similar to that of
    H. resemble those of
    J. is like

15. **A.** NO CHANGE
    B. opening them up to charges of malpractice
    C. giving patients grounds for suing the doc-
        tors
    D. OMIT the underlined portion.

Passage 2

The World's Worst Nuclear Accident

On April 26, 1986, Nuclear Reactor #4 at

Chernobyl in the former USSR (now Ukraine)

<u>overheated excessively and suddenly exploded</u>. The
                    16
explosion, history's <u>most worse</u> nuclear
                        17
accident, created a fireball that spewed tons of

radioactive material into the atmosphere. Winds

spread the radioactivity across Earth's

Northern Hemisphere. Thirty people died in the

<u>explosion; many more were to die later</u> in Ukraine,
                    18
neighboring Belarus, and Russia. More than

135,000 people had to be evacuated from their

homes and farms. To this day, many <u>thousands, had</u>
                                         19
<u>not returned yet</u>.
    19

16. **F.** NO CHANGE
    G. overheated and exploded.
    H. overheated excessively, and afterward
        exploded suddenly
    J. suddenly, exploded after overheating exces-
        sively

17. **A.** NO CHANGE
    B. most worst
    C. worst
    D. terrible

18. **F.** NO CHANGE
    G. explosion, many more were to die later
    H. explosion. Many more had died later
    J. explosion; much more died later

19. **A.** NO CHANGE
    B. thousands have not returned
    C. thousands, haven't yet returned
    D. thousands are still not returned

The Ukraine Radiological Institute reported that radiation poisoning <u>might have caused</u> more than
₂₀
2,500 deaths within a few months of the accident.

<u>Their studies also find that</u> the incidence of
₂₁
<u>cancer, especially thyroid cancer</u> increased by 64
₂₂
percent among people who lived within a 20-mile radius of the reactor as well as among the "liquidators" (that is, the men and women <u>who helped</u>
₂₃
<u>clean up after</u> the accident). Masses of people
₂₃
suffered long-term psychological disorders from the trauma and stress of the experience. They became depressed and overcome with feelings of extreme hopelessness, leading to social withdrawal and isolation. [24]

Now, a generation later, the accident's aftereffects are still being felt. Belarus contains some of the most contaminated places on the globe. Much of the land is still <u>radioactive, in fact,</u> in <u>only a 1 percent</u>
₂₅   ₂₆
<u>fraction</u> of the region's farmland has contami-
₂₆

20. F. NO CHANGE
    G. might of caused
    H. could of caused
    J. could cause

21. A. NO CHANGE
    B. Their studies also found that
    C. It's studies also found that
    D. It also found

22. F. NO CHANGE
    G. cancer—especially thyroid cancer—
    H. cancer; especially thyroid cancer,
    J. cancer, cancer of the thyroid,

23. A. NO CHANGE
    B. which helped clean up after
    C. that have helped afterward to clean up
    D. who helped clean from

24. Which of the following true statements, if added here, would provide that best evidence to support the assertion that residents close to the accident suffered from psychological problems?
    F. The suicide rate increased by 30 percent during each of the five years after the accident.
    G. In Ukraine, clinics and hospitals were built rapidly to treat victims of the blast.
    H. Many more students in medical colleges throughout the country began to specialize in the treatment of mental diseases.
    J. Alcohol consumption remained higher than ever, and the life expectancy of men fell from 62 to 58 years.

25. A. NO CHANGE
    B. radioactive, that
    C. radioactive; in fact,
    D. so radioactive that in fact

26. F. NO CHANGE
    G. just that 1 percent
    H. a 1 percent fraction
    J. only a fraction

nation <u>cooled off sufficient to let</u> farmers to plant
²⁷
and grow rye, barley, and other crops. Although

horse breeding has begun, and cattle are being

raised for beef, dairy farming hasn't returned

because of <u>people's fear toward</u> radiated milk.
²⁸
Health authorities still warn people not to eat wild

game, mushrooms, or berries, which absorb high

levels of radiation. <u>Fish caught</u> in lakes and streams
²⁹
are toxic, and the honey produced by local bees is

unsafe.

    [1] Chernobyl's legacy is bound to continue for a

long time. [2] Ever so slowly the people of the area

are trying to reclaim lands and enjoy the lifestyle of

pre-Chernobyl days. [3] Complete normalcy, how-

ever, isn't likely to return until the 22nd century, if

ever. [30]

27. **A.** NO CHANGE
    B. cooled off sufficient for
    C. cooled down sufficiently so as to let
    D. cooled sufficiently for

28. **F.** NO CHANGE
    G. people's fear of
    H. the peoples' fear to
    J. people's fear with respect of

29. **A.** NO CHANGE
    B. Fishing
    C. Catching fish
    D. The fish catched

30. The writer is considering the addition of the
following true sentence to the last paragraph:

    Radioactive materials such as censium-137
    take decades to lose their potency.

Should the sentence be added to the paragraph, and if so, where should it be placed?
    F. Yes, before sentence 1.
    G. Yes, after sentence 2.
    H. Yes, after sentence 3.
    J. The sentence should NOT be added.

Grammar Tests: ACT

Passage 3

Ghosts in the House

The majority of Americans don't believe in
<u>31</u>
UFOs, in Elvis sightings, making contact with dead
<u>31</u>
ancestors, and most other supernatural phenom-
<u>31</u>
ena. Yet, a large percentage—over a third of the
31
adults interviewed during a recent Gallup Poll—

admitted believing that ghosts reside <u>among us and</u>
<u>32</u>
<u>haunting</u> many of our houses.
32

[1] A case in point is the Zamora family of

Cypress, Texas. [2] <u>The day in 2003</u> that Harry and
33
Lesli Zamora moved into their home on a dead-

end street, they have been tormented by mysterious

visions, unusual flashes of light, a door that locks

itself, and appliances <u>that ran</u> when nobody is
34
home. [3] The Zamoras claim to keep losing

things. [4] They leave their car keys on the kitchen

counter, but later <u>they show up</u> in a bedroom. 36
35
Mrs. Zamora says that she has felt hands brushing

31. At this point in the essay the writer wants to show that Americans are not a terribly superstitious people. Given that all of the choices are true, which one best conveys that idea?
   A. NO CHANGE
   B. For years, reports of UFOs, ESP, Elvis sightings, and making contact with dead relatives have made headlines in newspapers and other media.
   C. Because people are fascinated by supernatural phenomena, publishers have made a great deal of money selling books that describe mysterious happenings.
   D. A vast number of otherwise rational people get excited by made-up stories of UFOs, ESP, Elvis sightings, and otherworldly occurrences.

32. F. NO CHANGE
   G. among us and haunt
   H. in, and haunt
   J. among us, and haunting

33. A. NO CHANGE
   B. On the day in 2003
   C. From the day in 2003
   D. Beginning in the day in 2003

34. F. NO CHANGE
   G. running
   H. having been run
   J. that run

35. A. NO CHANGE
   B. the keys show up
   C. it shows up
   D. they appear

36. For the sake of clarity, the writer is considering a change in the ending of sentence 4. Which of the following would best clarify the meaning of the sentence?
   F. NO CHANGE
   G. . . . bedroom; where they were taken by a ghost.
   H. . . . bedroom; after the keys are moved there.
   J. . . . bedroom; ghosts presumably relocated it.

her as she moves around the house. <u>An ominous</u>
<u>black-clad figure behind her husband when he was</u>
₃₇
<u>emerging from the shower was once seen by her.</u>
₃₇
She also recounts an episode in early 2005: While
she chatted on the phone with a friend, a strange
white dog with a pink collar darted through the
room. Explaining what occurred, <u>the previous</u>
₃₈
<u>occupant, who died</u> in the house, owned a dog that
₃₈
had left deposits of white hair all over the premises.
<u>The Zamoras' since then</u> have bought a dog of their
₃₉
<u>own; but he or she avoids</u> certain areas of the
₄₀
backyard where police cadaver dogs have detected
human remains buried <u>in what once has been</u> the
₄₁
cemetery for the plantation <u>standing on the</u>
₄₂
<u>property long ago in the nineteenth century.</u>
₄₂

37. **A.** NO CHANGE
    B. She once saw an ominous black-clad figure behind her husband when he was emerging from the shower.
    C. Emerging from the shower, her husband once had an ominous black-clad figure behind him, and Mrs. Zamora had seen it.
    D. Once, as he emerged from the shower, an ominous black-clad figure seen by Mrs. Zamora.

38. **F.** NO CHANGE
    G. the former owner had died
    H. she recalls that the previous occupant, who had died
    J. Mrs. Zamora makes clear that the former owner died

39. **A.** NO CHANGE
    B. The Zamora's since then
    C. Since then, the Zamoras
    D. Since, the Zamoras'

40. **F.** NO CHANGE
    G. own, he or she avoids
    H. own it avoids
    J. own, but it avoids

41. **A.** NO CHANGE
    B. in formerly what had been
    C. in what once had been
    D. in what previously in former times was

42. **F.** NO CHANGE
    G. standing on the property long ago in the nineteenth century
    H. that they had on the site long ago
    J that stood on the site in the nineteenth century

Irrespective of the years, science has been
43
unable to explain the events occurring in the
43
Zamoras' home. The Zamoras are not a wacky,

delusional couple out to perpetuate a hoax.

A toughly minded realist Harry Zamora is a well-
44
respected Houston police officer. But a researcher

from a group that studies the paranormal says,

"Once an idea that a place is haunted takes hold

with susceptible people, things are no longer acci-

dental." Consequently, "she is confident that the
45
Zamoras are on the level."
45

43. Given that all the choices are true, which of the following provides the most effective opening for the last paragraph of the passage?
   A. NO CHANGE
   B. For some people, they might say that science is unable to account for
   C. Starting in 2003, then, no one is smart enough to fully explain
   D. Science can't explain

44. F. NO CHANGE
   G. Tough and realistic
   H. As a toughly minded realist
   J. Realistically and toughly minded

45. A. NO CHANGE
   B. With confidence, therefore, the researcher says that the Zamoras are "on the level."
   C. "Consequently," the researcher says, "she is confident that the Zamoras are on the level."
   D. Therefore, she believes "that the Zamoras are on the level," she says confidently.

Passage 4

Pros and Cons of Child Care

[1] Being a worrisome issue for many working
46
parents, both single dads and moms as well as

couples, is how to care for their young children, age

two to four, on days when they can't be at home. [2]

Parents deal with this problem in many different

ways, one of the most common, is public child care
47
programs. [3] Whether children thrive by such
48

46. F. NO CHANGE
   G. A worrisome issue
   H. Worrying an issue
   J. Worry about the issue

47. A. NO CHANGE
   B. common, is
   C. common: are
   D. common being

48. F. NO CHANGE
   G. on
   H. in
   J. for

programs <u>is long been</u> an unanswered question.
49

[4] Recent studies, however, have found mixed results that are both comforting and alarming at the same time. ☐50

The most hopeful data show that group child care ultimately leads to higher skills in math and <u>reading, the greatest gains are being recorded</u> by
51
children from poor families. <u>Unlike poor children,</u>
52
<u>the</u> gains by children from middle-class homes are
52
more modest, and <u>an affluent child from the most</u>
53
<u>well-to-do families standing</u> to gain least from
53
group child care, probably because their home environments <u>had already given</u> them a head start
54
in early language and mathematical learning.

Studying the long-term effects of group child care, a research team from the National Institute of Child Health and Human Development <u>have</u>
55
<u>followed</u> the progress of thousands of children
55
from preschool through the primary years. <u>It was</u>
56
<u>found</u> that youngsters who spend 30 or more
56

49. **A.** NO CHANGE
    B. is long
    C. has long been
    D. has been long

50. For the sake of logic and coherence in the first paragraph, where should Sentence 4 be located?
    F. NO CHANGE.
    G. After Sentence 1.
    H. After Sentence 2.
    J. DELETE it from the passage.

51. **A.** NO CHANGE
    B. reading, and the greatest gains are being recorded
    C. reading, with the greatest gains recorded
    D. reading the greatest gains recorded

52. **F.** NO CHANGE
    G. In contrast with
    H. Different from
    J. DELETE the underlined words and begin the sentence with *Gains by.*

53. **A.** NO CHANGE
    B. an affluent child stands
    C. children from well-to-do families stand
    D. an affluent child from a well-to-do home stands

54. **F.** NO CHANGE
    G. have given
    H. already gives
    J. already gave

55. **A.** NO CHANGE
    B. followed
    C. following
    D. in order to follow

56. Which of the following alternatives to the underlined words is NOT acceptable?
    F. They found
    G. The findings reveal
    H. The study provides evidence
    J. An analysis of the research confirms

hours a week in group child care <u>scored more</u>
57
<u>higher</u> academically than those cared for in other
57
ways. After third grade, however, the differences

between the groups diminish, and other factors,

such as <u>some had greater natural ability, family</u>
58
<u>income, and the educational level</u> of parents, seem
58
to have a greater bearing on in-school performance.

On the downside, children in early child care

programs experience slower social development

than peers who are cared for at home or in other

settings. Their behavior is more aggressive and

negative, especially among the offspring of the

wealthiest parents. But by third grade, these differ-

ences by and large disappear.

These findings suggest a need for changes

that <u>will encourage greater public support for early</u>
59
<u>child care programs, regardless of the income</u>
59
<u>level</u>. The caregivers in the programs may also
59
need more advanced training in group <u>management</u>
60
<u>because of modifying</u> the behavior of socially
60
challenged youngsters while giving all children a

chance to grow and excel.

57. **A.** NO CHANGE
   B. scored more highly
   C. score higher
   D. have scored high

58. **F.** NO CHANGE
   G. some have greater natural ability, or family income or educational level
   H. natural ability, family income, and the educational level
   J. greater natural ability; higher family income; and more advanced education

59. Given that all the choices are valid, which one contains ideas that are most crucial to the development of the essay as a whole?
   A. NO CHANGE
   B. leave no child behind, including those in private and parochial schools
   C. provide nicer experiences for all young children, rich and poor alike
   D. make early child care programs beneficial to all young children regardless of their income level

60. **F.** NO CHANGE
   G. management in order to modify
   H. management, for modification of
   J. management. This modifies

Passage 5

Cinderella: A Rags to Riches Story

If you <u>drop by a toy store, recently, as I did,</u> to buy
₆₁
a gift for my kid sister, you will probably see

Cinderella in every nook and corner. <u>Nevertheless,</u>
₆₂
she's not the Cinderella I remember from my

childhood, <u>the one that once was a TV musical.</u>
₆₃
Only the intervention of a fairy godmother gave

her <u>a temporary and short-lived moment of relief</u>
₆₄
from a life of drudgery and abuse. Her transforma-

tion into a beautiful debutante wearing eye-

catching <u>clothes last only</u> a few hours. At midnight,
₆₅
back in <u>rags, she sits</u> humbly in the dust.
₆₆

As everyone knows, her story doesn't end there.

The Prince, smitten by the anonymous beauty he

danced with at the ball, sends out his aides to locate

the one foot in all the land that will fit into the

glass slipper she left behind. The foot belongs to

<u>Cinderella, of course, all ends happily</u> ever after.
₆₇

61. **A.** NO CHANGE
    B. recently drop by a toy store, as I did,
    C. drop by recently, as I did, a toy store,
    D. drop by a toy store, as I did recently,

62. **F.** NO CHANGE
    G. Furthermore,
    H. As a consequence,
    J. OMIT the underlined word.

63. Given that all the following choices are valid, in the context of the passage which one best defines the character that the narrator remembers from childhood?
    A. NO CHANGE
    B. the poor, soot-covered young waif, cowering in fear of her wicked stepmother and tyrannical stepsisters.
    C. a symbol of social and economic deprivation
    D. the one that my mother said brought back sad memories of her own girlhood.

64. **F.** NO CHANGE
    G. moment of relief
    H. temporary moment of relieved
    J. temporarily, a short-lived moment of relief

65. **A.** NO CHANGE
    B. clothes that last only
    C. clothing that only lasts
    D. clothes lasts only

66. **F.** NO CHANGE
    G. rags, sitting
    H. rags and she sits
    J. rags she is sitting

67. **A.** NO CHANGE
    B. Cinderella, of course, and all ends happily
    C. Cinderella, of course all ends happily
    D. Cinderella of course, and all ends happy

As I've already said, I was on a shopping expedition
68
to a toy store. Knowing that two- to six-year-old
68
girls would be unable to resist a line of Cinderella

products, the Disney company has evidently turned

Cinderella into a commercial bonanza. Naturally,
69
Cinderella dolls for sale and the Cinderella video,
69   **70**
for playing on their pink and blue Cinderella TVs
70
and DVD players. You can buy Cinderella costumes

complete with sparkly tiaras and glass slippers. The

shelves are packed with Cinderella games, puzzles,

tea sets, toy coaches, coats for dogs, even a waffle

iron that can stamp an image of a smiling

Cinderella right into the batter. [71]

Using this approach, amid all the Cinderella
72
glitter, hardly a trace of the wonderful old fairy tale

can be found. The original Cinderella, a patient,

68. Given that all the choices are valid, which one would serve most effectively as the introductory sentence of the paragraph?
   F. NO CHANGE
   G. My sister usually likes the presents I give her.
   H. In the store, I found Cinderellas by the hundreds.
   J. When I was growing up, Barbie was the doll of choice among little girls.

69. A. NO CHANGE
   B. Selling Cinderella dolls naturally,
   C. Naturally, that sale of Cinderella dolls
   D. Cinderella dolls are for sale, naturally,

70. F. NO CHANGE
   G. video, to be played on
   H. video to be played by
   J. video for the playing on

71. The writer is considering the addition of the following true statement:

   For $70 you can take home Magical Talking Vanity, among a multitude of other products.

   Should the writer make the addition here?
   A. Yes, because it is important for readers to know the cost of toys.
   B. Yes, because it helps the reader develop a deeper understanding of what the narrator observed in the toy store.
   C. No, because it's unclear that a Magical Talking Vanity has anything to do with Cinderella.
   D. No, because it is anticlimactic; the writer has already proved that a multitude of Cinderella products is available.

72. F. NO CHANGE
   G. Explicitly
   H. Hopefully
   J. Sad to say

modest, good-hearted lass who <u>has befriended</u>
₇₃
mice and scrubbed floors until she dropped,

possessed virtues that little girls might have emu-

lated. Now, however, she's been transformed into

an elegant socialite, <u>whom</u> promotes only crass
₇₄
materialism among the legions of her fans and

admirers. ⬚75⬚

73. **A.** NO CHANGE
    B. has made friends with
    C. befriended
    D. befriending

74. **F.** NO CHANGE
    G. who
    H. which
    J. DELETE the underlined word

75. Given that all the choices are valid, which one would provide the most fitting conclusion to the essay as a whole?
    A. Stunned by the makeover, I bought my sister the biggest Cinderella doll I could find.
    B. Depressed, I left the store empty-handed.
    C. As a girl, I don't remember many such opportunities coming along.
    D. The array of Cinderella products will no doubt inspire many shoppers like me to reread the story.

ANSWER KEY

1. D	11. B	21. D	31. A	41. C	51. C	61. D	71. D
2. G	12. J	22. G	32. G	42. J	52. J	62. J	72. J
3. C	13. A	23. A	33. C	43. D	53. C	63. B	73. C
4. H	14. H	24. F	34. J	44. G	54. G	64. G	74. G
5. B	15. D	25. C	35. B	45. B	55. B	65. D	75. B
6. H	16. G	26. J	36. F	46. G	56. F	66. F	
7. D	17. C	27. D	37. B	47. D	57. C	67. B	
8. G	18. F	28. G	38. H	48. H	58. H	68. H	
9. C	19. B	29. A	39. C	49. C	59. D	69. D	
10. F	20. F	30. J	40. J	50. F	60. G	70. G	

ANSWER EXPLANATIONS

Passage 1

1. **D** Because the perils of running are described as *common*, the underlined words, which are awkwardly expressed and confusing, are unnecessary. Choice B is a complete sentence that creates a comma splice and is neither grammatically nor logically related to the sentence that comes next in the passage. Choice C is a participle phrase that has no logical connection with the sentence it modifies.

2. **G** In Choice F the plural verb *surprise* disagrees in number with the singular pronoun, *one*. Choices H and J incorrectly shift the verb tense away from the present, the tense in which the passage is written.

3. **C** The word *however*, when used as a transitional word between two contrasting ideas, must be set off by commas.

4. **H** Choice F uses *Its*, the possessive pronoun, instead of *It's*, the contraction meaning *it is*. Choice G contains a comma splice. Choice J lacks punctuation between *dangerous* and *threats*, where a comma is needed.

5. **B** Choices A and C contain commas that unnecessarily separate the noun *athletes* from the phrase *in virtually every sport*. The meaning of Choice D suggests that runners are different from athletes, an idea that the writer certainly didn't intend.

6. **H** Because the topic being discussed is the amount that marathoners drink while racing, Choice H contributes most to the paragraph's coherence.

7. **D** The use of *to* in Choice A is nonstandard, unidiomatic English. Likewise, Choice B misuses the preposition *in*. Choice C misstates the writer's intent by describing health and well-being as *risky*.

8. **G** Choice F improperly shifts the text, written in third person, to second person. Choice H shifts the text from present to the past tense. Choice J changes both the verb tense from present to present perfect and the use of pronouns from third person to second person.

9. **C** Only Choice C uses understandable language that accurately conveys meaning.

10. **F** In Choice G the singular subject *word* fails to agree in number with the plural verb *have been*. Choice H is an incomplete sentence because the construction lacks a main verb. Choice J includes an improperly placed comma between the subject *authorities* and the verb *say*.

11. **B** Choice A contains a redundancy because *limit* and *restrict* have essentially the same meaning. Choices C and D contain similar redundancies.

12. **J** Choice F uses the singular *that* to refer to the plural *situations*. Choice G improperly uses a verb in the present progressive tense instead of a verb in the past tense. Choice H uses the objective case pronoun *them* instead of the subject pronoun *those*.

13. **A** Choice B uses *then* instead of *than*. Choice C leaves out the comma needed to separate the clauses of the sentence. Choice D improperly uses a semicolon instead of a comma to separate the independent and dependent clauses of the sentence.

14. **H** Choice F contains *similar with*, an unidiomatic, nonstandard phrase. In Choice G, the singular *that* refers to the plural *symptoms*. In Choice J the singular verb *is* lacks agreement in number with its subject *symptoms*.

15. **D** Choices A, B, and C contain ideas only marginally related to the subject of the passage.

Passage 2

16. **G** Note that *overheated* and *excessively* are redundant, as is *suddenly exploded* because explosions are always sudden; they never

happen gradually. Choices F, H, and J contain these redundancies. Choices H and J also include superfluous commas.

17. **C** The problem with Choice A lies in the use of *most* with an adjective in the comparative instead of the positive degree. Choice B contains the same error as A, except that an adjective in the superlative degree has been used. Choice D makes little sense in the context because the adjective *terrible* implies that history has seen but one terrible nuclear accident—implying that other accidents were not terrible.

18. **F** Choice G contains a comma splice. Choice H improperly shifts the verb tense from the past tense to the past perfect. Choice J contains an error in word choice. The phrase *much more* applies to mass quantities—quantities that cannot be counted, such as water and wheat. Because deaths can be counted, the proper phrase is *many more*.

19. **B** Because the situation being described still exists, the present perfect tense should be used, and Choice A improperly uses the past perfect tense. Choice C contains an unnecessary comma between the subject and verb. It also contains a redundancy: The word *yet* is virtually identical in meaning to the phrase *to this day*. Choice D, which substitutes *still* for *yet*, contains a redundancy similar to that in Choice C.

20. **F** The word *of* in Choices G and H is nonstandard English usage. Choice J inappropriately shifts the verb tense from the past perfect to the future, as if to say that someday the deaths may occur.

21. **D** Choice A contains the plural pronoun *Their*, which lacks agreement with its singular antecedent, *Institute*. It also shifts the

verb tense of the passage from past to present. Choice B contains the same problem in pronoun-antecedent agreement as A. Choice C uses the contraction meaning *it is* instead of the possessive pronoun *its*.

22. **G** *Especially thyroid cancer* is an explanatory phrase that must be set off by equivalent marks of punctuation. In Choice G the second comma has been omitted. Choice H uses two different punctuation marks to set off the phrase. Choice J uses the proper punctuation, but the repetition of *cancer* is a stylistic flaw.

23. **A** In Choice B, the relative pronoun *which* may not be used to refer to people. (Instead, use *who* or *that*.) Choice C improperly shifts the verb tense from the past to the present perfect. Choice D includes the phrase *clean from*, a substandard, unidiomatic construction.

24. **F** Choice F provides the most relevant evidence to support the idea that many people felt hopeless and isolated.

25. **C** Choice A contains a comma splice between *radioactive* and the phrase *in fact*. Choice B is a mixed construction in which the clause beginning with *that* has no grammatical relationship with the previous part of the sentence. Choice D lacks the necessary commas to set off the phrase *in fact*, and it also contains a clause (beginning with *that*) whose meaning is not logically related to the previous part of the sentence.

26. **J** Choice F is redundant because *fraction* and *1 percent* express essentially the same meaning, even though *fraction* is a less precise word. Choice G contains the pronoun *that*, which fails to refer to a specific noun or other pronoun. Choice H contains the same redundancy as F.

27. **D** Choice A incorrectly uses an adjective, *sufficient*, instead of an adverb to modify the verb *cooled*. Choice B is the same as A. Choice C is wordy. Because the word *sufficiently* and the phrase *so as* are somewhat redundant, one or the other—preferably the phrase—should be deleted.

28. **G** Choice F contains an error in diction. In this context, *toward* is an unidiomatic choice. The apostrophe in Choice H is misplaced; put it before the *-s*. Also, the word *to* is not idiomatic in this context. Choice J contains an error in diction. Correct usage calls for *with respect to* instead of *with respect of.*

29. **A** In Choice B, the subject *Fishing* is not logically or grammatically related to the remainder of the sentence. In addition, the singular subject fails to agree with the plural verb *are*. Choice C contains the same problems as B. Choice D includes an incorrect form of the verb: *Caught* is the past tense of *to catch.*

30. **J** Because Choice F changes the paragraph's topic sentence, it is a poor choice. The paragraph relates generally to the long-term influence of Chernobyl, not to the properties of radioactive materials. Choice G would cause the proposed sentence to intrude on the discussion of the effort to restore life as it once was. Choice H would turn the sentence into an irrelevant afterthought. If the sentence were to be located between sentences 1 and 2, it would not be out of place, but since that is not an option, the sentence shouldn't be included at all.

Passage 3

31. **A** In one way or other, Choices B, C, and D support the idea that people in large num-

bers accept the validity of supernatual phenomena. Because the paragraph's second sentence begins with *Yet*, a word that introduces a contrasting idea, none of these choices is appropriate.

32. **G** Choice F contains an error in parallel structure. Because coordinate sentence parts should be in the same grammatical form, *haunting* should be *haunt*—that is, parallel to *reside*. Choice H includes a misplaced and unnecessary comma. Choice J, like F, contains an error in parallel structure, and, like H, contains a superfluous comma.

33. **C** Choice A introduces a construction that lacks a grammatical relationship with the second clause of the sentence. Choice B limits the scope of the Zamoras' experience to one day, although the rest of the sentence indicates an ongoing problem. Choice D contains unidiomatic usage; the correct phrase is *Beginning on.*

34. **J** Choices F, G, and H improperly shift the verb tense away from the present. In F, the tense changes to the past, in G to the present progressive, and in H to the present perfect.

35. **B** The pronoun *they* in Choice A refers ambiguously to either the keys or to the Zamoras. In Choice C the pronoun *it* lacks agreement in number with its antecedent, *keys*. Choice C is the same as A.

36. **F** Considering the alternatives, the writer should leave the sentence as it is. Choice G can be interpreted in two ways: that the ghost carried the keys to the bedroom or that the bedroom is where the ghost picked up the keys. Choice H muddies the meaning still further by implying that the keys were moved either by a ghost or by a

Zamora. The clarity of Choice J is questionable because it says that the ghosts relocated the bedroom—a meaning that the writer could not have intended. All these choices also misuse a semicolon, which, when used correctly, separates independent clauses.

37. **B** Choice A is written in the passive voice, a stylistic flaw that dilutes the impact of what must have been a chilling experience. Choice C is a compound sentence in which the coordinate clauses are not equivalent. The fact that Mrs. Zamora had seen the figure would be more effectively expressed in a subordinate clause or even in a phrase embedded in the main clause. Choice D is a sentence fragment because it lacks a main verb.

38. **H** Choice F contains a dangling modifier. The phrase *Explaining what happened* should modify or refer to a person doing the explaining—i.e., Mrs. Zamora—not *previous occupant*. In Choice G, the phrase *Explaining what happened* incorrectly modifies *former owner* instead of *Mrs. Zamora* or *she*. Choice J is a construction that causes a subsequent mismatch of sentence parts.

39. **C** The apostrophe in Choice A improperly turns *Zamoras'* into a plural possessive noun. Choice B is a possessive noun in a context where there is no need for one. Choice D includes both a superfluous comma and an unnecessary apostrophe.

40. **J** Choice F contains the awkward usage *he or she*, a phrase often used when the gender of human beings is uncertain. For a dog the usage is inappropriate. Choice G contains a comma splice. Lacking punctuation to separate two independent clauses, Choice H is a run-on sentence.

41. **C**   Choice A improperly shifts the verb tense from the past to the present perfect. Choice B is redundant because the verb *had been* implies a former condition, making the adverb *formerly* unnecessary. Choice D, which includes both the adverb *previously* and the phrase *in former times*, is redundant in the extreme.

42. **J**   Choice F improperly shifts the verb tense from the past to the present progressive. Choice G contains a redundancy; in this context *nineteenth century*, almost by definition, implies *long ago*. Choice H uses *they*, a pronoun without an antecedent.

43. **D**   Choice A includes *Irrespective of the years*, a phrase that in this context makes no sense. Choice B begins with a vague and meaningless phrase that is not grammatically related to the remainder of the sentence. Choice C is confusing because the word *then* suggests a relationship with a previous idea that does not exist.

44. **G**   Choices F and H use an adverb (*toughly minded*) instead of an adjective (*tough-minded*) to modify the noun *realist*. Choice J uses adverbs instead of adjectives to modify the pronoun *he*.

45. **B**   Choices A and C improperly put quotation marks around an indirect quote. Choice D places the quotation marks properly but contains the redundant phrase, *she believes* and *she says*. One or the other, but not both, may be used.

Passage 4

46. **G**   Choice F creates a sentence fragment because the construction lacks a grammatical subject to go with the verb *is*. Choice H contains a grammatical mismatch of sentence parts that garbles meaning. Choice J is unclear and confusing. It refers to *the issue*, when no issue has been mentioned.

47. **D**   Choice A is a comma splice. Choices B and C include superfluous commas. Also, the colon in Choice C is improperly used.

48. **H**   Choices F, G, and J include a preposition that violates standard English idiom.

49. **C**   Choice A incorrectly uses *is* instead of *has*. Choice B contains a present tense verb in a context that calls for a verb in the past perfect. Choice D is not idiomatic English.

50. **F**   To move the sentence from its present location makes little sense because, if the order of sentences was changed, the transitional word *however* would become meaningless. Therefore, G and H are poor alternatives. Choice J is not acceptable because Sentence 4 is needed to introduce the main subject of the essay—that studies of child care programs have been conducted.

51. **C**   Choice A is a construction containing a comma splice. Choice B is grammatically correct, but stylistically weak because the two coordinate clauses of the compound sentence lack equivalence. The sentence would be strengthened by subordinating one of the clauses to the other. Choice D lacks the required comma between *reading* and *the greatest*.

52. **J**   In Choice F *children* are being compared with *gains*, an illogical and meaningless comparison. Choice G is essentially the same as F and, in addition, contains nonstandard, unidiomatic construction: use *to* instead of *with*. Choice H leads to a construction that contains mismatched grammatical parts, resulting in a totally confusing message.

53. **C** Choice A contains an incorrect form of a verb. In context, the simple present tense of the verb *to stand* is called for. Choice B is grammatically correct but uses a singular noun, *child*, that fails to agree in number with the pronoun *their* that follows. Choice D contains a redundancy: *affluent* and *well-to-do* have essentially the same meaning.

54. **G** Choice F improperly shifts the verb tense from the present to the past perfect. Choice H uses a singular verb, *gives*, that lacks agreement with the plural subject, *environments*. Choice J incorrectly shifts the verb tense from the present to the past.

55. **B** In Choice A the plural verb *have followed* fails to agree in number with *team*, the singular subject of the sentence. Choice C is a sentence fragment because it lacks a verb. The word *following*, as a participle, may not function as the main verb. Choice D is a sentence fragment because it lacks a main verb. *To follow* is an infinitive and may not serve as the main verb in a sentence.

56. **F** Choices G, H, and J are grammatically correct and appropriate phrases to use in the context. Choice F is not correct because the pronoun *they* does not agree in number with its antecedent, *team*.

57. **C** Choice A is an incorrectly worded comparison. The word *more* (or *less*) is not needed when the adjective in the positive degree is a one-syllable word, such as *high*. Choice B uses an adverb, *highly*, in a phrase that calls for an adjective (*scored higher*). Choice D does not fit the context because it fails to make a comparison.

58. **H** Choice F contains a problem in parallel structure. The clause *some had greater nat-*

ural ability is not grammatically parallel to the phrases *family income* and *educational level*. Choice G contains a problem in parallel structure (see F). Choice J misuses semicolons, which should not be used in a series of phrases unless the phrases contain commas, as in *Seattle, Washington; Las Vegas, Nevada; and Roanoke, Virginia.*

59. **D** Choice A raises an issue—public support for child care programs—that is not discussed in the passage. Choices B and C bring up matters that are unrelated to the content of the essay.

60. **G** Choice F creates an illogical cause-and-effect relationship. *Group management* is meant to modify *behavior*, not *because of modifying the behavior*. Choice H comes close to a valid answer, but the phrase *for modification of* is vaguely worded. Choice J contains the pronoun *This*, which has no clear antecedent. It also uses the present tense of the verb where the context calls for a verb in the future (*will modify*) or future conditional (*would modify*) tense.

Passage 5

61. **D** Choice A contains confusing and unidiomatic English because *recently* refers to past action, whereas *drop by* refers to present or future action. Choice B is an illogical statement: "If you recently drop by a toy store" takes liberties with time sequence that make no sense. Choice C is similar to B. "If you drop by recently" conveys a garbled message.

62. **J** In this context, Choices F, G, and H are *non sequiturs*. That is, they fail to create a meaningful transition between sentences. Therefore, it would be best to delete them altogether.

63. **B** Choices A, C, and D may be interesting, but they digress from the purpose of the paragraph, which is to describe the character rather than to add a piece of miscellaneous information about the tale of Cinderella.

64. **G** Choice F is full of redundancies. *Temporary* and *short-lived* mean essentially the same thing, and a *moment*, by definition, is a brief period of time. Choices H and J, being variations of F, are equally redundant.

65. **D** In Choice A the plural verb *last* fails to agree in number with the singular subject *transformation*. Choices B and C are sentence fragments because the subject *transformation* lacks a verb.

66. **F** Lacking a verb, Choice G is an incomplete sentence. Choice H contains mismatched sentence parts. The conjunction *and* introduces a clause that is grammatically unrelated to the previous part of the sentence. Choice J lacks the comma after *rags* that is needed to separate the phrase *back in rags* from the main clause of the sentence.

67. **B** Choice A contains a comma splice between *course* and *all*. The structure of Choice C confuses the reader because it is unclear whether the phrase *of course* ends the first clause or starts the second. Either way, however, the construction contains an error. It is a run-on sentence if you assume that the phrase comes at the end of the first clause, and it contains a comma splice if you put *of course* at the beginning of the second. Choice D lacks a comma between *Cinderella* and *of*.

68. **H** Choice F needlessly repeats information given earlier in the passage. Choice G has only a remote connection to the ideas expressed in the rest of the paragraph. Choice J raises a new topic that is not related to the substance of the paragraph that follows.

69. **D** Because a verb is missing from Choice A, it is a sentence fragment. Choice B is a participle without a noun to modify. In addition, using the adverb *naturally* to modify *Selling* is a puzzle. What is the meaning of "selling naturally"? Choice C is a problem not only because the construction lacks a verb, but also because it refers to *that sale*, an event that hadn't been mentioned earlier in the passage.

70. **G** Choice F includes a pronoun, *their*, that has no antecedent. Choice H contains an error in word choice: In standard English, videos are not played *by* TVs but *on* TVs. Choice J is an example of an unidiomatic, awkward expression.

71. **D** It would be hard to justify Choice A because the price of toys is irrelevant to the point of the passage. Choice B may be a tempting answer, but the writer has already discussed the abundance of Cinderella products available. Choice C is not valid because the writer has already listed at least one product—the coats for dogs, for example—that seems unrelated to Cinderella.

72. **J** Choice F is meaningless in this context and should be cast aside quickly. Choice G seems like a possibility, but the remainder of the sentence is hardly explicit; indeed, it is a rather general observation concerning the erosion of the original story of Cinderella. Choice H contradicts the writer's feelings, which are far from hopeful.

73. **C** In Choices A and B the verb tense has inappropriately shifted from the past to the present perfect. Choice D contains an error in parallel structure. The verb *befriending* should be in the past tense—in the same grammatical form as the verb *scrubbed.*

74. **G** Choice F uses a pronoun in the objective case when the context calls for a pronoun in the nominative case: Use *who* instead of *whom.* Choice H uses the pronoun *which* that is meant to refer to things rather than to people. Choice J leaves the sentence with two grammatical segments unrelated to each other.

75. **B** Discard A as a choice because the writer was stunned negatively, not in a way to inspire the purchase of a big doll. Choice C raises a matter unrelated to the passage. Choice D makes an assumption that cannot be supported by anything in the essay. If anything, the writer seems to have been repelled by the mass of Cinderella products, justifying Choice B as the best answer.

Chapter 6

Grammar Tests for
High School Graduation

Every state has them. In New York they're called Regents. California calls them the High School Exit Examination. Florida administers a Comprehensive Assessment Test. To graduate from high school in the United States, a student must pass a state test or a battery of tests.

These so-called "exit" exams differ from state to state. But there is one thing you can count on: In one way or another, you must show a degree of proficiency in grammar to earn a diploma.

The tests administered by most states require students to write an essay of some kind. The topic is usually general enough to elicit a response from virtually anyone of high school age or older. What you write and how you write it reveals whether you've learned not only how to organize and develop ideas, but also how to use the conventions of standard English—the kind of English generally used by literate people in our society. An essay shows, for example, whether you can write complete sentences, whether you use verbs, pronouns, and other parts of speech appropriately, and whether you can correctly spell, punctuate, and capitalize. No state will keep you from graduating if you misspell a few words or make a grammatical error or two, but an essay that is so full of mistakes that a reader can't understand it will definitely work against you.

Because essay writing is part of most high school exit exams as well as the SAT and ACT (for some students), the next (and last) chapter of this book discusses what you need to know about writing an essay in a relatively short time, say, in less than an hour. (Some states limit the time to 25 or 30 minutes; others give you all day if you need it.)

Several states require only an essay, but some also include multiple-choice questions about grammar. The questions themselves come in a variety of formats, such as those on the SAT and ACT. Students are given sentences with blank spaces to be filled in with grammatically correct words or phrases. Or they are presented with sentences that must be properly punctuated or revised in some way. The most common type of question, however, asks students to spot errors in sentences and pick the correct version from a list of three to five choices.

Rest assured that, regardless of the question format, the exams in every state cover the very same grammatical problems and pitfalls listed in Chapter 3 and discussed in greater detail in Chapters 1 and 2 of this book.

PRACTICE FOR HIGH SCHOOL EXIT EXAMS

A book as short as this one can't possibly include every type of grammar question found on the exit exams of all 50 states. Yet, using several samples, it *can* give you a taste of the questions you may encounter in your own state. What matters most in the end is not the format of the questions but their content—whether you can recognize grammatical errors and whether you know how to correct them. Ideally, therefore, your grasp of grammar should be firm enough to successfully complete the exercises that make up the rest of this chapter. After doing each exercise, check your answers and read the explanations at the end of this chapter.
Good luck!

Checkpoint 1. SUBJECT-VERB AGREEMENT

INSTRUCTIONS: Look for the ERROR in each of these sentences. That is, identify the choice in which the subject and verb DO NOT agree.

1. One of our airplanes _____ missing.
    A. is
    B. are
    C. was
    D. has been

2. The skulls of every human being _____ 22 bones.
    A. are made up of
    B. have
    C. contain
    D. has

3. Fourteen of the bones _____ the face and jaw.
    A. are used to form
    B. serves as the
    C. make up
    D. shape

4. The gym's supply of available exercise machines, including treadmills and stationary bikes, _____ running low.
    A. is
    B. has been
    C. have been
    D. seems to be

5. The most convincing evidence at both trials _____ reports from eyewitnesses who claim to have seen the muggings.
    A. appears to be
    B. is likely to come in the form of
    C. was a series of handwritten
    D. were provided by

6. An arm and a hand, comprising the most flexible and complex bone system in the body, _____ 32 bones.
    A. are composed of
    B. is made up of
    C. consist of
    D. have

7. Neither one of these keys _____ this lock.
    A. work in
    B. fits
    C. opens
    D. goes into the keyhole of

8. The principal or one of the assistant principals always _____ our dances.
    A. attends
    B. chaperone
    C. comes to
    D. shows up at

9. Either of those buses _____ to Baker Field.
   A. gets you
   B. follows the route
   C. take you
   D. goes to

10. There _____ a doctor and a crew of nurses looking after the patient.
    A. were never
    B. are
    C. have been
    D. is

11. On the radio, the news _____ : tomorrow, we'll have sunshine and temperatures in the 70s.
    A. were good
    B. sounds promising
    C. was favorable
    D. is the best yet

12. The human skeleton, which _____ vital organs from harm, also allows us to stand up straight and _____ our size and build.
    A. protect . . . determine
    B. protects . . . influences
    C. shelters . . . governs
    D. guards . . . affects

13. In the second act, a little boy, along with his brothers and sisters, _____ a song that brings the audience to its feet.
    A. plays
    B. performs
    C. sing
    D. whistles

14. The head of every animal with a backbone, from the largest elephants to the smallest mice, _____ a skull.
    A. contains
    B. has
    C. encloses
    D. have

15. It is hard to tell whether the passengers or the bus driver _____ the accident.
    A. is responsible for
    B. is going to be held accountable for
    C. are guilty of causing
    D. was telling the truth about

Answers on page 215

For more details on subject-verb agreement, turn to page 30.

Checkpoint 2. VERB TENSES AND FORMS

INSTRUCTIONS: Choose the CORRECT VERB for each sentence.

1. All of the mail carriers _____ especially hard during the holiday season.
   A. works
   B. work
   C. has worked
   D. working

2. The teacher and I _____ my term paper for two hours yesterday afternoon.
   A. discusses
   B. is discussing
   C. discussing
   D. discussed

3. Mitch planned _____ them, but he had to change his schedule.
   A. accompany
   B. accompanying
   C. to accompany
   D. to accompanied

4. If you brush regularly, you _____ no cavities.
   A. will get
   B. will have gotten
   C. won't get
   D. got

5. I _____ happy when my friend Dexter visits me.
   A. be
   B. been
   C. am
   D. is

6. Last night, my cousin's lateness _____ us to miss the train.
   A. causes
   B. has caused
   C. will cause
   D. caused

7. The dead fish _____ to the bottom of the tank.
   A. sink
   B. has sunk
   C. has sunken
   D. sanked

8. Hessie and Mike _____ a box of chocolates when they came for dinner.
   A. brought
   B. brang
   C. bring
   D. have brought

9. If Melissa _____ her mind, she still has a good job at the insurance company.
   A. changes
   B. change
   C. have changed
   D. will have changed

10. It seemed likely that Lucy _____ a cold from her baby sister last September.
    A. catches
    B. catched
    C. has caught
    D. caught

11. Every morning last summer, we _____ with the sun.
    A. awake
    B. woke
    C. has awaked
    D. have awakened

12. They should _____ for a walk before the rain started.
    A. have went
    B. have gone
    C. of went
    D. go

13. The patients' constant whining _____ the nurse out of her mind.
    A. drived
    B. has drove
    C. have drove
    D. has driven

14. The infant started to cry as soon as the balloon _____.
    A. busted
    B. bursts
    C. is bursting
    D. had burst

15. Last winter, fuel prices _____ more than 50 percent in some parts of the country.
A. has risen
B. rose
C. are rising
D. raised

Answers on page 215

For details on verb forms and tenses, turn to page 21.

Checkpoint 3. INCOMPLETE SENTENCES

INSTRUCTIONS: Choose the word or words that make the sentence complete and grammatically correct.

1. _____ about the bears in Yellowstone National Park.
A. A fascinating talk
B. Fascination
C. Lloyd worries a great deal
D. A great deal of worrying

2. Amelia remembered that today _____.
A. was her mother's birthday
B. could have been
C. her mother's birthday
D. to go to a birthday party

3. _____ get to the library when it opened.
A. Maria
B. Hope to
C. Maria hopes to
D. Maria hoped to

4. Because of the storm, the valley _____.
A. had been completely flooded
B. had been
C. completely flooded
D. having been flooded completely

5. Running short of time on the test, _____.
A. all the questions couldn't be answered
B. questions not answered
C. I couldn't answer all the questions
D. left some questions blank by me

6. They finally _____ the bridge across the bay.
A. after years of trying to build
B. finishing the building of
C. finished building
D. building

7. Team confidence _____ after each win.
A. that was building up after each win
B. was building
C. building
D. to be built up

8. When the rock hit the window, _____.
A. in Mr. Strickman's house
B. the first time
C. on Halloween night
D. Mr. Strickman had a fit

9. Fragments of pottery, a valuable source of information, _____.
   A. were found in the ruins of Pompeii
   B. along with ancient coins and jewelry
   C. colorfully decorated
   D. that were worth millions of dollars

10. After she lost her job _____.
    A. Mrs. Johnson
    B. became emotionally upset
    C. Mrs. Johnson's husband
    D. Mrs. Johnson's life fell apart

11. _____ pieces of glass lying on the road at the site of the accident.
    A. Several
    B. The crew sweeping up
    C. There were
    D. Seeing the

12. _____ hitting a high C and cracking the crystal goblet on the table.
    A. In order to be
    B. Kiri had no trouble
    C. When she was
    D. The singer,

13. With the storm dumping two feet of snow on the roads and having a whole day with nothing to do except watch TV, _____.
    A. I got plenty of rest
    B. and do a 1500-piece jigsaw puzzle
    C. a well-stocked refrigerator was good company
    D. a perfect snow day

14. Because the grocery bag that fell on the sidewalk contained a glass bottle of tomato juice, _____.
    A. and because I had spent my last dime at the store
    B. a mess on my hands
    C. that night we drank cranberry juice instead
    D. walked away and left the debris where it lay

15. To write a unified essay you must be sure that all the paragraphs _____.
    A. support the main idea of the essay
    B. from start to finish
    C. full development of the thesis statement
    D. relating to the main idea of the essay

Answers on page 216

For details on complete sentences, turn to page 57.

Checkpoint 4. PRONOUN CHOICE

INSTRUCTIONS: In each sentence, fill in the blank with the correct word or phrase.

1. Roger and _____ went to the party wearing Jay Leno masks.
   A. me
   B. I
   C. them
   D. her

2. _____ created quite a stir and livened the place up.
   A. Us
   B. They
   C. They're
   D. Them

3. Between _____, the party was a flop anyway.
   A. you and me
   B. you and I
   C. me and they
   D. I and you

4. When it ended, Francie volunteered to drive _____ home.
   A. we and they
   B. us girls
   C. them girls
   D. we girls

5. When it was over, _____ wanted to play poker with _____.
   A. Carolyn and me . . . Hank and her
   B. me and Carolyn . . . Hank and she
   C. Carolyn and I . . . her and Hank
   D. I and Carolyn . . . she and Hank

6. How could anyone enjoy _____ arguing the whole time?
   A. they
   B. she and he
   C. them
   D. their

7. The job never could have been completed without _____.
   A. him and I
   B. he and I
   C. him and me
   D. he and me

8. _____ are much better singers than _____.
   A. Shirley and him . . . them
   B. She and Shirley . . . they
   C. Shirley and I . . . Frank and him
   D. Me and you . . . she and he

9. That's a question for _____ to decide.
   A. Jack and he
   B. he and Jack
   C. me and Jack
   D. Jack and I

10. _____ women take sexual harass-ment more seriously than _____.
    A. Us . . . they
    B. Us . . . them
    C. We . . . they
    D. We . . . them

11. Following a long talk with both Clint and Chloe, the doctor understood _____ better than he understood _____.
    A. him . . . her
    B. him . . . she
    C. he . . . her
    D. he . . . she

12. _____ ended up in Times Square at midnight on New Year's Eve.
    A. Me and Jamie
    B. Jamie and myself
    C. Jamie and I
    D. Myself and Jamie

13. Mother was upset about _____ opening the presents too soon.
    A. your
    B. you
    C. them
    D. him

14. _____ planned to spend the weekend working at the homeless shelter near the stadium.
    A. Ourselves
    B. We
    C. Him and Margaret
    D. Margaret and them

15. I never spoke to them, nor _____.
    A. did they speak to myself
    B. to me
    C. they to me
    D. them to me

Answers on page 218

For details on pronoun choice, turn to page 6.

Checkpoint 5. PRONOUN-ANTECEDENT AGREEMENT

INSTRUCTIONS: Fill in the correct word or phrase in each sentence.

1. Applicants must have _____ school transcripts sent to the admissions office.
   A. his or her
   B. their
   C. one's
   D. your

2. If you ride your bike recklessly, _____ could have an accident.
   A. he
   B. one
   C. you
   D. they

3. I love eating chocolate chip cookies, but _____ must control myself.
   A. we
   B. one
   C. he or she
   D. I

4. Everyone who missed the bus had to find _____ own way home.
   A. their
   B. his or her
   C. its
   D. your

5. Students who like to read increase _____ chances of doing well in English class.
   A. their
   B. your
   C. our
   D. one's

6. Neither Whitney nor Jason said _____ left a jacket in the locker room.
   A. one
   B. he
   C. they
   D. they're

7. When a person hasn't eaten in days _____ a hamburger, not a glass of water.
   A. they want
   B. one wants
   C. he wants
   D. you want

8. One must accept responsibility for _____ own actions.
   A. your
   B. their
   C. his or her
   D. its

9. After a trial that dragged on for three months, the jury will render _____ verdict today.
   A. their
   B. they're
   C. its
   D. it's

10. Our team won. That's why _____ celebrating.
    A. we are
    B. one is
    C. you're
    D. he or she is

11. Please consider the alternatives before _____ decide to spend $300 on a pair of shoes.
A. their
B. you
C. he or she
D. she or he

12. If you plan to leave the country, _____ must have a passport.
A. you
B. one
C. they
D. I

13. The girls' chorus is looking for new members, and _____ need any prior experience.
A. I don't
B. they don't
C. she doesn't
D. you don't

14. The astronauts, _____ had been waiting for hours, were launched into space at noon.
A. whose
B. which
C. who
D. whom

15. The committee complained that _____ was overworked and underappreciated.
A. they
B. you
C. it
D. we

Answers on page 219

For details on pronoun-antecedent agreement, turn to page 10.

Checkpoint 6. ADJECTIVES VS. ADVERBS

INSTRUCTIONS. Identify the word or phrase that SHOULD NOT BE USED in each sentence.

1. On ice-covered roads, you should drive _____.
A. slowly
B. careful
C. with care
D. cautiously

2. Wally looked _____ at his sick hamster.
A. glumly
B. sad
C. sadly
D. gloomily

3. Ruthie took a _____ picture with the digital camera in her cell phone.
A. good
B. beautiful
C. lovely
D. well

4. The audience remained _____ Ms. Hunt's frightening story.
A. calmly about
B. indifferent to
C. unmoved by
D. apathetic to

5. That old bicycle doesn't ride as
   _____ as it used to.
   A. smoothly
   B. smooth
   C. quietly
   D. well

6. Ma has felt _____ ever since Pa tumbled
   into the well.
   A. strange
   B. bad
   C. badly
   D. good

7. At the auto factory you'll see the most
   _____ designed assembly line in
   the world.
   A. efficiently
   B. clever
   C. intelligently
   D. well

8. The weather forecasters are kept on their toes
   by _____ changing winds.
   A. ever
   B. constantly
   C. always
   D. perpetual

9. If I am interpreting this poem
   _____, the narrator envies the
   swan.
   A. in the proper manner
   B. correctly
   C. right
   D. as the poet intended

10. The fumes of burning rubber smelled
    _____ down in the tunnel.
    A. awfully
    B. dreadful
    C. unpleasant
    D. awful

11. The newpaper printed _____
    account of the meeting in Garden City.
    A. a nearly complete
    B. an almost completely
    C. a close to complete
    D. a thorough, unbiased

12. A(n) _____ mystery writer
    spoke to our creative writing class about devel-
    oping a plot for a short story.
    A. internationally-recognized
    B. world-renowned
    C. best-selling
    D. famous prominently

13. I'm glad that you went to a counselor who
    could analyze your problem _____.
    A. calm and thoughtfully
    B. carefully and with objectivity
    C. without prejudice
    D. quickly and accurately

14. After a hectic week of school and work, she
    was overjoyed to float _____ the river
    on a raft.
    A. without a worry down
    B. quietly along
    C. serene down
    D. peacefully on

15. Although he looked _____,
    Dennis never showed his _____ side in
    the classroom.
    A. mischievously . . . mischievous
    B. mischievous . . . mischievous
    C. naughty . . . naughty
    D. impish . . . rascally

Answers on page 220

For more details on adjective and adverb usage, turn
to page 34.

Checkpoint 7. PARALLEL STRUCTURE

INSTRUCTIONS: Choose the word or words that complete the sentence correctly.

1. Smoking has been banned in many public places because it harms people's health, _____, and offends with its unpleasant smells.
   A. people have a right to breathe clean air
   B. deprives nonsmokers of clean air
   C. clean air is something everyone wants and needs
   D. pollution adversely affects the air we breathe

2. Archie enjoys canoeing, driving, _____, and writing.
   A. to read
   B. reading
   C. reading is his favorite pastime
   D. to spend an evening reading

3. As a teacher, Ms. Barkley is interesting, humorous, and _____.
   A. she inspires the class to do better
   B. a knack for inspiring us to do better
   C. the class is inspired by her
   D. inspiring to everyone in the class

4. Since entering her art history course, I've not only worked harder but also _____.
   A. fewer parties
   B. longer hours
   C. at home
   D. improved my grades

5. I like to go to bed early and _____.
   A. to get up at early in order to study
   B. getting up early to study
   C. have studied early in the morning
   D. turned into an early riser

6. I haven't yet made up my mind whether to be an art historian or _____.
   A. commercial art
   B. a commercial artist
   C. learning about commercial art
   D. training in commercial art

7. Either way, I plan to move to the country because I like to wander in the woods, live simply, and _____ than in the city.
   A. have fewer expenses
   B. save money
   C. more cheaply
   D. spend less money

8. My ideal house would be located on a dirt road, near a river or lake, and _____.
   A. hidden by pine trees
   B. pine trees would cover the property
   C. in a grove of tall pine trees
   D. very private

9. My experience in carpentry and interior design would allow me to build the house myself and _____.
   A. decorating it would be no problem
   B. decorate it
   C. decoration would be easy, too
   D. its decoration is going to be a breeze

10. On the other hand, hearing no car horns, seeing no people, and _____ may cause me to grow bored.
    A. to be miles from friends
    B. friends would be miles away
    C. I'd have to travel miles to see friends
    D. being miles from friends

11. In the long run, maybe I'll have an apartment in the city, a house in the country, and

    _____.

    A. get a job in the suburbs
    B. a job in the suburbs
    C. find a suburban job
    D. jobs in the suburbs are plentiful

12. Early in the morning Charlene is usually glum, moody, grumpy, and _____.
    A. a grouch
    B. irritable
    C. wants to sleep some more
    D. she wears a frown

13. By practicing five hours a day and _____, Jim became a champion figure skater.
    A. because he made up his mind to succeed
    B. parents who supported his effort
    C. he was convinced that he could do it
    D. by sacrificing many ordinary pleasures

14. Martha works in New York City, lives in Bedford, and _____.
    A. she is a frequent traveler
    B. frequently travels around the country
    C. frequent travel is part of her job
    D. a week never goes by without travel

15. This book has not only helped me to analyze sentences more skillfully _____.
    A. but also to write more competently
    B. but a more competent writer
    C. and to write more competently
    D. but also writing more competently

Answers on page 220

For details on parallelism, turn to page 65.

Checkpoint 8. CAPITALIZATION

INSTRUCTIONS: Choose the answer containing ALL the words that require capitalization in each sentence.

1. camp minisink is located on fairview lake in new jersey.
   A. Minisink . . . New Jersey
   B. Camp Minisink . . . Fairview . . . New Jersey
   C. Camp Minisink . . . Fairview Lake . . . New Jersey
   D. Camp Minisink . . . Lake . . . New Jersey

2. after the pilgrims crossed the ocean, they landed at plymouth rock and became acquainted with local indian tribes.
   A. After . . . Pilgrims . . . Ocean . . . Plymouth . . . Indian Tribes
   B. After . . . Pilgrims . . . Plymouth Rock . . . Indian
   C. After . . . Ocean . . . Plymouth Rock . . . Local Indian
   D. After . . . Pilgrims . . . Plymouth Rock

3. when the president of the united states addresses congress, he invariably states that his roots are in the south.
   A. When . . . President of the United States . . . Congress . . . South
   B. When . . . United States . . . The South
   C. President Of The United States . . . Congress . . . The South
   D. When . . . President of the United States

4. the medieval period is called the dark ages in m. crawford's textbook that is used in our history class.
   A. The Medieval Period . . . Dark Ages . . . M. Crawford's . . . History
   B. The Medieval . . . the Dark Ages . . . M. Crawford's
   C. The . . . Dark Ages . . . M. Crawford's
   D. The . . . Crawford's . . . History

5. the author of the article on capital punishment in missouri is justice andrew ryan, chief judge of the court of appeals in the ninth district.
   A. The . . . Capital Punishment . . . Missouri . . . Andrew Ryan . . . Court of Appeals . . . District
   B. The . . . Missouri . . . Justice Andrew Ryan, Chief Judge . . . Court of Appeals . . . Ninth District
   C. The Author . . . Capital Punishment . . . Missouri . . . Andrew Ryan, Chief Judge . . . Court Of Appeals
   D. The . . . Missouri . . . Justice Andrew Ryan . . . Appeals . . . Ninth District

6. every day, including sunday, members of st. monica's roman catholic church distribute copies of the bible to passers-by in downtown fresno, california.
   A. Every Day . . . Sunday, Members . . . St. Monica's Roman Catholic Church . . . Bible . . . Fresno, California
   B. Every . . . Sunday . . . St. Monica's . . . Church . . . Fresno, California
   C. Every . . . Sunday . . . St. Monica's Roman Catholic Church . . . Copies . . . Bible . . . Downtown Fresno, California
   D. Every . . . Sunday . . . St. Monica's Roman Catholic Church . . . Bible . . . Fresno, California

7. my grandmother gave me a book entitled *the dragon's teeth* and told me that, as a lifeguard at jones beach during the summer, I would have plenty of time to read it.
   A. My . . . Grandmother . . . *The Dragon's Teeth* . . . Lifeguard . . . Summer
   B. My . . . Grandmother . . . *Dragon's Teeth* . . . Jones . . . Summer
   C. *The Dragon's Teeth* . . . Lifeguard . . . Jones Beach
   D. My . . . *The Dragon's Teeth* . . . Jones Beach

8. the high school track coach advised me to go to the doctor, but when I got to the brookfield medical group's waiting room, dr. henderson was too busy to see me.
   A. The . . . Brookfield Medical Group's . . . Dr. Henderson
   B. The . . . High School Track Coach . . . The Brookfield Medical Group's . . . Dr. Henderson
   C. The . . . Track Coach . . . Doctor . . . Brookfield Medical Group's Waiting Room . . . Dr. Henderson
   D. The . . . Coach . . . Doctor . . . Brookfield Medical Group's . . . Dr. Henderson

9. en route home, larry stopped at safeway, the local supermarket, to pick up rye bread, cheerios, a package of bounty paper towels, and two blueberry muffins.
   A. En . . . Larry . . . Safeway . . . Supermarket . . . Rye Bread, Cheerios . . . Bounty Paper Towels . . . Blueberry Muffins
   B. En . . . Larry . . . Supermarket . . . Bread . . . Cheerios . . . Package of Bounty Paper Towels . . . Blueberry Muffins
   C. En . . . Larry . . . Safeway . . . Cheerios . . . Bounty
   D. En . . . Larry . . . Safeway . . . Supermarket

10. in their english classes juniors at ridgemont high school are assigned *the grapes of wrath*, a novel by john steinbeck about the plight of migrant farmers during the great depression.
    A. In . . . Ridgemont . . .*The Grapes of Wrath* . . . John Steinbeck . . . Great Depression
    B. In . . . English . . . Ridgemont . . . *Grapes of Wrath* . . . John Steinbeck . . . Migrant . . . Depression
    C. In . . . English . . . Juniors . . . Ridgemont High School . . . *The Grapes of Wrath* . . . Novel . . . John Steinbeck . . . Great Depression
    D. In . . . English . . . Ridgemont High School . . . *The Grapes of Wrath* . . . John Steinbeck . . . Great Depression

Answers on page 221

For details on capitalization, turn to page 86.

Checkpoint 9. PUNCTUATION

INSTRUCTIONS: Choose the sentences that are correctly punctuated.

1. A. We were told, that the school's roster of students is kept in the office.
   B. We were told that the schools roster of students is kept in the office.
   C. We were told that the school's roster of students is kept in the office.
   D. We were told that the schools' roster of student's is kept in the office.

2. A. Mike Poole, the second-string shortstop, however hit a home run.
   B. Mike Poole, the second-string shortstop however hit a home run.
   C. Mike Poole the second-string shortstop however, hit a home run.
   D. Mike Poole, the second-string shortstop, however, hit a home run.

3. A. The traffic backs up, when its' raining.
   B. The traffic backs up when it's raining.
   C. The traffic backs up when its' raining.
   D. The traffic backs up when its raining.

4. A. If you're not coming to work today, then you wont be paid.
   B. If your not coming to work today then you won't be paid.
   C. If youre not coming to work today then you won't be paid.
   D. If you're not coming to work today, then you won't be paid.

5. **A.** It was hot, so very hot, therefore, the city streets were empty.
   B. It was hot; so very hot; therefore, the city streets were empty.
   C. It was hot, so very hot; therefore, the city streets were empty.
   D. It was hot! so very hot therefore the city streets were empty.

6. **A.** Dave, unfortunately, couldn't climb the cliff because he had left his boots at home.
   B. Dave, unfortunately couldn't climb the cliff, because he had left his boots at home.
   C. Dave unfortunately couldn't climb the cliff because, he had left his boots at home.
   D. Dave, unfortunately, couldn't climb the cliff; because he had left his boots at home.

7. **A.** The term paper requires: a title page, a table of contents, and a bibliography.
   B. The term paper requires a title page, a table of contents, and a bibliography.
   C. The term paper requires a title page; a table of contents; and a bibliography.
   D. The term paper requires: a title page, a table of contents and a bibliography.

8. **A.** The store's policy is to guarantee two years free maintenance with all computers.
   B. The store's policy is to guarantee two years' free maintenance with all computers.
   C. The stores policy is to guarantee two year's free maintenance with all computer's.
   D. The stores policy is to guarantee two year's free maintenance with all computers.

9. **A.** The trees' leaves all over town turned brown instead of red and yellow.
   B. The trees leaves all over town, turned brown instead of red and yellow.
   C. The tree's leaves all over town turned brown instead of red and yellow.
   D. The trees' leaves, all over town, turned brown instead of red and yellow.

10. **A.** Jim Herndon, a Virginian, joined Lewis and Clark on their journey to the West.
    B. Jim Herndon—a Virginian, joined Lewis and Clark on their journey to the west.
    C. Jim Herndon—a Virginian—joined Lewis and Clark, on their journey to the west.
    D. Jim Herndon, a Virginian joined Lewis and Clark on their journey to the West.

11. **A.** Our guest's coat's got spattered with paint, which upset everyone but Josh.
    B. Our guests coats got spattered with paint, which upset everyone, but Josh.
    C. Our guests' coats got spattered with paint, which upset everyone but Josh.
    D. Our guests coat's got spattered with paint which upset everyone, but Josh.

12. **A.** The infant was frightened by the thunder. She cried in her crib.
    B. The infant was frightened by the thunder; She cried in her crib.
    C. The infant was frightened by the thunder she cried in her crib.
    D. The infant was frightened by the thunder, she cried, in her crib.

13. **A.** Larry's computer is in the shop; where it will be repaired.
    B. Larry's computer is in the shop, where it will be repaired.
    C. Larrys' computer is in the shop: where it will be repaired.
    D. Larry's computer, is in the shop where it will be repaired.

14. **A.** "Hey, man, can you spare a dollar," asked the panhandler.
    B. "Hey man, can you spare a dollar"? asked the panhandler.
    C. "Hey man, can you spare a dollar" asked the panhandler?
    D. "Hey, man, can you spare a dollar?" asked the panhandler.

15. **A.** Janie said that "the diamond was originally her grandmother's."
    B. Janie said, "that the diamond was originally her grandmothers."
    C. Janie said that the diamond was originally her grandmother's.
    D. Janie said, that the diamond was originally her Grandmothers'.

Answers on page 222

For details on punctuation, turn to page 81.

Checkpoint 10. EFFECTIVE SENTENCES

Choose the most effectively expressed sentences among the choices below. Avoid choosing sentences containing unnecessary words, awkward usage, incorrect word choice, or faulty grammar.

1. **A.** Bodybuilders have a habit of always looking at themself in the mirror.
   B. Bodybuilders don't do nothing but always look at themself in the mirror.
   C. Bodybuilders always look at themselves in the mirror.
   D. Bodybuilders is always looking at themselves in the mirror.

2. **A.** Martha was startled to find an unexpected surprise package on the doorstep leading into her house.
   B. Martha startled by an unexpected surprise package on the doorstep leading into her house.
   C. To her surprise, Martha found an unexpected package on her doorstep.
   D. Martha was surprised to find a package on her doorstep.

3. **A.** Guidance counselors help students plan their future.
   B. Guidance counselors, which belong to the guidance department, help students plan the future.
   C. The counselors, that are members of the guidance department, helps students plan the future.
   D. The counselors of the guidance department help student while planning for the future.

4. **A.** Snorkeling is when one swims underwater wearing a mask on your face.
   B. Snorkeling is where you swim underwater with a mask on your face.
   C. Snorkeling is swimming underwater while wearing a mask.
   D. Snorkeling is like swimming underwater with a mask on.

5. **A.** In my opinion, an apartment in the city is preferable to a rural type of a life.
   B. I think that living in the city is preferable to living in the country.
   C. In my opinion, an apartment in the city is more better than a rural type of a life.
   D. In my personal opinion, an apartment in the city is more better place to a rural type of a life.

6. **A.** My grandmother's house built where the train depot was.
   B. My grandmother's house was built where the train depot was.
   C. My grandmother's house was built where the train depot had been.
   D. My grandmother's house was built where the train depot is.

7. **A.** Getting rich is easy all you have to do is win the lottery.
   B. To get rich easy, win the lottery.
   C. It's easy to get rich, by winning the lottery.
   D. It's easy to get rich; win the lottery.

8. **A.** All the flags are waving from white poles in front of the building.
   B. Each of the flags are waving from white poles in front of the building.
   C. Each flag is waving from their white poles in front of the building.
   D. All the flags on the white poles in front of the building.

9. **A.** For as many as thirty years and more Babe Ruth's home run record was held.
   B. Babe Ruth held the home run record for more than thirty years.
   C. Babe Ruth, for a little over thirty years and more the home run record had been held by him.
   D. For as many as thirty years and then some, the home run record was held by Babe Ruth.

10. **A.** The electric trolley originated in 19th century Richmond, and many guess that it was Boston or New York.
    B. The electric trolley originated in 19th century Richmond, many people guessing that it was Boston or New York.
    C. The electric trolley originated in 19th century Richmond, however many people guess Boston or New York.
    D. The electric trolley originated in 19th century Richmond, not, as many people guess, Boston or New York.

11. **A.** Many impressive sports arenas, from Maine to California, coming from corporate donations.
    B. Many impressive sports arenas, from Maine to California, they come from corporate donations.
    C. Many impressive sports arenas, from Maine to California, came from corporate donations.
    D. Many impressive sports arenas, from Maine to California, which came from corporate donations.

12. **A.** During the rush hour, a truck carrying honey spilled its contents on the freeway, sticking many commuters in a traffic jam.
    B. During the rush hour, a truck filled with honey spilled its contents on the freeway, and it thereby caused many commuters stuck in traffic.
    C. During the rush hour, a tanker truck carrying honey spilled its contents on the freeway, by which many commuters got therefore stuck.
    D. During the rush hour, a truck filled with honey spilled its contents on the freeway, and, therefore, sticking many commuters in a traffic jam.

13. **A.** The photographer traveled all over the world, going from America first he went to Tibet, then eventually to Russia from Australia.
   B. The photographer traveled all over the world, the first trip he took was leaving America when he went to Tibet, and eventually to Russia from Australia.
   C. The photographer traveled all over the world, first from America to Tibet and then from Australia to Russia.
   D. The photographer traveled all over the world, first from America he went to Tibet and wound up in Russia after leaving Australia.

14. **A.** Fear is different than cowardice because some can conquer it while the other can't be.
   B. Fear differs from cowardice, for fear can be conquered whereas cowardice cannot.
   C. Fear is not the same as cowardice; because it is conquerable.
   D. Fear is far different than cowardice. The first can be overcome but the last one is not.

15. **A.** A new athletic center is run by the department of recreation, it contains three gyms, a weight room, and two swimming pools.
   B. A new athletic center is run by the department of recreation, containing three gyms, a weight room, and two swimming pools.
   C. A new athletic center to contain three gyms, a weight room, and two swimming pools, and to be run by the department of recreation.
   D. A new athletic center, containing three gyms, a weight room, and two swimming pools, is run by the department of recreation.

Answers on page 223

For more details on sentence style and expression, see page 70.

ANSWERS AND EXPLANATIONS

Subject-Verb Agreement, page 198

1. **B** *One* is the singular subject of the sentence. Choices A, C, and D are singular verbs. Only Choice B contains a plural verb and is, therefore, the answer to this question.

2. **D** The subject of the sentence is *skulls*, a plural noun. Choices A, B, and C are plural verbs. Therefore D, the only choice containing a singular verb, is the answer to this question.

3. **B** The plural word *Fourteen* is the subject of the sentence. Because Choice B contains the singular verb, *serves*, it is the correct answer to this question.

4. **C** *Supply*, a singular noun, is the subject of the sentence. All the choices except C are also singular, making C the correct answer.

5. **D** The singular word *evidence* is the subject of the sentence. Because *were* is plural, D is the correct answer.

6. **B** Because the sentence has a compound subject, *arm and hand*, it requires a plural verb. The verb in Choice B is singular, making B the correct answer.

7. **A** *Neither one* is a singular phrase that requires a singular verb, supplied by all the choices except A.

8. **B** Only Choice B contains a verb that is not in agreement with the *principal*, the singular subject of the sentence.

9. **C** *Either* is a singular word. Choice C is plural, and, therefore, is the correct answer.

10. **D** In this inverted sentence, the plural subject, *doctor and crew*, comes after the verb. Choice D is singular, making it the correct answer. (The sentence would sound better if the subject were *a crew of nurses and a doctor*.)

11. **A** The noun *news*, although it sounds plural, is singular. All the choices except A (the correct answer) contain a singular verb.

12. **A** Only Choice A contains plural verbs that fail to agree in number with the singular subject, *skeleton*.

13. **C** *Boy*, a singular noun, is the subject of the sentence. Because *along with his brothers and sisters* is a prepositional phrase, it may not be part of the subject. All the choices are singular verbs except C.

14. **D** The verb in D lacks agreement in number with *head*, the singular subject of the sentence.

15. **C** When a plural noun and a singular noun make up the subject, the verb must agree with the nearer subject—in other words, *the bus driver*. Only Choice C uses a plural, instead of a singular, verb.

Verb Tenses and Forms, page 199

1. **B** Choices A and C are singular verbs that lack agreement with the plural subject of the sentence. Choice D is nonstandard usage.

2. **D** Choice A is incorrect because the sentence calls for the past tense of the verb. Choice B is in the present progressive and is also a singular verb that lacks agreement with the plural subject of the sentence. Choice C is nonstandard usage.

3. **C** The sentence requires the infinitive form of the verb. The other choices are nonstandard usages.

4. **A** The sentence requires a verb in the future tense. Choice B is incorrect because it is in the future perfect tense. Likewise, Choice D

uses the past tense instead of the future. Choice C is a double negative.

5. **C** Choices A, B, and C are nonstandard usages.

6. **D** The sentence requires a verb in the past tense. Choice A is in the present tense. Choice B is in the present perfect, and Choice C is in the future tense.

7. **B** Choice A is a plural verb that lacks agreement with *fish*, the singular subject of the sentence. Choices C and D are nonstandard verb forms.

8. **A** Choice B is nonstandard usage. The sentence requires a verb in the past tense. Because C is in the present tense, and D is in the present perfect tense, A is the correct answer.

9. **A** Choices B and C are plural verbs that lack agreement with *Melissa*, the singular subject of the sentence. Choice D, a verb in the future perfect tense, is wrong because the sentence requires a verb in either the present or the past tense.

10. **D** The sentence requires a verb in the past or past perfect tense. Choice A is in the present tense, and Choice C is in the present perfect tense. Choice B is a nonstandard usage.

11. **B** The sentence requires a verb in the past tense. Choice A is in the present tense, and Choice D is in the present perfect tense. Choice C is a nonstandard usage.

12. **B** Choices A and C are nonstandard usages. Choice D, a verb in the present tense, is incorrect because the sentence describes action that occurred in the past.

13. **D** Choices A, B, and C are nonstandard usages.

14. **D** Choice A is a nonstandard usage. Choice B, a verb in the present tense, is incorrect because the sentence is cast in the past tense. Likewise, Choice C is a verb inconsistent with the tense of the sentence.

15. **B** Choice A is wrong because the singular verb fails to agree with *prices*, the plural subject of the sentence. Choice C, a verb in the present progressive tense, is not appropriate in a sentence cast in the past tense. Choice D is an example of faulty word choice.

Incomplete Sentences, page 201

1. **C** Choice C provides a subject (*Lloyd*) and a verb (*worries*) that make the sentence complete. Choices A, B, and D provide subjects but no verbs.

2. **A** Choice A provides a verb, *was*, to complete the clause that begins with *that*. Choice B provides a verb but leaves the clause incomplete: *could have been* what? Choice C leaves out the verb that is needed to complete the clause. Choice D is not grammatically related to the rest of the sentence.

3. **D** Choice D has a subject and verb in the proper tense to make the sentence complete. Choice A leaves the construction without a verb. Choice B leaves the construction without a subject. Choice C has a subject and verb, but the verb is in the present instead of in the past tense.

4. **A** Choice A provides the sentence with a correct verb and completes the thought being conveyed. Choice B provides a verb but fails to complete the thought. Choice C lacks the verb needed to make a sentence complete. Choice D lacks a main verb because the *-ing* form of a verb (*having been*) may not serve as the main verb in a sentence.

5. **C** Choice A contains a dangling modifier. The phrase *Running short of time* should modify the person who is taking the test, not *questions.* Choice B is an incomplete construction that makes little sense. Choice D is made up of sentence parts that are grammatically unrelated.

6. **C** Choice C provides the verb that properly completes the sentence. Choice A consists of prepositional phrases that leave the sentence incomplete. Choices B and D contain *-ing* verbs that may not serve as the main verb of a sentence without the addition of a helping verb, as in *are finishing* or *will be building.*

7. **B** Choice B supplies the verb needed to complete the sentence. Choice A is a subordinate clause, a construction that never contains the main verb of a sentence. Choice C uses the *-ing* form of a verb, which may not be used as the main verb of a sentence without a helping verb, as in *was building.* Choice D uses the infinitive form of a verb, which may not serve as the main verb of a sentence.

8. **D** A subject and verb in an independent clause are needed to make the given subordinate clause part of a whole sentence. Choice D, an independent clause, properly completes the sentence. Choices A and C are prepositional phrases. Choice B is a phrase modifying *hit.*

9. **A** The subject *Fragments* lacks a verb, which is provided by Choice A. Choice B is a prepositional phrase. Choice C is a phrase that describes the subject. Choice D is an adjective clause that modifies the subject.

10. **D** The given construction is only a prepositional phrase. A subject and verb—provided by Choice D—are needed to make the sentence complete. Choices A and C provide only a subject. Choice B provides a verb but no subject.

11. **C** Only Choice C provides a verb to go with the subject *pieces.* Choice A is an adjective modifying the noun *pieces.* Choice B gives the sentence a new subject, *crew,* but it lacks a verb. Choice D turns the construction into a participial phrase.

12. **B** Choice B adds a subject, *Kiri,* to the sentence, and also the verb, *had.* Choice A does no more than add an adverbial clause to the construction. Choice C is a phrase that turns the construction into a subordinate clause. Choice D adds a subject, *singer,* but no verb.

13. **A** Choice A completes the sentence with a subject, *I,* and a verb, *got.* Choice B simply adds another detail to the construction without changing the grammatical structure of the sentence fragment. Choice C is a dangling modifier because the phrase that starts *with having a whole day* modifies *refrigerator* instead of the person who had all day with nothing to do. Choice D is grammatically unrelated to the rest of the sentence.

14. **C** Choice C completes the sentence with an independent clause. Choice A merely adds another detail to the given subordinate clause. Choice B is a phrase that cannot complete the sentence because it lacks a verb. Choice D cannot complete the sentence because it fails to provide a subject for the sentence.

15. **A** Choice A completes the thought that makes the sentence whole. Choice B is a phrase that leaves the construction incomplete. Choice C is grammatically unrelated to the earlier part of the sentence. Choice D is an adjectival phrase that fails to complete the thought.

Pronoun Choice, page 202

1. **B** Pronouns serving as sentence subjects should be in the nominative case. Choices A, C, and D are in the objective case.

2. **B** Pronouns serving as sentence subjects must be in the nominative case. Choices A and D are objective case pronouns. Choice C is a contraction of *they are*, a usage that makes no sense in the context.

3. **A** Pronouns that serve as objects of a preposition (*between*) should be in the objective case. Choices B, C, and D include at least one pronoun in the nominative case.

4. **B** The nominative case pronouns in Choices A and D may not be used as the object of the verb *drive*. Choice C includes *them*, ordinarily a pronoun in the objective case. But in the phrase *them girls*, it is not being used as a pronoun but as an adjective modifying *girls*. Because standard usage calls for the phrase to be *those girls* instead of *them girls*, Choice C is incorrect.

5. **C** A pronoun in the nominative case should be used in the subject; a pronoun in the objective case is used as the object of the preposition *with*.

6. **D** A possessive pronoun (*my, our, your, his, her, their*) is used before the gerund *arguing*. Gerunds are nouns that looks like verbs because of their *-ing* ending.

7. **C** Objective case pronouns are needed as objects of the preposition *without*.

8. **B** The objective case pronouns in Choices A and D may not be used in the subject of a sentence. The last word in Choice C should be *he*, a subject pronoun used to correctly complete a comparison containing *than*. In other words, use the pronoun that goes with the verb that would follow naturally if

the construction were complete, as in ". . . better singers than Frank and *he* (are)."

9. **C** An objective case pronoun is needed in the prepositional phrase beginning with *for*. Choices A, B, and D are incorrect because each contains a subject pronoun.

10. **C** Choices A and B improperly use the objective case pronoun *Us* in the subject of the sentence. Choice D incorrectly includes *them*, an objective case pronoun in a comparison using *than*. Use the pronoun that goes with the verb that would follow naturally if the construction were complete, as in ". . . more seriously than *he* (does)."

11. **A** Objective case pronouns are needed as objects of the verb *understood*.

12. **C** Choice A uses *me*, an objective case pronoun that may not be used as the subject of a sentence. Choices B and D use the reflexive pronoun, *myself*. Such pronouns (*myself, yourself, herself*, etc.) may not be used as the subject of a sentence. Rather, they can be an object but only when the subject and the object refer to the same person, as in Tanya swears that she wrote the paper *herself* or The chief *himself* showed up at the rally.

13. **A** A possessive pronoun (*my, our, your, his, her, their*) rather than a personal pronoun should be used before a gerund, a noun that looks like a verb because of its *-ing* ending.

14. **B** Choice A is a reflexive pronoun that may not be used as the subject of a sentence. Choices C and D contain objective case pronouns that are unsuitable for use in the subject of a sentence.

15. **C** Choice A is wrong because reflexive pronouns, including *myself*, may not be used as a substitute for *me* or for any other personal pronoun. Choice B uses the proper pronoun but is an incomplete construction

that makes little sense. Choice D uses an objective case pronoun where a nominative case pronoun is needed. Had every word of the sentence been spelled out, it would read *nor did they speak to me.*

Pronoun-Antecedent Agreement, page 204

1. **B** A third-person plural pronoun is needed to agree with the antecedent *Applicants.* Choices A and C are singular. Choice D is a second-person pronoun.

2. **C** The sentence requires a pronoun in the second person. Choices A, B, and D are third-person pronouns.

3. **D** The sentence calls for a first-person singular pronoun. Choices A, B, and C are third-person pronouns. In addition, Choice A is plural.

4. **B** The sentence calls for a third-person singular pronoun to agree with the antecedent *Everyone.* Choice A is plural. Choice C may not be used to refer to people. Choice D is a second-person pronoun.

5. **A** The sentence calls for a third-person plural pronoun. Choice B is in the second person. Choice A is in the first person. Choice D is singular.

6. **B** The sentence requires a singular third-person pronoun that agrees with the antecedent *Neither . . . nor.* Choice A is a possible answer, but the shift from personal to impersonal pronouns is awkward. Choices C and D are plural.

7. **C** The sentence requires a third-person singular pronoun. Choice A is plural. Choice B is a possible answer, but the shift from personal to impersonal pronouns is awkward. Choice D is in the second person.

8. **C** The sentence calls for a third-person singular pronoun. Choice A is in the second person. Choice B is plural. Choice D is not appropriate for referring to people. In a formal context, *one's* might have been a good alternative to the correct answer, but *his or her* is perfectly acceptable here.

9. **C** The sentence calls for a third-person singular pronoun. Choice A is plural. Choices B and D are contractions.

10. **A** The sentence calls for a plural pronoun in the third person. Choices B and D are in the third person but are singular. Choice C is in the second person.

11. **B** The sentence requires a second-person pronoun. Choices A, C, and D are in the third person. Note that the pronoun's antecedent is not stated, but is understood as "you" because the sentence makes a request.

12. **A** The sentence calls for a pronoun in the second person. Choices B and C are third-person pronouns. Choice D is in the first person.

13. **B** The sentence requires a third-person plural pronoun. Choice A is in the third person. Choice C is a third-person singular pronoun. Choice D is in the second person.

14. **C** Choice A is nonstandard usage. Choice B should not be used to refer to people. Choice D is incorrect because the context calls for a pronoun in the nominative rather than the objective case.

15. **C** The sentence requires a third-person singular pronoun. Choice B is in the second person. Choice D is plural. In everyday speech, Choice A would be acceptable, but in strictly grammatical terms, the plural pronoun *they* does not agree with the singular antecedent *committee.*

Adjectives vs. Adverbs, page 205

1. **B** The sentence needs an adverb or an adverbial phrase to modify the verb *drive*. Because *careful* is an adjective, it is incorrect.

2. **B** In what manner did Wally look at his pet hamster? The answer must be stated with an adverb. All the choices are adverbs except B, which is an adjective.

3. **D** The context requires an adjective to modify the noun *picture*. D is an adverb, however, and, therefore, is the correct answer.

4. **A** The sentence needs an adjective to describe the audience. Because *calmly* is an adverb, Choice A is the correct answer.

5. **B** An adverb is needed to modify the verb *ride*. *Smooth* is an adjective.

6. **C** Because *felt* is a linking verb, it should be followed by an adjective. Because *badly* is an adverb, C is the answer.

7. **B** An adverb is needed to modify the verb *designed*. Because *clever* is an adjective, B is the right answer.

8. **D** The context calls for an adverb to modify the adjective *changing*. Since *perpetual* is an adjective, D is the correct answer.

9. **C** The context calls for an adverb or an adverbial phrase to fill in the blank. Only Choice C does not qualify because *right* is an adjective.

10. **A** Because *smelled* is used as a linking verb in this sentence, it must be modified by an adjective. Choice A is the answer because *awfully* is an adverb.

11. **B** The blank may be filled with one or more adjectives or with an adjective preceded by an adverb. Choice B, because it consists of two adverbs, is the answer.

12. **D** The blank must be filled in with one or more adjectives or with an adjective preceded by an adverb. Choice D contains an adjective and an adverb but not in the proper order.

13. **A** The context calls for one or more adverbs or an adverbial phrase. Choice A incorrectly pairs the adjective *calm* with an adverb.

14. **C** The context calls for an adverbial phrase or one or more adverbs followed by a preposition. Choice C is nonstandard usage because it uses an adjective instead of an adverb.

15. **A** The construction calls for an adjective in each blank because in this sentence *looked* is a linking verb. Because A uses an adverb, it is the correct answer.

Parallel Structure, page 207

1. **B** Choices A, C, and D are independent sentences, not phrases that are parallel to *harms people's health* and *offends with its unpleasant smells*. Only Choice B begins with a verb and cites a reason for the ban on smoking in public places.

2. **B** Only Choice B is parallel to *canoeing, driving, . . . and writing*. All are nouns, or to be more precise, gerunds. Because Choices and A and D are infinitives, and C is a complete sentence, none of them has the same structure as the items in the list of Archie's pleasures.

3. **D** In the given sentence, a series of adjectives describes Ms. Barkley. Only Choice D contains an adjective, *inspiring*, that is parallel to *interesting* and *humorous*.

4. **D** The use of the correlative conjunctions *not only . . . but also* means that ideas must be stated in parallel form. Only *improved my*

grades is parallel to *worked harder* because both phrases start with the past tense of a verb.

5. **A** Choice A contains the infinitive *to get*, which is parallel to the verb *to go*. None of the other choices are structured in parallel form. In everyday language the *to* in the phrase *to get up early* is optional.

6. **B** Only Choice B names an occupation that is parallel to *art historian*. The other choices refer to the field of commercial art, not to a job within the field.

7. **D** The correct answer must begin with a verb and be grammatically parallel to *wander in the woods* and *live simply*. Only D qualifies. Choice B also begins with a verb, but it makes no sense in the context of the sentence.

8. **C** To be correct, the phrases that follow the verb *located* must begin with prepositions, such as *on* and *near*. Only Choice C begins with a preposition—*in*.

9. **B** The correct answer must be parallel to the phrase *to build the house*—the infinitive form verb followed by a noun or pronoun. Choice B omits the word *to*, but it is understood.

10. **D** In order to be grammatically parallel to *hearing no car horns* and *seeing no people*, the correct answer must begin with the *–ing* form of a verb.

11. **B** The phrases *an apartment in the city* and *a house in the country* contain a noun followed by a prepositional phrase. Only Choice B has a similar structure.

12. **B** A series of one-word adjectives describes Charlene. Only Choice B adheres to that pattern. Choice A is a noun phrase, and Choices C and D are clauses.

13. **D** Only Choice D is parallel to *by practicing five hours a day*. Both are prepositional phrases.

14. **B** Only Choice B consists of a verb followed by a prepositional phrase, a structure that makes it parallel to *works in New York City* and *lives in Bedford.*

15. **A** Look for infinitives that are parallel to *to analyze sentences.* You'll find one in both Choice A and Choice C. Choice C, however, incorrectly uses *and* instead of *but also* to complete the construction that begins with *not only. . . .*

Capitalization, page 208

1. **C** Capitalize the first letter of sentences and of proper names.

2. **B** Capitalize the first letter of sentences and of proper nouns, but not the nouns that don't use an actual name, such as *ocean.*

3. **A** Capitalize the first letter of sentences and of proper nouns, such as official titles, the names of institutions, and specific areas of the country. In titles, capitalize only the important words, including the first and last words. Don't capitalize articles (*the, an, a*), coordinating conjunctions, or prepositions of fewer than five letters.

4. **C** Capitalize the first letter of sentences and of proper nouns. Don't capitalize a subject studied in school unless it is the actual name of the course.

5. **B** Capitalize the first letter of sentences and of proper nouns, including official titles and the names of institutions and states.

6. **D** Capitalize the first letter of sentences and of proper nouns, including days of the week, book titles, and the names of institutions and states.

7. **D** Capitalize the first letter of sentences and of proper nouns, including place names and book titles, but not nouns that do not stand for an actual name, such as *my grand-mother*.

8. **A** Capitalize the first letter of sentences and of proper nouns, including official titles and the actual names of institutions, but not their general description, such as *high school* and *track coach*.

9. **C** Capitalize the first letter of sentences and of proper nouns, including the actual names of people, businesses, and products, such as *Cheerios* but not the type of business (*supermarket*) or product (*paper towels*).

10. **D** Capitalize the first letter of sentences and of proper nouns, including the names of languages, schools, books, people, and historical periods.

Punctuation, page 210

1. **C** To turn singular nouns into possessives, add *–'s*. If the noun ends in *–s*, the apostrophe goes after the *–s*. No commas are needed in this simple declarative sentence.

2. **D** Commas are needed before and after appositives and before and after conjunctive adverbs like *however*.

3. **B** Only Choice B uses the correct contraction *it's* as a substitute for *it is*. Don't confuse *it's* with *its*, a possessive pronoun.

4. **D** The contractions *you're* and *won't* are used in place of *you are* and *will not*. Also insert a comma between independent clauses and after dependent clauses that begin with *If*.

5. **C** Semicolons are used to separate independent clauses. Also commas are needed before and after the conjunctive adverb *therefore* to separate it from the clause it modifies.

6. **A** Commas are needed before and after a conjunctive adverb that falls between the subject and verb of a sentence.

7. **B** Colons are not used after incomplete sentences. Use commas, not semicolons, to separate items in a list of three or more items. A comma before the last item is optional.

8. **B** To turn the singular noun *store* into a possessive, add *–'s*. To turn the plural noun *years* into a possessive, put an apostrophe after the final *–s*.

9. **A** To turn plural nouns such as *trees* into possessives, put an apostrophe after the final *–s*. If the noun does not end in *–s* (as in *children*), add *–'s*. No commas are needed in this simple declarative sentence.

10. **A** Commas are needed before and after the appositive, *a Virginian*. Also, the *West* is the name of a place, and as a proper noun, it should be capitalized.

11. **C** To turn the plural noun *guests* into a possessive, put an apostrophe after the final *–s*. A comma is needed to separate the independent clause from the dependent clause that begins with *which*.

12. **A** When two independent clauses are separated by a period, both begin with capital letters. If a semicolon is used, the second clause begins with a lowercase letter.

13. **B** To turn the proper noun *Larry* into a possessive, add *–'s*. A comma is needed to separate the independent clause from the dependent clause that begins with *where*.

14. **D** Commas are needed after the interjection *Hey* and after various forms of address, such as *Hey, man*. For a quote that asks a question, put the question mark inside the quotation marks.

15. C An indirect quotation is not enclosed by quotation marks. Capitalize *grandmother* only when it is used as the person's name.

Effective Sentences, page 212

1. C Choice A is ineffective for two main reasons. First, it is wordy. By definition, a habit is something that is always done. Therefore, you don't need *have a habit* and *always* in the same sentence. And second, the pronoun *themself* is an example of nonstandard English.

Choice B, like A, uses the nonstandard pronoun *themself* instead of *themselves*. It also contains *don't do nothing*, a double negative.

Choice D uses a plural subject (*Bodybuilders*) and a singular verb (*is.*)

2. D Choice A contains redundancies. Because surprises, by their nature, are unexpected, it makes no sense to say *unexpected surprise*. Similarly, because doorsteps serve as access to a house, the phrase *leading into her house* is unnecessary.

Choice B is similar to A. It is also a sentence fragment because in this context the verb *startled* needs a helping verb, such as *is* startled or *was* startled, to be complete.

Choice C includes the same redundancy as A. That is, *surprises*, by definition, are unexpected.

3. A Choice B is incorrect because the pronoun *which* should not be used to refer to people. The wording in the sentence also suggests that students plan the future—not their own future, but the general future, an idea that the writer could not have intended to convey.

Choice C is not altogether clear because the clause beginning with *that* should not be set off by commas. Also, the plural subject, *counselors*, does not agree with the singular verb, *helps*.

Choice D is nonstandard because *student* should be *students*. More important, it's unclear whether it is the students or the counselors who are planning for the future.

4. C The problem with Choice A is that it defines snorkeling by using *is when* rather than by simply stating the definition. Furthermore, an improper shift in pronoun person, from *one* to *you*, occurs within the sentence.

The problem with Choice B is that it defines snorkeling by using *is where* rather than by simply stating the definition. Moreover, the sentence contains *on your face*, an unnecessary phrase because masks are worn nowhere else but on the face.

Choice D uses *like*, a word that makes the sentence a comparison instead of a definition.

5. B Choice A is a poor choice because it illogically compares an apartment to a rural type of life. Also, the standard phrase is *type of life*, not *type of a life*.

Choice C contains the same faulty comparison as Choice A. In addition, using *more* with the comparative word *better* is redundant.

Choice D contains the same weaknesses as Choices A and C. Also, in the phrase *my personal opinion*, the word *personal* is unecessary because opinions, by definition, are personal.

6. C Choice A is a sentence fragment because the verb *built* needs a helping verb such as *is* or *was* to be grammatically complete.

Choice B concludes with a verb in the past tense instead of the past perfect tense. By failing to differentiate between tenses, the writer has said that the house and depot occupied the same site at the same time— obviously a physical impossibility.

Choice D uses an illogical combination of past and present tense that makes the sentence meaningless.

7. **D** Choice A is a run-on sentence. Punctuation is needed betweeen *easy* and *all*.

Choice B uses the adjective *easy* instead of the adverb *easily* to modify the verb *To get*.

Choice C contains an unnecessary comma that divides the sentence into two unrelated grammatical units.

8. **A** Choice B uses a singular subject, *Each*, that lacks agreement with the plural verb, *are waving*.

Choice C contains the plural pronoun, *their*, that does not agree with its singular antecedent, *flag*.

Choice D is a sentence fragment because it lacks a verb.

9. **B** Choice A uses the construction *as many as thirty years and more*—a confusing phrase that makes no sense because it suggests that Babe Ruth's record was held for both less than thirty and more than thirty years. Although the writer certainly intended to say that Babe Ruth held the home run record, the passive sentence construction leaves up in the air who it was that actually held Babe Ruth's record.

Choice C leaves uncertain how long the home run record had been held. Also, a misleading shift in sentence structure leads to the awkwardly expressed phrase *had been held by him*.

Choice D is constructed in the passive voice. It also includes *thirty years and then some*, a phrase that can easily be tightened to *more than thirty years* or some other equivalent phrase.

10. **D** Choice A has two main faults. Its two coordinate clauses suggest that each contains information of equal significance, when the writer probably intended to convey a different message. Also, the antecedent of the pronoun *it* is unclear. The writer meant the pronoun to refer to the origin of the trolley, but the sentence does not use *origin* or any other equivalent noun.

Choice B contains the pronoun *it*, which in the context has no specific antecedent. Moreover, it's unclear which people guessed about the origins of the trolley. Were they from Richmond in the 19th century? Or does the writer mean more contemporary people?

Choice C contains a comma splice. Instead of a comma after Richmond, a period or semicolon is needed to indicate that the construction is made up of two independent sentences.

11. **C** Choice A is a sentence fragment because it lacks a complete verb. The *-ing* form of a verb may not be used as the main verb in a sentence without a helping verb, such as *were coming* or *have been coming*.

Choice B is poorly constructed because the subject of the sentence switches from *arenas* to *they* halfway through. As a result, the sentence contains two grammatically unrelated sentence parts.

Choice D is a sentence fragment because it lacks a main verb.

12. **A** Choice B contains the awkward and non-standard construction that begins, "*it thereby....*"

Choice C includes the redundancy *by which ... therefore*, a construction that is also awkwardly phrased in nonstandard English.

Choice D uses a construction (*sticking many commuters in a traffic jam*) that is grammatically unrelated to the previous part of the sentence.

13. **C** Choice A is a construction made up of sentence parts that do not go together grammatically. It can be read as two sentences with a comma splice between them. Or it may be a single sentence that is awkwardly expressed. In either case, it lacks parallel structure, which it desperately needs.

Choice B contains a comma splice between *world* and *the*. The second sentence also is poorly structured because *trip he took* is awkwardly described by *leaving America when he went to Tibet*.

Choice D contains a comma splice between *world* and *first*, and the second sentence is in need of parallelism.

14. **B** Choice A uses *different than* instead of the standard phrase *different from*. The antecedent of the pronoun *it* is ambiguous. Does it refer to fear or to cowardice? Finally, the phrases that follow *because* should be stated in parallel form.

Choice C uses a semicolon improperly. A semicolon should separate two independent clauses, but the construction beginning with *because* is a sentence fragment.

Choice D uses *different than* instead of the standard phrase *different from*. It also uses the adjective *last*, suggesting that a comparison of more than two things is being made.

15. **D** Choice A contains a comma splice between *recreation* and *it*.

Choice B uses modifying phrases (*containing three gyms*, etc.) that are too far from the noun (*center*) that they are meant to modify. That's why the phrases seem to modify *department of recreation*.

Choice C is a sentence fragment because it lacks a main verb.

Part III

Essay Writing on the SAT and ACT

Chapter 7

Writing a Grammatical Essay

Hey, wait a minute! What is a chapter on essay writing doing in a grammar book?

A fair question, and one with a fairly simple answer: The SAT, ACT, and high school exit exams administered in most states include an essay question that tests whether students can **express themselves in standard English**. Essay questions also give students a chance to show that they have the brainpower to organize and present ideas clearly and coherently. In addition, the grammar sections of every SAT and ACT, as well as many exit exams, contain multiple-choice questions about the essentials of essay writing: organization, style, tone, unity, word choice, and so on.

In a word, then, grammar is important, but it isn't everything. The overall quality of an essay depends equally, if not more so, on the manner in which ideas are presented and developed.

AN ESSAY-WRITING PROCESS

Essay questions on most tests give you a time limit (25 minutes on the SAT, 30 minutes on the ACT). An essay completed in half an hour or less is bound to be shorter than the take-home essays you've written for English or other classes. Yet, it doesn't take hours to prove that you have what it takes to demonstrate your writing competency. Indeed, it's important to keep in mind that no one expects you to produce an immortal essay on the SAT or ACT, only to show that you have a reasonable command of essay-writing skills.

Essay tests usually begin with a question, often called a *prompt*, to which you must respond. A prompt may consist of a quotation with which you are asked to agree or disagree. Another may ask for your opinion on a given issue or a set of circumstances. Rest assured that the issue will be general and open-ended enough to elicit a response from all students who have been more or less awake during their high school years.

Although you can't predict what the prompt will say, every test includes a set of instructions for writing the essay likely to contain the following information:

> Write an essay in reponse to the topic. As you write, develop your thoughts clearly and effectively. Try to include examples and specific evidence to support your point of view. A plain, natural writing style is best. The length of the essay is up to you, but remember that quality takes precedence over quantity.
> Be sure to write only on the assigned topic.

Develop your thoughts clearly and effectively.

Because you don't have much time to reflect on the issue, you must quickly take a position on the issue. There is no right or wrong answer. You won't be penalized for an unusual or unpopular point of view. All parts of an essay should work together to make a single point. If the evidence you provide wanders from the main idea, the effect of the essay will be diluted. Above all, you don't want readers to come to the end of your essay in doubt about what point you were trying to make.

Include examples and specific evidence to support your point of view.

This guideline urges you to support your main idea with specific examples. It's easy to write in generalities, but the heart of an essay is its details. The development of specific supporting evidence reveals more about the depth of your thinking than almost anything else in the essay.

A plain, natural writing style is best.

A plain, natural style makes you sound like a real, flesh-and-blood person with something to say. Avoid using complex words except when they are the only ones that say exactly what you mean and will add something to the essay's tone and meaning that would otherwise be lost. Elegant words have their place, but to use them merely to sound more mature is pretentious— and if the meaning is not exactly right, foolish.

The length of the essay is up to you.

Keep in mind that the purpose of a writing test is to show your ability to think and express yourself. A short essay of, say, 250 or 300 words can produce such evidence. A brief essay allows you to devote more attention to choosing each word and crafting each sentence. It also leaves time for revising and polishing your work. But don't be satisfied with an abbreviated one-paragraph essay that might suggest your head is an empty vessel. Just remember that effective development of the main idea matters more than word count.

SAMPLE SAT WRITING TEST TOPICS

1. The following quotation comes from a newspaper editorial: "If you are like most people, your sadness over losing, say, $1,000 would be twice as great as your happiness at winning $1,000. That all-too-human tendency to feel the pain of loss more deeply than the joy of gain is called 'loss aversion.'"

   Essay topic: Do you think that negative feelings are generally stronger than positive ones?

2. After rescuing a dozen men and women from a burning office building in Chicago, Jim Burns, a firefighter, said, "Courage is just a matter of luck—of being at the right place at the right time."

   Essay topic: Is Jim Burns correct? Is courage a widespread human quality that most people never get a chance to demonstrate? Or is courage of the Jim Burns variety a rarity?

SAMPLE ACT WRITING TEST TOPICS

1. Students in greater numbers are choosing to take time off between high school and college. Some use the time for public service or charity work. Others travel, find internships, or earn money.

   Supporters of this trend say that experiences away from the classroom contribute to personal growth and maturity. Opponents argue that students are bound to lose their urge to study and to continue with their education later on.

   In your opinion, should students take time off between high school and college?

2. In an effort to improve discipline and the learning environment, many schools have implemented dress codes for students. The codes ban, among other things, tank tops, ragged jeans, short shorts, and T-shirts with provocative or obscene messages. One day a week in many schools has been designated dress-up day, when students are required to wear clothing that would be appropriate for occasions such as a job or college interview.

   Those who object to the measure claim that dress codes violate students' rights and create an oppressive atmosphere.

   In your opinion, should schools be allowed to impose dress codes on their students?

MAKING EVERY SECOND COUNT

In general, the essay-writing process consists of three main stages:
1) prewriting, 2) composing, and 3) revising and proofreading.

The first stage, called *prewriting*, consists of everything that needs to be done before you actually start scribbling words on paper:

- Analyzing the topic
- Narrowing the topic
- Choosing a main idea
- Gathering and arranging ideas

In a half-hour test, prewriting should consume perhaps five or six minutes at most.

During the second stage, *composing*, you choose the words and form the sentences that express your thoughts. At full throttle, you'll be

- Introducing the main idea
- Developing paragraphs
- Choosing the best words for meaning and effect
- Structuring sentences effectively
- Writing a conclusion

Again, in a 30-minute test, you should expect to compose your essay in about 20 minutes.

And during the third stage, *revising and proofreading*, you devote five to eight minutes to polishing and refining the essay word by word, making the text clear, correct, and graceful.

Just how much time to allot to each step in the essay-writing process is up to you, of course. Neither this nor any other book can hand you a foolproof plan, but here is a general schedule for you to follow:

Prewriting	3–5 minutes
Composing	15–20 minutes
Proofreading	
and Editing	3–5 minutes

The plan that works for you will be different from the one that works for others. Besides, the three stages of the process are not all that discrete. They overlap and blend indiscriminately. Writers compose, revise, and proofread simultaneously. They jot down sentences during prewriting, and even late in the process sometimes weave new ideas into their text. In fact, no stage really ends until the final period of the last sentence is put in place—or until time is up and the test booklets are closed.

Three Effective Techniques to Improve Your Writing.

Experience has shown that the three best ways for anyone to prepare for writing a good essay are to 1) practice, 2) practice, and 3) practice some more.

The rewards of regular practice include

1. Greater fluency and self-confidence as a writer.
2. The growth of the skills needed to answer grammar and writing questions on the SAT, ACT, and other exams.

Regardless of the blurry boundaries between stages, however, it's worth keeping in mind the functions of each stage as you become familiar with several essential principles of essay writing.

Prewriting
Analyzing the Topic

At the risk of stating the obvious, be sure to read the assigned essay topic very carefully. Read it two or three times, or until you are certain what is being asked of you.

Some topics won't turn you on right away. Nevertheless, you have no choice but to deal with them. With a bit of luck, you'll think about your topic and soon begin bursting with ideas.

Narrowing the Topic

An essay focused on a narrow topic will always turn out better than one that tries to cover too much ground in just a few paragraphs. If your topic is too broad, the essay is likely to consist of little more than a few vague and superficial generalities. A narrow topic, on the other hand, offers you the opportunity to say something sensible, meaningful, provocative, and interesting. And never doubt that an interesting essay will work on your behalf.

Your first task, then, is to think small—to reduce the topic to a size snug enough to fit into a short essay. For example, let's say the prompt describes a situation in which faulty communication causes a misunderstanding between two people. The general topic, therefore, might be *communications.* To downsize this broad and rather abstract term for a short essay, create a ladder of abstraction that quickly makes the broad term more specific.

Communications	Highest level of abstraction
Functions of communication	Way too broad for a short essay
Communication technology	Still too broad
Electronic and digital communication	Better, but still too broad
Widespread use of cell phones	Getting there, but still very broad
Using cell phones for sending and receiving text messages	Close, but not there yet
Advantages and disadvantages of texting as a form of communication	A reasonable topic
Why texting should be permitted during the school day	Yes, the best topic yet for a short essay

Some writers find that an efficient way to narrow a topic is to begin writing. After a few sentences, they pause to reread their words. If the lines they've composed strike them as dull or disappointing, they may realize that the topic they chose was too vague, too broad, too boring (if the writer is bored, imagine what the essay will do to a reader), and they find themselves in a cul-de-sac. Then they have no choice but to turn to another topic and start over. Because of time constraints on most standardized tests, you'd be lucky to have more than one chance to start over. Therefore, a minute or so spent narrowing the topic before you start composing may be the most important 60 seconds of the exam.

Choosing a Main Idea

Once you've narrowed the topic sufficiently, it's time to decide what to say about the topic. That is, you must search for an idea that will become the purpose, or point, of your essay. An essay may not simply be "about" something—about the law, music, or field hockey. What counts is the statement your essay will make about the topic—about the law, music, or field hockey—in other words, your main idea.

The point, or main idea (also called the ***thesis***) is the thought to lock on to as you write. Every piece of the essay, from its opening sentence to the conclusion, should contribute to its development. Any material that wanders from the main idea should be left out. It not only wastes words but detracts from the unity and impact of your essay.

Obviously, the main idea will depend on the topic you are given to write on. If you are asked to agree or disagree with a particular point of view, the essay's main idea will be a statement of your opinion. For instance, if the topic happened to relate to required dress codes in high school, a main idea might be any of the following:

1. Yes, high schools should impose dress codes on students.
2. No, high schools should not impose dress codes on students.
3. High schools should impose dress codes on freshmen and sophomores but not on juniors and seniors.

Using one of these main ideas as your starting point, the essay would then go on to prove the validity of your opinion.

If possible, choose a main idea that matters to you personally, one that truly reflects your thinking. Essay evaluators won't fault you for stating opinions with which they disagree, so there's no good reason for choosing a main idea that makes you sound politically correct or one that you think will please or flatter the reader. Likewise, because you don't want to sound pompous or pretentious, avoid picking a main idea solely to demonstrate your intellectual superiority. A truthful essay that comes from the heart will serve you best.

Gathering and Arranging Ideas

While preparing to write your essay, do yourself a favor by gathering and arranging specific ideas, arguments, anecdotes, examples—whatever you can think of—to support and develop your thesis. Search your knowledge and experience. List your thoughts on paper as they occur to you—just a word or two for each idea. These jottings, in effect, will become the working outline of your essay. Once the flow of ideas has slowed to a trickle, sort through your notes by drawing circles around key words, connect related ideas with arrows, cross out the rejects, or just underline the thoughts you'll definitely use.

With ideas assembled, put them in some kind of order. Decide what should come first, second, third, and so on. In most essays, the best order is the one a reader can follow with the least effort. But, just as a highway map may show several routes from one place to another, there is no single way to get from the beginning to the end of an essay. The route you plan depends on the purpose of the trip.

Each purpose will have its own best order. In storytelling, the events are often placed in the sequence in which they occur. To explain a childhood memory or define an abstract term takes another organization. An essay that compares and contrasts two books or two people may deal with each subject separately or discuss point-by-point the features of each. No plan is necessarily superior to another, provided there's a valid reason for using it.

The plan that fails is the aimless one, the one in which ideas are presented solely according to how they popped into your head. To guard against aimlessness, rank your ideas in order of importance. Then work toward your best point, not away from it. Giving away your *piece de resistance* at the start is self-defeating. Therefore, if you have, say, three good ideas to support your thesis, save the strongest for last. Launch the essay with your second best, and sandwich your least favorite between the other two. A solid opening draws readers into the essay and creates that all-important first impression, but a memorable ending is even more important. Coming last, it is what readers have fresh in their minds when they assign the essay a grade.

An essay containing three good pieces of supporting information may be just about right. Why three? Well, because three suggests that you know what you are talking about. One is feeble and two only slightly better, but three indicates thoughtfulness. Psychologically, three also creates a sense of rhetorical wholeness, like "blood, sweat, and tears," and "of the people, by the people, and for the people."

It shouldn't be difficult to divide a main idea into three secondary ideas. A narrative essay, for instance, naturally breaks into a beginning, middle, and end. A process is likely to have at least three steps, some of which may be broken into substeps. In an essay of comparison and contrast, you should be able to find at least three similarities and differences to write about. A similar division into thirds applies to essays of cause and effect, definition, and description, and certainly to essays of argumentation—the kind most often given on SATs, ACTs, and other writing tests.

Each of three ideas may not require an equal amount of emphasis, however. You might dispose of the weakest idea in just a couple of sentences, whereas each of the others gets a whole paragraph. But whatever you emphasize, be sure that each idea is separate and distinct. The third idea mustn't simply rehash the first or second in the guise of something new.

The Formula

The five-paragraph essay formula is a simple, all-purpose plan for arranging ideas into clear, easy-to-follow order. You may well have used it in school for answering essay questions on tests, for analyzing a poem, or reporting on lab work. It's a technique you can rely on any time you need to set ideas in order. Its greatest virtue is clarity. Each part has its place and purpose.

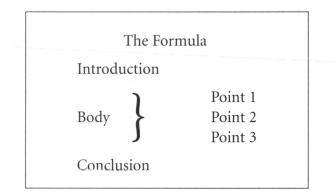

When writing an essay, you needn't follow the formula slavishly. In fact, you're not likely ever to find an essay in print that adheres strictly to this five-paragraph arrangement. Yet, many essay writers, even those who take a roundabout path between the beginning and end, use some version of it. In the *introduction*, they tell readers what they plan to say. In the *body* they say it, and in the *conclusion*, they tell the reader what they've been told. Since all writers differ, however, you find endless, often surprising, variations within each step.

Composing

Introducing the main idea

Introductions let readers know what to expect, but don't make a formal announcement of your plan, as in

> This discussion will show the significance of television as an influence on the learning of children from age 3 to 12. Distinctions will be made between early childhood (age 3–7) and middle childhood (8–12).

Such announcements are appropriate for term papers but are out of place in a short essay. Readers will recognize the topic soon enough, even without a separate statement of your intention.

Here, for example, is the opening of an essay on the rights of high school students:

> On Monday morning, October 20th, I arrived in school to find every locker door in my corridor standing ajar. Over the weekend, school officials had searched through students' lockers for drugs and alcohol. I believe that this illegal action was a violation of both my civil rights and the civil rights of every other student in the school.

This opening sets the essay's boundaries. The writer couldn't include everything about students' rights or about the duties and responsibilities of school authorities, so she concentrated instead on one issue raised by her personal experience on that Monday morning.

The best essays usually begin with something catchy, something to lure the reader into the piece. Think of the opening as a hook—a phrase, a sentence, or an idea that will grab your readers' interest so completely that they'll want to keep reading. Hooks must be very sharp, very clean, simple and brief, and should relate directly to the main subject of the essay.

To do its job, a hook mustn't be dull:

> **Drugs and alcohol are a problem for many young people in today's society.**

What dulls this hook is a statement so obvious and general that no one would be moved to continue reading. Here's a sharper hook on the same subject:

> **When sixth-graders get drunk and 13-year-olds smoke pot every Friday night, society's got a problem.**

This hook states a problem by using a compelling image of adolescents out of control. It provokes curiosity. The reader wants to know more about the "problem."

Numerous techniques for hooking readers have been devised. A brief account of an incident, such as that of the weekend locker search, can be all that it takes to lure the reader into an essay. Others include

- Stating a provocative idea in an ordinary way or an ordinary idea in a provocative way.

> **As any football hero will tell you, on the field brains count for more than brawn.**

This unconventional idea may cause readers to wonder whether the writer has lost touch with reality. Or it may lead readers to question their own preconceptions about football players.

- Using a quotation—not necessarily a famous one—from Shakespeare, a popular song, or your grandmother. Whatever the source, however, its sentiment must relate to the essay's topic.

> **"You can take people out of the country but you can't take the country out of the people."**

This opening gives a clever new twist to a common adage and introduces the essay's main idea—the futility of changing people's basic personality and core values.

- Refuting a commonly held assumption or defining a word in a new and surprising way.

> **Even though she's never written a rhyme or verse, my boss at Safeway is just as much a poet as Shelley or Keats.**

By inviting readers to imagine how someone who has written neither rhymes nor verses can be a *poet*, the writer hints at a new and perhaps surprising meaning of the word. That the label "poet" applies to her boss is even more intriguing because you don't often find poets working as supermarket managers. In short, the opening quickens our interest in reading an essay on an unlikely topic.

- Asking an interesting question or two that you will answer in your essay.

> **Why are stories of crime so fascinating?**

This opening question has wide appeal because it pertains to many of us who are riveted to both fictional and real accounts of criminal acts. We read the police blotter in the newspaper, tune to news channels that emphasize crime stories, talk about the latest murder, watch *Law and Order* on the tube. Presumably the essay will explain our fascination with the subject.

When writing an essay for practice or for real, you don't always need a super-catchy opening. A direct, clearly worded statement of the essay's main idea could serve just as well. But if a sharp hook occurs to you, use it. Work hard to get it right, but not too hard, because an opening that seems forced may sound phony. Beware also of an introduction that's too cute, too shocking, or too coarse. Be thoughtful and clever, yes, but not obnoxious. Also, keep it short. An opening that makes up, say, more than a quarter of your essay reflects poorly on your sense of proportion.

Developing paragraphs

Each paragraph of a well-written essay is, in effect, an essay in miniature. It has a purpose, an organizational plan, and a progression of ideas. You can scrutinize a paragraph just as you would scrutinize a complete essay. You can study its structure and development, identify its main idea and its purpose. The indentation that marks the beginning of a new paragraph alerts readers to get ready for a shift of some kind, somewhat like a car's directional blinker that tells other drivers that you're about to turn.

Yet, not every new paragraph signals a drastic change. The writer may simply want to nudge the discussion ahead to the next step. Some paragraphs spring directly from those that preceded them. The paragraph you are now reading, for instance, is linked to the one before by the connecting word *Yet*. The connection is meant to prepare you for a change in thought, but it is also intended to remind you that the two paragraphs are related.

Abrupt starts are useful from time to time because sudden turns keep readers on their toes. But writers must guard against a whole string of surprises. By shifting too often, they may lose readers and transform surprise into confusion. Connecting words, on the other hand, while diluting the impact of the surprise, integrate paragraphs into the essay. They create a sense of belonging.

Another function of paragraphs is that they permit readers to skip rapidly through your work, particularly when each first or last sentence summarizes the rest of the paragraph, as they often do in textbooks. Readers may then focus on paragraph openings and closings and skip what's in between. Readers in a hurry will appreciate that, but you can force readers to linger a while by varying the location of the topic sentence, the most important idea in each paragraph.

In an essay, most paragraphs play a primary role and one or more secondary roles. An *introductory paragraph*, for instance, launches the essay and makes the intent of the essay clear to the reader. The *concluding paragraph* leaves the reader with a thought to remember and provides a sense of closure. Most paragraphs, however, are *developmental*. That is, they are used to carry forward the main point of the essay. In one way or other, developmental paragraphs perform any number of functions, including:

- adding new ideas to the preceding discussion
- continuing or explaining in more detail an idea presented earlier
- reiterating a previously stated idea
- citing an example of a previously stated idea
- evaluating an opinion stated earlier
- refuting previously stated ideas
- turning the essay in a new direction
- providing a new or contrasting point of view
- describing the relationship between ideas presented earlier

Essay Writing

- providing background material
- raising a hypothetical or rhetorical question about the topic
- serving as a transition between sections of the essay
- summarizing an argument presented earlier

Whatever its functions, a paragraph should contribute to the essay's overall growth. A paragraph that fails to amplify the main idea of the essay should be revised or deleted. Similarly, any idea within a paragraph that doesn't contribute to the development of the paragraph's topic needs to be changed or eliminated. Incidentally, the SAT and ACT almost always include multiple-choice questions about paragraph development and paragraph unity. In addition, these tests frequently throw in questions about the role and placement of paragraphs within an essay.

Topic and supporting sentences

Every now and then, readers need to find sentences that help them know where they are. Such guiding sentences differ from others because they define the paragraph's main topic; hence the name *topic sentence.*

Most, but not all, paragraphs contain topic sentences. The topic of some paragraphs is so obvious that to state it would be redundant. Then, too, groups of paragraphs can be so closely knit that one topic sentence states the most important idea for all of them.

> Topic sentences help readers stay focused on the point of your essay.

What all topic sentences have in common is their helpfulness. They mark the turning points of an essay, telling readers the direction they'll be going for a while. Because no rule governs every possible use of a topic sentence, use as a guide your sense of what readers need in order to understand your essay. If in doubt, grasp your readers' hands too firmly rather than too loosely. Follow the principle that if there is a way to misunderstand or misinterpret your words, readers will most certainly find it.

Of the second kind, the *supporting sentences,* there are likely to be several. Supporting sentences provide the particulars needed to develop topic sentences. Some supporting sentences themselves need support, provided by minor supporting sentences. The following paragraph contains examples of each kind:

> [1] The Industrial Revolution changed the manner in which products were manufactured. [2] Before the revolution, most manufacturing was done by skilled workers very knowledgeable about every aspect of the product they made. [3] A barrel-maker, for example, had the ability to construct a barrel from start to finish. [4] He knew his materials, had the tools, and understood the entire process. [5] With the growth of factories, assembly lines began to produce the same goods with less skilled workers, each of whom may have mastered only one step in the process. [6] One worker may have become an expert stave cutter, another a specialist in manufacturing the metal hoops that hold barrels together.

Sentence 1 is the topic sentence of the paragraph. Each supporting sentence adds evidence to prove its validity—that the Industrial Revolution caused change in manufacturing practices. Sentence 2 is a supporting sentence that requires additional support, provided by sentence 3. Similarly, sentence 6 supports sentence 5, and taken altogether, sentences 2–6 support sentence 1.

Topic sentences are usually stated first in a paragraph, but they show up in other places, too. Also, they are not always separate and independent grammatical units, but rather are woven into a supporting sentence as a clause or a phrase. (In the paragraph you are now reading, for instance, the topic of the paragraph is stated in the second clause of the first sentence—*they show up in other places, too.*) Writers frequently vary the location of topic sentences to avoid monotony. A topic sentence saved for the end of a paragraph may stand out boldly as the climax to which the supporting sentences lead.

In some kinds of writing—particularly narrative and descriptive—the topic sentence may be left out because the main idea is implied by accumulated details and ideas. For instance, the writer who sets down several observations of a fast-food restaurant, including the crowd, the noise, the overflowing garbage cans, the smell of cooking oil, the lines of people, the crumb-strewn Formica tables, and so on, creates the impression of a frenetic place. It would have been superfluous to state explicitly, "It was a busy day at Burger King."

The key to unlocking a paragraph's purpose usually lies in the topic sentence. If a reader fails to catch the main idea, the meaning of the entire paragraph could be lost. Instead of a coherent unit of meaning, the paragraph may seem like a collection of unrelated sentences. The overall effectiveness of a paragraph, therefore, is tied to its supporting details. A loose or ambiguous connection erodes the effectiveness of both the paragraph and the entire essay.

Like essays, paragraphs should have a discernible organization. As always, clarity and intent should govern the sequence of ideas. In a coherent paragraph each sentence has its place and purpose. Disjointed paragraphs, on the other hand, consist of sentences arranged in random order. Or they contain ideas only vaguely related or irrelevant to the development of the main idea.

Some paragraphs contain transitional sentences—sentences that link the thought in one paragraph to those in the previous or subsequent paragraphs. Transitional sentences, in other words, serve as bridges. In fact, the first sentence of the paragraph you are reading is a transitional sentence that ties the previous paragraph to this one. The sentence provides an example of how to achieve coherence in an essay—the topic of the preceding paragraph.

As luck would have it, the English language brims with transitional words and phrases that can tie ideas together—among the most common: *for example, also, but, on the other hand, moreover, however, next,* and *nevertheless.* By using transitions like these you do readers a favor. You assure them of a smooth trip through your essay. Without such help, or when every sentence stands unconnected to the next, readers lurch from one idea to another. Before long, they'll either give up or get lost like travelers on an unmarked road. Although many sentences won't contain transitions, three or four sentences in succession without a link of some kind may leave readers confused, if not doubtful, that their trip is worth taking.

Links between sentences aid writers, too. They help writers stick to the topic and avoid inadvertent detours that may disorient even the most careful readers. Ideas that fail to connect with others around them or are unrelated to the paragraph's main idea should be revised, moved, or discarded. Take note: The SAT and ACT are fond of asking questions about irrelevant sentences.

Choosing the Best Words

To write clearly, use plain words. Never use a complex word because it sounds good or makes you seem more sophisticated. A writing test is not a place to flaunt your vocabulary. Use an elegant word only when it's the only word that will let you add something to the essay that you can't achieve in any other way. Why? Because an elegant word used merely to use an elegant word is bombastic . . . er . . . big-sounding and artificial.

Besides, simple ideas dressed up in ornate words often obscure meaning. Worse, they make writers sound phony, if not foolish. For instance, under ordinary circumstances you'd never utter the words, "Let's go to our domiciles" at the end of a day at school. Nor would you call your teachers *pedagogues* or your dog a *canine*. Yet, the following overblown sentence appeared in a student's essay:

> Although my history pedagogue insisted that I labor in my domicile immediately upon arrival, I was obliged to air my canine before commencing.

How much clearer and direct it would have been to write:

> I had to walk the dog before starting my history homework.

Fortunately, English is loaded with simple words that can express the most profound ideas. A sign that says STOP! conveys its message more clearly than CEASE AND DESIST. When a dentist pokes at your teeth, it *hurts*, even if dentists call it "experiencing discomfort." Descartes, the famous French philosopher, said, "I think. Therefore, I am," a statement that forever afterward shaped the way we think about existence. Descartes might have used more exotic words, of course, words more in keeping with the florid writing style of his time, but the very simplicity of his words endows his statement with great power. In fact, a sign of true intelligence is the ability to convey deep meanings with simple words.

> Trendy words have their place, but their place is not your SAT or ACT essay.

Simple doesn't necessarily mean short. It's true that plain words tend to be the short ones, but not always. The word *fid* is short, but it's not plain unless you are a sailor, in which case you'd know that a fid supports the mast on your boat. On the other hand, *spontaneously* is five syllables long. Yet it is a plain and simple word because of its frequent use.

Ernest Hemingway called a writer's greatest gift a "built-in, shock-proof crap detector." Hemingway's own detector worked well. He produced about the leanest, plainest writing in the English language—not that you should try to emulate Hemingway. (That's already been done by countless imitators.) But an efficient crap detector of your own will encourage you to choose words only because they express exactly what you mean.

Euphemisms

Of course, there are occasions when the plainest words won't do. English, as well as other languages, contains innumerable euphemisms—expressions that soften or mitigate painful, unsavory, or objectionable truths. For example, there are scores of euphemisms for the verb "to die" (*pass away, pass on, be deceased, rest, expire, meet one's maker*, and so on) and for bathroom (*restroom, ladies'/men's room, W.C., lounge*), and for drunkenness, vomiting, and everything else that might upset a prissy sensibility. Pussyfooting with words has its place. We do it all the time, but in your essay writing, use euphemisms only when you have a valid reason for doing so.

Don't interpret this advice to use plain words as justification for using current, everyday slang or street talk. Spoken language overflows with colorful, trendy words and expressions like *hulk out, cop some z's, awesome*, and *total babe*. Such words have their place, but the place is not your SAT or ACT essay unless you definitely need current lingo to create an effect that you can't produce in any other way. Also, avoid words and abbreviations that are popular in e-mails, texting, and tweets—such as *LOL, BFF, CU, B4*, and *GR8*. Of course you are free to write as though you are wired, but don't highlight your digital usages with quotation marks. Why call attention to your nonstandard usage? If to make a point you let txt msgs creep in2 your essay, be sure to show your mastery of conventional English at least in part of your piece. After all, the purpose of an essay test is to see whether you can write good, standard prose.

A plain, conversational style will always be appropriate. The language should sound like you. In formal essays, custom requires you to remove yourself from stage center and focus on the subject matter. But the essays given on the SAT, ACT, and other tests encourage more casual responses in which references to yourself are perfectly acceptable. It's not essential to use first-person singular pronoun, but using *I* is often preferable to using the more impersonal *one*, as in "When *one* is writing an essay, *one* sometimes writes funny," or *you*, as in "Sometimes *you* feel like a dope," or by avoiding pronouns altogether. But an essay that expresses the writer's personal opinion will sound most natural when cast in first-person singular.

The point is, don't be phony! Essay evaluators are old hands at spotting pretense in students' writing, so let your genuine voice ring out, although the way you speak is not necessarily the way you should write. Spoken language is often vague, clumsy, repetitive, confused, and wordy. Consider writing as the everyday speech of someone who speaks exceedingly well. It's grammatically correct and free of pop expressions and clichés. Think of it as the kind of speech expected of you in a college interview or in serious conversation with the head of your school. Or maybe even the way this paragraph sounds. You could do a lot worse!

Precise language

Precise words are memorable, whereas hazy, hard-to-grasp words fade as quickly as last night's dream. Tell your garage mechanic vaguely, "This car is a lemon," and he'll ask for more information. Say precisely, "My car won't start in freezing weather," and he'll raise the engine hood and go to work. If a patient in the E.R. says, "I feel pain," a surgeon might at least like to know exactly where it hurts before pulling out her scalpels. In other words, precise language is more informative, more functional, and thus, more desirable.

In the first draft of an essay about a day he'd like to forget, Jeff, a high school junior, wrote this paragraph:

> It was an awful day outside. Everything was going wrong. I felt terrible. Things weren't going well in school. I got a below-par grade on a paper, and I was sure that I had failed my science quiz. I also had lots of things to do at home and no time to do them. My mother was in a bad mood, too. She yelled at me for all kinds of things. Then Penny called, and we got into a disagreement. I had trouble with my computer's disk player, and I couldn't pay for repairs. I went to bed early, hoping that tomorrow would be better.

Reviewing the essay a few days later, Jeff realized the paragraph begged for more precise writing. Yes, the day had been dreadful, but his account needed details to prove it. The next draft took care of that:

> It had been a cold and rainy November day, and my life was as miserable as the weather. I felt chills all day, and my throat was sore. In school I got a D on a history paper about the Bubonic Plague, and I was sure that I had failed the chemistry quiz. The homework was piling up—two lab reports, over 150 pages to read in <u>Wuthering Heights</u>, a chapter in the history text, and about a hundred new vocabulary words in Spanish. I didn't have time or energy to do it all, especially when my mother started to pick at me about my messy room and the thank-you letters I'm supposed to write to my grandparents. Just as she was reminding me that my registration for

Essay Writing

the ACT was overdue, Penny called to tell me that she wouldn't be coming over for Thanksgiving after all, and we argued about loyalty and trust and keeping promises. I'd hoped to watch *Lord of the Rings* again, but when I put the disk into my computer, it kept skipping scenes. The repairman said he would charge $100 just to look at the damn thing, but I don't have that kind of money. By 9:00 PM I was in bed, hoping that tomorrow would be better.

In this version Jeff included many precise details that vividly illustrate the wretchedness of that miserable day. And he's made clear why he picked that day as the subject of his essay.

Of course, not every essay topic calls for such detail. Some topics invite you to write more vaguely, more abstractly, perhaps more philosophically. For example, *loyalty, trust,* and *keeping promises,* as well as *love, freedom, spirit, fairness, conformity, satisfaction,* and countless other words stand for concepts that exist in our hearts and minds. The power to express principles, ideas, and feelings is unique to humans, and such a gift shouldn't go untapped, but an essay consisting solely of abstractions will leave readers at sea. However amorphous the topic, therefore, an essay's success depends on precise, hard-edged, concrete words.

Undoubtedly, vague, shadowy words are easier to think of. But they are often meant to cover up a lack of clear and rigorous thinking. It's a cinch to pass judgment on a book by calling it "good" or "interesting." But what readers want to know is precisely why you thought so. How simple it is to call someone an "old man" without bothering to show the reader a "stooped, white-haired gentleman shuffling along the sidewalk." A writer who says her teacher is "ugly" sends a different image of ugliness to each reader. If the teacher is a "shifty-eyed tyrant who spits when she talks," then, by golly, say it. Or if the teacher's personality is ugly, show her ill-temper, arrogance, and cruelty as she scolds her hapless students.

Good writers understand that their words must appeal to the readers' senses. To write precisely is to write with pictures, sounds, and actions that are as vivid on paper as they are in reality. Exact words leave distinct marks; abstract ones, blurry impressions. As the following pairs of sentences illustrate, precise writers turn hazy notions into vivid images:

HAZY:	Skiing is a fun sport. The mountains are pretty, and it takes skill.
PRECISE:	On the ski slope, I marvel at the snow-decked pines and brilliant sky and thrill to the challenge of weaving gracefully down steep mountains.

HAZY:	Rather violently, Carolyn expressed her anger at the other team's player.
PRECISE:	Carolyn snarled, "Get out of my face" as she punched the Tigers' goalie in the nose.

HAZY:	My parents were happy when I got accepted to college.
PRECISE:	The letter thrilled my parents. Their worried looks suddenly disappeared, they stopped nagging me about homework, and because the question had been answered, they never again asked what would become of me.

Clearly, the precisely worded sentences are richer than the hazy ones. But they are also much longer. In fact, it's not always desirable or necessary to define every abstraction with precise details. Each time you mention *dinner,* for instance, you don't have to recite the menu. When you use an abstract word in an essay, ask what's more important—to give readers a more detailed account of your idea, or to push on to other matters. The context, as well as your judgment of the readers' intelligence, will have to determine how abstract your essay can be. Remember, though, it's punishing to read an essay that never deals concretely with anything.

Writing a conclusion

At the end of your essay you can lift your pen off the paper and be done with it. Or, if you have the time, you can present your readers with a little gift to remember you by—perhaps a surprising insight, a bit of wisdom, a catchy phrase—something likely to tease readers' brains, tickle their funny bones, or make them feel smart.

Choose the gift carefully. It should fit the content, style, and mood of your essay and spring naturally from its contents. A good essay can easily be spoiled by a grating conclusion. A serious essay shouldn't end with a joke. Steer clear of endings that are too common or too cute, such as: *that's it; a good time was had by all; tune in next time—same time, same station; it was a dream come true; good night and God bless,* and many other equally trite expressions. Such banal endings will leave readers thinking that you either lack imagination or are too lazy to choose a more thoughtful gift. In short, don't spoil a fresh essay with a stale conclusion.

Because it comes last, the final paragraph leaves an enduring impression. A weak, apologetic, or irrelevant conclusion may dilute or even obliterate the effect that you tried hard to create. Above all, stay away from summary endings. When an essay is short to begin with, it's insulting to review for readers what is evident on the page in front of them. Readers are intelligent people. Trust them to remember what your essay says.

A catchy conclusion isn't always necessary, but even a short ending may be preferable to none at all. Effective endings leave readers fulfilled, satisfied that they have arrived somewhere. A judiciously chosen ending may sway readers to judge your essay somewhat more leniently than otherwise. There are no guarantees, of course, but readers are bound to be touched by a memento of your thinking, your sense of humor, or your vision. Even an ordinary thought, uniquely expressed, will leave an agreeable afterglow.

You might try any one of these common techniques:

- Have a little fun with your conclusion; try to put a smile on your reader's face.

    Essay Topic: Growing Old

    Purpose: To show that old people can still act young, the essay concludes with an anecdote about an elderly gray-haired man of about seventy on a crowded city bus.

    Conclusion: He carried bundles of packages and almost fell down as the bus lurched to a stop. At one point a young, gum-chewing woman stood up and pointed to the unoccupied seat. "Here, Pops, take this."
    He looked at her in amazement. "Cool it, girlie," he said, "I still run marathons," and he stood all the way to his stop.

    Essay Topic: Extending compulsory education to age 19

    Purpose: To argue against forcing teenagers to attend school until at least age 19. The essay ends with a hypothetical consequence of having a much older classmate.

    Conclusion: When you're assigned to interview an "old person," it shouldn't be the guy who sits behind you.

- End with an apt quotation drawn from the essay itself, from the prompt, or from another source.

    Essay Topic: Survival Training

> Purpose: To describe an incident in which the writer found herself in need of a safe shelter.
>
> Conclusion: At that point I knew by instinct, "This is the place."
>
> Essay Topic: Computer Glitches
>
> Purpose: To show that, because many consumers are uninformed, they waste lots of money when purchasing personal computers.
>
> Conclusion: To paraphrase an old saying, "What you don't know can hurt you."

- Finish by clearly restating your essay's main point but using new words. If appropriate, add a short tagline, a brief sentence that creates a dramatic effect.

> Essay Topic: Sexism
>
> Purpose: To decry the male chauvinism that exists in the school administration.
>
> Conclusion: As long as positions of authority are given to sexists, women must be prepared to fight against gender abuse in this institution.
>
> Topic: Twitter
>
> Purpose: To explain the value and importance of Twitter to teenagers. The writer concludes with a sample of tweeting language.
>
> Conclusion: At the end of the day, I can't go 2 bed B4 tweeting at least 6 of my BFFs.

- Bring your readers up to date or project them into the future. Say something about the months or years ahead.

> Essay Topic: Vandalism in School
>
> Purpose: To condemn the daily carnage of smashed windows, graffiti, and broken ceiling tiles. The essay ends with a few questions about the future.
>
> Conclusion: How long can this go on? How can we turn away meekly? How much longer can we let the vandals make us their victims?
>
> Essay Topic: Fighting AIDS
>
> Purpose: To explain why it is imperative to rid the world of the scourge of AIDS.
>
> Conclusion: When the history of the 21st century is written, let us hope that AIDS will have gone the way of the dinosaurs.

Although an effective conclusion will add luster to an essay, don't feel obliged to add an ending just for the sake of form. Readers will have developed a fairly accurate sense of your writing ability before reaching your essay's last word. Rest assured that a good but incomplete piece of writing will be graded according to what you have done well, instead of what you haven't done at all.

Revising and Proofreading

To understand your essay, a reader needs the kind of help that only you can provide. As you write and revise, therefore, keep asking yourself, "Which words will guarantee that my message will be clear?" If you yourself don't fully grasp the meaning of your own words—if you've written something fuzzy or included an idea expressed in a way that doesn't quite convey what is in your mind—you can't expect readers to understand it. That's why, once you've finished composing your essay, you should use the remaining time to edit it for clarity and correctness. Give it a clean sweep, tossing out anything that might interfere with clear communication.

Because many words have multiple meanings, check each word for clarity. Ask yourself whether any reader might misconstrue a word or find it ambiguous. Penny O. wrote an essay about students who cut classes. One of her sentences read: "The last thing parents should do is talk to their kids." Coming upon that sentence, readers might wonder whether Penny means that parents should talk to their kids only as a last resort, or that in a list of what parents ought to do, the final step is talking to their kids.

Later in the essay Penny wrote: "Eileen told her friend Debbie that she had made a serious mistake by cutting gym class for two weeks." Penny no doubt understood what she intended to say, but readers can't tell whether Eileen took a dim view of Debbie's actions or whether Eileen herself had second thoughts about her own absence from gym class. Granted, these sentences have been quoted out of context, but the point remains: What may seem like a perfectly clear sentence to the writer may send a puzzling message to the reader.

Because clarity is worth striving for, careful writers work hard to arrange their words in the clearest order and they watch out for grammatical perils—the very same perils discussed in detail in the first three chapters of this book.

ESSAY SCORING

SAT and ACT essays are read twice and judged "holistically." That is, each reader decides the score according to the essay's overall impression rather than by an item-by-item analysis of what the writer did or did not do well. The general qualities that contribute to or detract from an essay's success are spelled out in the following chart.

Both the SAT and the ACT use a scale from 1 (low) to 6 (high) for rating essays. *Note:* Because two readers evaluate your essay, a 12 represents the highest possible score.

6 = outstanding, the highest quality
5 = very good, well above average
4 = good, above average
3 = fair, below average
2 = poor, far below average
1 = very poor, unacceptable

Purpose of the essay

6   Very clearly focused and insightful
5   Mostly clear, focused, and insightful
4   Fairly clear and with evidence of insight
3   Somewhat clear, but with some confusing aspects
2   Generally unclear, unfocused, and confusing
1   Extremely confusing, virtually incomprehensible

Organization and development

6 Well organized and fully developed with excellent supporting material
5 Generally well organized and developed with appropriate supporting material
4 Reasonably organized and partly developed with supporting material
3 Barely adequate organization; inappropriate or weak supporting material
2 Some evidence of organization; thin development
1 Lack of organization and development; virtually incoherent

Use of sentences

6 Varied and engaging sentence structure
5 Sufficiently varied sentence structure
4 Some sentence variation
3 Little sentence variation; minor sentence errors
2 Frequent sentence errors, with some loss of meaning
1 Severe sentence errors; meaning obscured

Word choice

6 Effective word choice
5 Competent word choice
4 Conventional word choice; mostly correct
3 Some errors in diction or idiom
2 Frequent errors in diction or idiom
1 Meaning obscured by word choice

Grammar and usage

6 Completely or virtually error-free
5 Occasional minor errors
4 Several minor errors
3 Some major errors
2 Frequent major errors
1 Severely flawed; meaning obscured

Overall impression

6 Evidence of competence and control; few, if any, errors
5 Reasonably consistent competence and control; occasional lapses
4 Adequate competence and control; some lapses in quality
3 Evidence of developing competence, but with several weaknesses
2 Suggestions of incompetence; significant weaknesses
1 Demonstration of incompetence; serious flaws

Index

A

absolute adjectives, 37
ACT
    essay writing, 229–246
    grammar questions, 140–149
active voice, 69, 102
adjectives
    about, 34
    absolute, 37
    compound, 34–35
    degrees of comparison, 35–36
    phrases and clauses, 35, 60
    vs. adverbs, 41, 101
adverbs
    about, 38–40
    comparisons, 41
    phrases and clauses, 39, 60
    vs. adjectives, 41, 101
among/between, 45
antecedents and pronoun agreement, 10–14, 97
apostrophes, 15, 81
appositives, 82
articles, 5, 34
as/like, 44
awkwardness, 74–75, 102

B

being (linking) verbs, 7
between/among, 45

C

capitalization, 86–88
case of pronouns, 6–7, 100
clauses
    about, 60
    adjective, 35, 60
    adverbial, 39, 60
    coordinate, 61, 100–101
    dependent, 47, 60
    independent or main, 47, 60
    noun, 60
    relative clauses, 16
    subordinate, 47, 100–101
collective nouns, 4
colons, 84
commas, 82–83, 98–99
comma splices, 64
comparative degree of comparison, 36
comparisons
    and adverbs, 41
    degrees of, 35–38
    faulty, 98
    and pronouns, 7
complex sentences, 61
composing stage of essay writing, 231–232, 235–244
compound adjectives, 34–35
compound-complex sentences, 61
compound sentences, 46–47, 61
conclusion of essay, 243–244
conjunctions, 46–48
coordinate clauses, 61, 100–101
coordinating conjunctions, 46
correlative conjunctions, 47

D

dangling participles, 63–64, 99
dashes, 84
definite articles, 5
degrees of comparison, 35–38
demonstrative pronouns, 18–19
dependent clauses, 47, 60
developing paragraphs for essay writing, 237–242
diction, 78–79, 97
direct objects, 59

E

essay writing, 229–246
euphemisms, 240
exclamation points, 86

F

faulty comparisons, 98
faulty diction, 78–79, 97
faulty idioms, 75–78, 101
fewer/less, 37
first-person pronouns, 9
five-paragraph essay formula, 235
future perfect tense, 21–22
future tense, 21–22

G

gathering and arranging ideas, 234–235
gender and pronoun/antecedent agreement, 10–11
gerunds, 15, 63
grammar
    ACT questions, 140–149
    high school graduation questions, 197
    importance of, vii
    pitfalls, 95–102
    SAT questions, 103–108

H

helping verbs, 21
high school graduation grammar questions, 197

I

ideas, gathering and arranging of, 234–235
identifying sentence errors, 106–108
idiomatic usage, 75–78, 101
improving sentences, 104–106
incomplete sentences (sentence fragments), 60, 62, 99
indefinite articles, 5
indefinite pronouns, 10
independent or main clauses, 47, 60
indirect objects, 59
infinitives, 29, 40, 63
interjections, 5
interrogative pronouns, 18
introduction to essay, 235–237
irregular verbs, 27–28

L

language usage, vii
less/fewer, 37
like/as, 44
linking (being) verbs, 7

M

main idea, 233–234
main (independent) clauses, 47, 60
mismatched sentence parts, 98
modifiers, misplaced, 35, 99

N

nominative case, 6–7
nonsentences, 60, 62, 99
noun clauses, 60
nouns, 3–4, 9, 102
number, 4, 10–11, 102

O

objective case, 6–7
object of the preposition, 44
object pronouns, 6–14
objects of the verb, 7, 59

P

parallel structure, 65–68, 97
participle phrases, 63
participles
    dangling, 63–64, 99
    and possessive pronouns, 15
parts of speech, 5
passive voice, 69–70, 102
past perfect tense, 21–22
past tense, 21–22
personal pronouns, 6–14
phrases
    adjective, 35
    adverbial, 39
    participle, 63
    prepositional, 7, 14
plural nouns, 4
plural verbs, 26
positive degree of comparison, 36
possessive pronouns, 15
predicate nominative pronouns, 7

predicate of a sentence, 57–59
prepositional phrases, 7, 44
prepositions, 43–46
present perfect tense, 21–22
present tense, 21–22
prewriting stage of essay writing, 231–235
prompts, 229
pronouns
    about, 5–6
    ambiguous references, 12, 97
    antecedent agreement, 10–14, 97
    case, 6–7, 100
    demonstrative, 18–19
    indefinite, 10
    interrogative, 18
    and noun combinations, 9
    object, 7, 59
    pairs, 8
    personal, 6–14
    possessive, 15
    predicative nominative, 7
    reflexive, 18
    relative, 16–17
    shifts in person, 9, 100
proofreading stage of essay writing, 231–232,
        245–246
proper nouns, 4
punctuation, 81–86, 146–147

Q
question marks, 85
quotations marks, 85

R
redundancies, 79–81
reflexive pronouns, 18
relative clauses, 16
relative pronouns, 16–17
revising stage of essay writing, 231–232, 245–246
rhetoric, 147–149
run-on sentences, 64, 100

S
SAT
    essay writing, 229–246
    grammar questions, 103–108

scoring
    of ACT, 245–246
    of SAT, 104, 245–246
second-person pronouns, 9
semicolons, 83, 98–99
sentence fragments, 60, 62, 99
sentence mechanics, 81–88
sentences *see also* clauses
    about, 57–59
    active and passive voice, 69–70
    capitalization, 86–88
    comma splices, 64
    complex sentences, 61
    compound, 46–47, 61
    compound-complex, 61
    construction, 101–102
    expression and style, 74–81,
        101–102
    faulty parallel structure, 65–68, 97
    identifying errors, 106–108
    improving, 104–106
    mismatched parts, 98
    nonsentences, 60, 62, 99
    predicate of a, 57–59
    problems, 62–70
    punctuation, 81–86
    run-on, 64, 100
    simple, 61
    structure, 70–74, 144–146
    subject of, 57–58
    topic and supporting, 238–239
    types of, 61
series, commas in, 83
simple sentences, 61
singular nouns, 4
singular verbs, 26
splitting infinitives, 40
state-of-being verbs, 7, 21–22
subject of a sentence, 57–58
subject pronouns, 6–14
subject-verb agreement, 30–34, 96
subjunctive mood, 29
subordinate clauses, 47, 100–101
subordinating conjunctions, 47, 61
superlative degree of comparison, 36
supporting sentences, 238–239

T
tenses, verb, 21–25, 96
that, 17
third person pronouns, 9–10
topic, analyzing and narrowing, 232–233
topic sentences, 238

U
usage, language, vii

V
verbals *see* gerunds; infinitives
verb forms, 25–29
verbs
    being or linking, 7, 21–22
    forms, 96
    helping, 21

infinitives, 29, 40, 43
irregular, 27–28
objects of, 7, 59
plural, 26
singular, 26
subject agreement,
    30–34, 96
subjunctive mood, 29
tenses, 21–25, 96
verb-subject agreement, 96

W
which, 17
who, 17
who/whom, 17
word choice, 239–242
wordiness, 79, 101

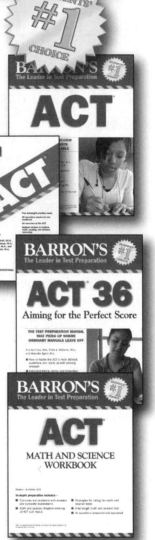

It's Your Personal Online Test Preparation Tutor for the SAT*, PSAT*, and ACT

Log in at: www.barronstestprep.com

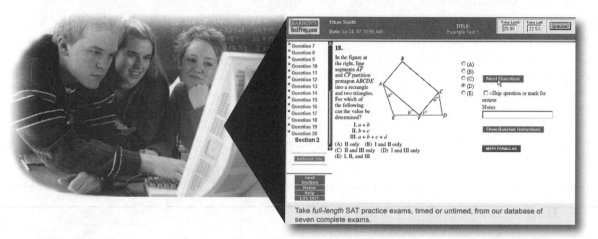

Take *full-length* SAT practice exams, timed or untimed, from our database of seven complete exams.

And discover the most comprehensive SAT, PSAT, and ACT test preparation available anywhere—

- Full-length sample SAT, PSAT, and ACT practice exams with automatic online grading.
- Your choice of two test-taking modes:

    Test Mode: Replicates actual test-taking conditions (timed or untimed). Students must complete one section before they can advance to the next.

    Practice Mode: User chooses the particular question type for practice and review— for instance, sentence completion, reading comprehension, quantitative comparisons, etc.— and chooses the number of questions to answer.

- Answers and explanations provided for all test questions.
- Performance evaluation given after each exam taken, and on the total exams taken by any one user. Students can get a comparative ranking against all other web site users.
- Extensive vocabulary list for practice and review.

Plus these great extra features—
- Test-taking advice in all areas covered by the exam
- Up-to-date SAT, PSAT, and ACT exam schedules
- Optional onscreen timer
- A personal exam library to evaluate progress

Site Licenses Available
- Schools and libraries can now give an unlimited number of students access to all three exams, SAT, PSAT, and ACT, on a per terminal basis.
- Administrator screen for reviewing student usage statistics such as time spent online, type and number of exams reviewed, average scores, and more ...

Start now with a click of your computer mouse
- Just $19.99 per subscription gives you complete preparation in all test areas
- Group Subscriptions Available

For Full Subscription Information
Visit our site at www.barronstestprep.com

All prices are subject to change without notice.

*SAT and PSAT are registered trademarks of the College Entrance Examination Board, which was not involved in the production of and does not endorse this product.

#104 R 6/10